T5-BQA-041

Library of
Davidson College

VOID

the shadows within

Gershon Shaked

the shadows within

essays on modern Jewish writers

The Jewish Publication Society
Philadelphia · New York · Jerusalem   *5748 / 1987*

809.8
S 5275

Copyright © 1987 by The Jewish Publication Society
First edition   All rights reserved
Manufactured in the United States of America
Library of Congress Cataloging in Publication Data

Shaked, Gershon.
  The shadows within.
  Bibliography: p. 191
  Includes index.
  1. Jewish literature—20th century—History and
criticism. 2. German literature—Jewish authors—His-
tory and criticism. 3. Hebrew literature, Modern—
History and criticism. 4. Israeli literature—History
and criticism. 5. Jews—Identity. I. Title.
PN842.S53 1987   809'.889'24   87–16849
ISBN 0–8276–0295–2

Designed by Adrianne Onderdonk Dudden

90-0263

To the memory of my uncles:
Salomon Mandel and Salomon Grossman

acknowledgments

Most of these essays have been published in various journals (such as *Ariel, Jerusalem Quarterly, Hebrew University Literary Studies, Modern Hebrew Literature,* and *Forum*). Some of them have appeared in literary collections (*The Great Transition,* published by the Center for Jewish Studies, Oxford; *Voices from Israel,* published by Herzl Press). An earlier version of "Shadows of Identity" will be published by Greenwood Press in 1988 as "An Essay on the Comparative Study of Themes in German, Hebrew, and American-Jewish Literatures" (in *Handbook of American-Jewish Literature: An Analytical Guide to Themes and Sources,* ed. Lewis Fried). I am grateful to the publishers for allowing me to include these essays in this collection.

Some of these essays were written originally in English, others in German, the majority of them in Hebrew. Most of the articles were translated by Jeffrey Green, some by Yael Lotan and Eleanor Lapin. Ruth Nevo and Malka Jagendorff have been more than just editors. I wish to thank each and every person who participated in the translation and editing of the different articles.

This collection would never have been published without the active participation of Sheila F. Segal, editor-in-chief of The Jewish Publication Society, and Ilene P. Cohen, the copy editor, who would not let me leave out any relevant detail and created stylistic unity. They have done their best; whatever the collection lacks is my responsibility.

G.S.
New York, 1987

contents

ACKNOWLEDGMENTS   *vii*

PREFACE   *xi*

Kafka, Jewish Heritage, and Hebrew Literature   3

The Wassermann Case   23

*The Grace of Reason and the Grace of Misery:
On the Zweig-Roth Correspondence   39*

*Shadows of Identity: A Comparative Study of
German Jewish and American Jewish Literature   57*

*Jewish Tradition and Western Impact in
Modern Hebrew Literature   83*

Jewish Heritage: Revolt and Transformation in Israeli Culture   97

The Great Transition   111

Bialik Here and Now   123

By a Miracle: Agnon's Literary Representation of Social Dramas 133

First Person Plural: Literature of the 1948 Generation 145

Questionable Exclamation Points: On the Political Meaning of Contemporary Israeli Fiction 165

No Other Place: On Saul Friedländer's When Memory Comes, *1979* 181

SELECTED BIBLIOGRAPHY 191

INDEX OF WRITERS 195

preface

Literary critics sometimes live under the illusion that they represent a rational conceptual approach to the realm of literary texts. In this conventional view, the texts themselves are regarded as intense fusions of unconscious primary processes and secondary conscious processes. The function of criticism seems to be only a secondary process: the objective reformulation of the fictitious world of imagination. Fiction has biographical and subjective sources, while criticism tries to be above and beyond the critic's personal life and biography.

This is of course a concept that does not pass the test of reality. Genuine criticism originates from the same sources and resources as authentic fiction. The difference is only the genre of communication: The literary text transforms personal and impersonal materials into a world of fiction; the critical text reformulates the world of fiction into a web of critical conceptual terms. The selection of texts, the extraction of critical issues, and the ideological arrangement of critical terms are as conditioned by the biographical, psychological, and ideological background of the critics as literary works are by those of the artist.

I emphasize the subjectivity of criticism at the outset of this volume in order to make it clear to the reader that in my analyses of the texts and contexts of various Jewish writers—writers who wrote in at least three languages and on three continents—I am trying to understand my own, and my generation's, identity as it is influenced by the major issues of our Jewish and human existence. The texts to which I refer are the texts of my intellectual biography; the continents where these writers have lived and written are the locations of my own physical wanderings; and the sources of the issues I evoke are of my own emotional life as depicted and delineated by some of the best Jewish writers of the last century.

This collection of essays tells the story of a spiritual emigration from Jewish Europe. It is an attempt to understand the transformations of the deracinated European Jew when he tries to strike roots in America and especially in Israel. It is the intellectual autobiography of a young immigrant who could sever neither his intellectual ties with his past nor his spiritual affinities with his brethren on the other side of the ocean, but has chosen Israel, definitively and unequivocally, as the location of his physical and spiritual present and future.

The image of the native-born Israeli, who emerged *ex nihilo* and bears no resemblances whatsoever to his Diaspora ancestors or relatives, is a literary falsification. Yet in the forties we "immigrants" also wanted to lose our identity and assimilate into the society of the native-born—into what seemed to be the majority. Those of us who remained "immigrants" in our souls felt like a silent minority among "real" Israelis. In the last two decades, however, the tables have turned, and we have become a voiceful majority. Now Israel's native-born are drawn into the more complex identities of the so-called immigrants, identities that have been, and remain, "the shadows within."

I don't know if a collection of literary essays really can describe the agonies and struggles of my generation. It may be that this could be done—if at all—only by art. But criticism is for the time being the only language in which I express myself, and it is at least a genuine attempt to convey a message in my own way.

This collection is dedicated to my relatives who came to the United States after World War II and passed away in this country. They have always been personal proof to me that even though we are an ocean apart we remain one family.

New York   1987

He left his people! What did he leave? Shattered bodies, shadows, just shadows. What do you see in the Jews except shadows? But those shadows dwell in his spirit, in his essence, and in everything within him.

(M. J. Berdyczewski, "The Stranger")

Kafka, Jewish heritage, and Hebrew literature

I

In Hebrew my name is Amschel, like my mother's maternal grandfather, whom my mother, who was six years old when he died, can remember as a very pious and learned man with a long, white beard. She remembers how she had to take hold of the toes of the corpse and ask forgiveness for any offense she may have committed against her grandfather. She also remembers her grandfather's many books which lined the walls. He bathed in the river every day, even in winter, when he chopped a hole in the ice for his bath.[1]

As a child I reproached myself, in accord with you, for not going to the synagogue enough, for not fasting, and so on. I thought that in this way I was doing a wrong not to myself but to you, and I was penetrated by a sense of guilt, which was, of course, always ready to hand.

Later, as a boy, I could not understand how, with the insignificant scrap of Judaism you yourself possessed, you could reproach me for not (if for no more than the sake of piety at least, as you put it) making an effort to cling to a similar insignificant scrap. It was indeed really so far as I could see, a mere scrap, a joke—not even a joke.[2]

What have I in common with Jews? I have hardly anything in common with myself and should stand very quietly in a corner, content that I can breathe.[3]

These three quotations from the personal writings of Franz Kafka shed light on several important aspects of his approach-avoidance relationship to Judaism. Whereas the religious faith of Eastern Jewry attracted him very much, he was repelled by the pharisaism of Western Jews. Despite profound hatred for his bourgeois, Western-style Jewish upbringing, Kafka always felt Jewish and often dwelt on his Jewish identity in his documentary writings, his correspondence and diaries. These texts also show that some of his friends, such as Hugo Bergmann, Max Brod and Felix Weltsch, were active Zionists. In addition, they reveal the deep impressions made on him by certain Jews, particularly Löwy and his Yiddish theater troupe. Kafka was always eager to improve his fragmentary knowledge of Judaism. To this end, he studied Heinrich Graetz's *History of the Jews* (*Diaries*, 1 Nov. 1911) and Meyer Pines's *History of Jewish* (i.e., Yiddish) *Literature* (*Diaries*, 1 Jan. 1912); he copied whole passages from the Old Testament into his diaries (Isaac, Abimelech, Abraham, *Diaries*, 14 July 1916; Moses, *Diaries*, 19 Oct. 1921). Sometimes these passages are transformed in such a way as to indicate that Kafka intended to use them as the basis for biblical reinterpretations. In fact, he frequently used ancient tales in his stories, such as "Poseidon" and "The City Coat of Arms," which describes the building of the Tower of Babel.

Numerous passages in Kafka's letters and diaries reflect his interest in the pious Jews from Eastern Europe. In some, he describes encounters and experiences with Hasidim from various groups and with rabbinic courts (*Diaries*, 18 Sept. 1912, 6 Oct. 1915, 19 Nov. 1915; *Letters to Felice*, 20, 21 Jan. 1913, 16 Jan. 1913). For Kafka, certain aspects of Eastern European Orthodox Jewish life were oddities that aroused his curiosity and opened up a new world for him: circumcision (*Diaries*, 3 Mar. 1912), the water for the ritual bath (*Diaries*, 21 Oct. 1911), talmudic seminaries, which he calls "yeshivas" (*Diaries*, 7 Jan. 1912), and Hasidic rabbis such as the rabbi from Belz (letter to Max Brod, July 1916).[4] The following passage from the *Diaries* is one example among many of his ironic, somewhat playful interest:

. . . custom, immediately after awakening, to dip the fingers three times in water, as the evil spirits have settled during the night on the second and third joints of the fingers. Rationalist explanation: To prevent the fingers directly touching the face, since, uncontrolled, during sleep and dreams, they could after all have touched every possible part of the body, the armpits, the behind, the genitals (27 Oct. 1911).

Kafka takes the trouble to note in minute detail superstitious Hasidic customs and manners—although his own "rational" explanation is also quite irrational. At times one detects an ironic tone in these descriptions. In general, however, one has the impression that this material could be a collection for use in a naturalistic, or possibly folkloristic, Jewish novel. Seen in that light, these preliminary notes serve to highlight a striking contradiction between Kafka the man and Kafka the artist. In his diaries and letters he reveals an almost perverse curiosity about the baffling mystery of Orthodox Jewry, whereas in his literary works he hardly ever deals with this world.

The absence of overt Jewish themes from Kafka's work is even more surprising since his interests extended, as well, beyond the older tradition and culture of Orthodox Judaism. He was also well versed in Yiddish and Hebrew literature and was familiar with the works of Sholem Aleichem, I. L. Peretz, and Sholem Asch (*Diaries*, 20 Oct. 1911; *Letters to Felice*, 26 Sept. 1916, 29 Sept. 1916). During his last years, with the help of his Hebrew teacher Puah Menzcel, he read the works of Y. H. Brenner, the foremost Hebrew author of the time. Kafka wrote to Robert Klopstock (*Letters*, 25 Oct. 1923) that he had read thirty-two pages of the novel *Shekhol ve-khishalon* (*Breakdown and Bereavement*) without great enthusiasm. Clearly he made every effort to become acquainted with the Jewish world; and although he always remained an outsider, he was a committed one, familiar with the literary works of his Jewish contemporaries.

Kafka's attitude toward the social and political life of the Jews was also ambivalent. His closest friends and his last lover and attendant, Dora Diamant, were Zionists. He too at times was sufficiently attracted to Zionism even to contemplate a trip to Palestine (*Letters*, to Robert Klopstock, Dec. 1921; to Else Bergmann, July 1923; *Diaries*, 12 Sept. 1912). More typically, however, he declined to espouse any one specific ideology, believing himself temperamentally unsuited to make such a commitment. In fact, some aspects of Zionism repelled him and always remained foreign to him. The following section from a letter to Felice clearly indicates his ambivalence:

Then I met an acquaintance, a Zionist student who is very sensible, keen, active, amiable, but at the same time, possesses a degree of composure I find altogether disturbing. He stops me, invites me to an especially important evening meeting (how many similar invitations has he not wasted on me in the course of the years!); at that moment my indifference to him as a person, or to any form of Zionism, was immense and inexpressible (*Letters to Felice*, 27–28 Feb. 1913).

Kafka's attitude toward Eastern Jewry was by and large more positive. He envied their naïveté (though he sometimes ridiculed it) and appreciated them for being an authentic religious community. They remained capable of a true belief in God and held to a sense of community—both of which were inaccessible to assimilated Western Jews like himself. The following excerpt from a letter to Max Brod shows how much Kafka actually hated his own social group:

Most young Jews who began to write German wanted to leave Jewishness behind them, and their fathers approved of this, but vaguely (this vagueness was what was outrageous to them). But with their posterior leap they were still glued to their father's Jewishness and with their wavering anterior leap they found no new ground. The ensuing despair became their inspiration (*Letters*, June 1921).

It is impossible within the context of this short survey to deal with, or even mention, all the nuances of Kafka's relationship with Judaism. Nevertheless, it is readily apparent from Kafka's letters and diaries over a period of years that he was preoccupied with the Jewish world and Jewish problems. Indeed, they are the focus of his personal and intellectual life.

II

As we have seen, there is a striking discrepancy between Kafka's letters and diaries, which betray an intense interest in Judaism, and his novels and stories, which lack any overt Jewish content. Characters such as Gregor Samsa, Karl Rossmann, Joseph K , and K. cannot be taken for Jews even in name. In the novel *Amerika*, which comes closer to realism than any other work by Kafka, the characters and their names are an international assortment, including: Germans (Rossmann, Brunelda, Therese Berchtold, Grete Mitzelbach, and Pollunder); Americans (Mac, Green); Hungarians (headwaiter Isbary); Russians (head doorman Feodor); Irish (Robinson); French (Delamarche, Renell); Slovaks (Butterbaum); and Italians (Giacomo). Only the student Mendel, who appears in chapter 7, has a Jewish name—perhaps his only Jewish trait. In this novel all of Europe has, as it were, been "exported" to America; it can thus be considered Euro-American, but certainly not Jewish.

It would seem, then, that Kafka led a double life. By his own testimony, in his daily life he felt himself to be intensely Jewish, in the spirit of the Amschel image of his diaries. In his literary opus, however, he completely repressed the world of his ancestors and never used the folkloristic and cultic material that he so studiously collected in his diaries. Kafka's work is almost *"judenrein"* at a time when authors such as Jakob Wassermann, Arthur Schnitzler, Stefan Zweig, and others who were far less self-consciously Jewish wrote so-called Jewish novels and dramas (Wassermann, *Die Juden von Zirndorf*; Schnitzler, *Die Weg ins Freie*; Zweig, *Jeremias*).

III

Nevertheless, there have been numerous critics—among them Max Brod, Hannah Arendt, Max Fürst, Walter H. Sokel, Hermann Pongs, and Walter Jens—who have tried to interpret Kafka's works within the context of Judaism. Most of their interpretations are feasible simply because Kafka's texts are so highly ambiguous, open, and often allegorical. Max Brod, for instance, summarizes his view of Kafka's Jewishness: "Kafka must be understood as a renewer of old Jewish religiosity, which demanded the whole man, the ethical deed and decision of the individual in the most secret part of his soul."[5] Sokel takes a different point of view: "What fascinated Kafka about Judaism above all, it seems, was its union of normally contradictory ideals—the ideal of radical asceticism, chastity and purity on the one hand, and the ideal of family life and generational continuity on the other. Kafka sought to obey both of these ideals and he was torn in this conflict."[6]

It is doubtful that the "ethical deed of the individual" or "ascetism and family life" can be called characteristic traits of Judaism. It is also difficult to discern them as the hallmarks of Kafka's life and work. Such attempts to interpret Kafka's works from the vantage point of Jewish theology and ethics are therefore not convincing. Looking to interpretations based on archetypes and on the sociology of literature seems to be a far more cogent approach. Hannah Arendt, for example, argues that Kafka's works hint at the failure of Jewish attempts to assimilate, and Pongs discovers in Kafka the archetype of Ahasuerus the wandering Jew. Both interpretations can be supported by analogies drawn between the autobiographical writings and the deeper substructure of the novels and short stories.

When one considers the significant role that Judaism and Jewish themes played in the "reality" of Kafka's day-to-day existence and in his interpretation of life as reflected in his diaries and letters, it seems reasonable to assume that these preoccupations are in some way manifest in the literary texts, albeit reappearing in transformed and transposed form, after having first undergone a process of repression. Our task, then, is to gain insight into the manner in which Kafka the artist deals with his Jewish experience.

IV

Lucien Goldmann's genetic-structuralist method offers a good base from which to launch this endeavor. Goldmann's basic hypothesis is "that the collective character of literary creation derives from the fact that the *structures* of the world of the work are homologous with the mental structures of certain social groups." However, "the reproduction of the immediate aspect of social reality and the collective consciousness in the work is, in general, all the more frequent when the writer possesses less creative force and is content to describe or recount his personal experience without transposing it."[7]

Kafka, one of the greatest writers of our century, tended to use "immediate aspects of social reality" less than most of his contemporaries. He transposed the social world so that the structure of the texts cannot be readily translated into socioeconomic terms. But the homology of the structure of his works with the social structure, that is, with the collective consciousness of a group, still exists.

The most obvious characteristic of Kafka's fictional world is its lack of temporality or locale. Standing outside of history and place, it is a world without extrafictional references, a world of abstractions. The characters inhabit a fictional never-never land, even when it is described in concrete detail. In *Amerika*, for example, the contours of the signified object are blurred so that the space of the American continent becomes unreal. Even historical time is not delimited: Kafka's universal world lacks nationality and history; its geography is uncertain. We may say that his works possess the bare minimum of Central European cultural semiotics required for communication: details such as clothes, gender, bureaucracy, and convention. Even these, however, are applied in a very erratic manner.

The homological method would thus be useful in trying to understand Kafka's world of man without history, man outside of time and space, who must be at home everywhere but who feels safe nowhere. This extrahistorical, homeless dimension seems to be homologous with the collective consciousness of the assimilated Diaspora Jew—one who severs his ties with the Jewish community but is never accepted by, nor admitted to, European society. He is cut off from the world of Jewish law without striking roots anywhere else. Kafka called this condition the absence of any firm "Jewish ground" (*Letters*, to Brod, 31 July 1922). Homology points to the consciousness of those uprooted Jewish loners who, despite their loneliness, actually formed a group of their own. The conditions of space without definition and time without history correspond to the situation of the Jews of the Diaspora: expelled from the safety of Jewish ritual time and the space of the shtetl into a timeless, spaceless existence.

Jens describes Kafka's image of space as "a Chagall world [in which] the scenery of Jewish folklore arises before the eyes of the reader."[8] But Kafka's abstract world is very different from Chagall's world of concrete Jewish symbols. Had Kafka used the material he collected in his diaries, he might have created something like the world of Chagall. But for the latter, the Eastern European milieu of the shtetl was an authentic reminiscence of his own youth; for Kafka it represented the alien world of his grandfather. Both attracted and repelled by that world, he never succeeded in making it his own.

Not only is the timeless, spaceless world of Kafka's fiction homologous with the collective consciousness of assimilated Diaspora Jewry, but also the basic situations of the plots correspond to the basic condition of the Jew in exile. This is especially striking in the novels.

The basic theme of the novel *Amerika* is the curse of exile: expulsion, migration, search for a secure haven, feelings of guilt, accusations, and, again, expulsion and migration. Karl Rossmann, the main character—driven from his home through no fault of his own—emigrates to an America that is more a symbol than an actual country: But even there he cannot find his place in the sun. He is an innocent victim who inevitably gravitates to those who persecute and dominate him. The social homology is fairly obvious: Eternal aimless migration is the quintessence of the unredeemed Diaspora.

This homology is even more apparent in *The Trial*. The questions that the main character asks himself (and, by implication, the reader) from the outset correspond again to the mental and social condition of the Jew. This is especially true of the novel's basic questions: Why is this "European" being persecuted? Of what is he guilty? Why does this innocent man accept the heavy burden of guilt and its consequences? Why is he actually put on trial? Why does he subject himself to this arbitrary law? All of this again points to a homology with "Jewish fate": impersonal, baseless persecution very often arising from the free-floating guilt and self-hatred of Western European Jews.

The Castle, too, has frequently been interpreted from this point of view. Pongs, for example, draws such a comparison: "The land surveyor K. who has first to create 'Earth, Air, Law' before he is able to survey, has too much of the wandering Jew, that Kafka felt himself to be."[9] It is also possible to interpret the land surveyor as a modern Ahasuerus, but this is still only another aspect of the broader Jewish problem. The formulation of the question and the mystery of the novel point toward the "Jewish condition" by means of homology. Why is this man never received in the castle and never admitted to the village community? Why is he condemned to the life of a pariah? Why does he have to fight for permission to stay in the village? Why can he approach the officials only indirectly? He is rejected by society because he is "different," but it is society that has differentiated him.

For Kafka, the problem of the Jew as rootless outcast is most effectively portrayed in an abstract manner—not called by its name—and thus open to metaphysical and deep psychological interpretations. (By contrast, when Max Frisch designated the race of his main character in *Andorra,* he committed "artistic treason," meaning a creative adaptation of the source of influence, against this notion.) Fundamentally, however, the situation described in Kafka's novels corresponds to the existential realities of the twentieth-century Jew. Even as Kafka transforms, transposes, and represses the psychosocial situation, one cannot avoid the fact that his themes of emigration, the struggle to obtain a residence permit, eternal wandering, persecution, and guilt feelings are all typical of the Jewish condition. The homologous relationship to the Jewish experience, therefore, cannot be denied, even though the "transformation" of this stark social reality deepened the meaning of the "fictional world" and made other interpretations possible.

v

At this point I would like to consider Kafka's relationship to Judaism from a completely different vantage point, that of Kafka and Hebrew literature. In particular, how did Hebrew authors receive Kafka and how did they understand him? Was there any mutual influence, and what differences and similarities exist? The analysis spans three generations of Hebrew authors, beginning with Kafka's contemporaries, who read him (if at all) in the German original.

Y. H. Brenner, whom Kafka read in the original Hebrew, was born in 1881 in Novi Mlini in the Ukraine and emigrated to Palestine in 1909, after living for a while in Polish Galicia and England. He was murdered by Arab marauders in 1921. As far as we know, he never read Kafka. In contrast to Kafka, who came from an assimilated Western European Jewish bourgeois background, Brenner came from the Orthodox Eastern European Jewish "proletariat." Whereas Brenner rebelled against the latter world, Kafka was profoundly attracted to it, remote though it was from his own experience. Brenner's characters, usually impotent and weak, move from the small towns of Eastern Europe to the big city, from the East to the West, from Europe to Palestine or America. Although

the locale changes, their fundamental nature remains unaltered—
even Palestine does not modify them (as in *Breakdown and Bereavement*, which Kafka read in 1923). The characters fail, on both the
ideological and the existential level, to realize their Zionist and
their personal ideals. They remain uprooted, alienated, and frightened. This fairly common social condition of shattered hope or
failed emigration found eloquent expression in Brenner's works.

There is no technical similarity between Brenner's works and
those of Kafka: Kafka was a great surrealist, Brenner a somewhat
good realist. The basic structures of their works are also different.
Even though Hebrew was at that time not yet a spoken tongue, but
only a literary language, Brenner's language and the world it described were firmly grounded in reality. Evolving as it was into language of a new society, Hebrew already had the capacity to depict
social realities. Kafka's world, by contrast, is static, representing a
kind of eternalization of the Diaspora situation. Regardless of his
despair, Brenner believed in the possibility of changing the Jewish
predicament. Kafka's letters reveal that he too was at times open to
Zionist ideas, but his works never reflect a belief that a Zionist future could change the Jewish condition.

Although, like Kafka, the Hebrew writers were full of doubts,
they still believed in the deeper meaning of history, in the viability
of secular messianism; and they were convinced that the Jewish nation had the right to demand for itself a place in history and space.
Even though Brenner's characters, like Kafka's, are tormented by
fear and feelings of guilt and persecution, their problems can still
be defined and solved within space and time. The differences,
therefore, between Kafka and most of his Hebrew-writing contemporaries—such as Brenner, Agnon, Shofman, and Steinberg—are
far greater than their similarities.

S. Y. Agnon, the Israeli writer who received the 1966 Nobel
Prize for Literature, was born in Buczacz, Galicia, in 1888, five
years after Kafka. (He died in Jerusalem in 1970.) Like Kafka, he
was a product of the Habsburg monarchy, but he was more Jewish
and less assimilated. Unlike Kafka, Agnon's mother tongues were
Hebrew and Yiddish, but German was his main European language and the primary source of his "general" culture. His formative years were spent as a young immigrant in Palestine (1908–1913)

and in Germany (1914–1924). Possibly the most important modern Hebrew writer, Agnon created a style of his own and a highly original narrative technique that constituted a unique contribution to the form of the modern novel. He probably read Kafka in the German original, although Hebrew translations were available as early as 1924. From the 1930s on, Agnon's works became increasingly surrealistic. Indeed numerous critics, including Baruch Kurzweil, Gabriel Moked, and Hillel Barzel, compared him with Kafka, although he himself always rejected this comparison, claiming that he had only occasionally read him and that his "roots" were very different. My analysis is based on a phenomenological approach; whether Agnon read Kafka or not is insignificant.

Most of Agnon's characters are Jews who, having lost their faith, are desperately searching for God and a true belief. Agnon employed the talmudic style of the sages, thus creating ironic contrasts between form and content. His work poses a basic situation that is, once again, quite similar to some aspects of Kafka's works, as will be elucidated in the following discussion of his novel *A Guest for the Night* (1939) and his novella *Ad henna* (Unto Here, 1952).

The novel, written before 1939, prophesies the destruction of European Jewry. Set in the late 1920s, it depicts the creeping decay of the Jewish community of Szybuscz (Polish Galicia), a small town whose collective fate is revealed in the stories of the lives of its numerous inhabitants. And, in turn, the fate of each is determined by the fate of the community. World War I, only recently ended, weighs heavily on the daily life of these people; and the future looms as a source of immense anxiety and uncertainty. Since it is structured around individual lives, the novel is in one sense fragmentary. Coherence is provided, however, by the common fate of the town and the unifying perspective of the narrator, a "narrating witness" returned from Palestine to his childhood home. The novel's form reflects the impossibility of a "classic plot," which, according to Aristotle, is coherent and unified, in a world in which man is the helpless victim of overpowering forces. The visions of terror and the nightmares depicted in this novel constitute a presentiment of approaching catastrophe, a vignette of the sad fate of a generation facing extinction. Agnon is unquestionably a master of portraying the dissolution, decay, and attrition of shtetl life.

His point of departure is the basic situation of the Jews. Given the similarities of mood, theme, and structure in Agnon's work to those in Kafka's, one may assume that Agnon was possibly influenced by him. (The obvious differences between these two master writers will be discussed subsequently.)

The novella *Ad henna* also bears a certain resemblance to Kafka's works. It is a first-person account of the life story of a lonely bachelor poet set during World War I in Berlin and Leipzig, where the protagonist tries to save old books. He witnesses the activities of war profiteers and the anguish of parents who have lost their sons in the war. (He himself takes home his landlady's seriously wounded son.) This stranger in a suicidal land is driven from rented room to rented room, the motifs of migration and uncertainty being basic to the structure of the novella. Although the main character appears to be a man without a home and native land, he has come from Palestine and ultimately returns there, the land functioning as a kind of deus ex machina. This story of homelessness is thus set against a background in which there exists the possibility of a secure haven. The following passage conveys Agnon's tone and technique:

And yet I fell asleep and slumbered. Where from, however, do I know that I slept? From the dream that I dreamt. But what did I dream? I dreamt that there was a great war in the world and that I had to go to war. I took our oath before God that I, when I return from this war safe and sound, would make him, who first comes towards me in front of my house when I come from the war, an offering. I returned safe and sound and lo! I myself came towards me![10]

This passage is a sad parody of the biblical tale of Jephthah's daughter (Judges 11). The grotesqueness of this reinterpretation derives from the reality that in this war there are no survivors. The living as well as the dead are victims of an impersonal situation. This excerpt therefore expresses the main motif not only of this novella but also of the aforementioned novel. The dream structure of the passage is a typical feature of Agnon's work, by which the narrator can depart from his description of geographical space and historical time in order to give an interpretive understanding of the outside world. The dream fulfills a metaphoric function, commenting on reality from the point of view of an inner vision. Thus, both the sense of fundamental anxiety and the plot dealing with the wanderings of an uprooted character—as well as the "technique of displacement" (dream technique)—suggest a similarity between Agnon and Kafka.

Their differences, however, are greater than their similarities. Whereas Kafka describes his abstract *universal world* in a detailed and concrete manner, Agnon, in his *surrealist* works, "transforms" a concrete, historical world. Jens's comparison with Chagall therefore applies to Agnon's structure rather than to Kafka's. Agnon did not need to make notes on the folklore and myths of everyday Jewish life and culture; they were part of his cultural heritage. Mythological and legendary allusions, as in the case of Jephthah's daughter, were the collective symbols of his people. Although he mourned the decline of the shtetl and described the new world in a grotesque fashion, Agnon never left the solid ground of history and Jewish culture. His characters are embedded—via allusions and quotes—in the cultural language of the holy texts of Judaism.

Even though his world and times appear to be godless, God exists, so to speak, in his language; and even though despair dominates the foreground, a shadow of hope still hovers in the background. In the two works discussed here, the narrator leaves the foreground of history—the shtetl or Germany, both in a sense accursed—to escape to the promised land, where a historical solution of the existential misery is possible. Similarly, Agnon's "Israeli novels" are neither naïve nor particularly optimistic. In these works dreams and ideologies also fail, but again in the background there exists a different historical option. Agnon's attitude toward history then is essentially positive (notwithstanding that it has often been seen as ambivalent).

Kafka transformed the Jewish condition into a new art form. By turning the need to stand outside of history into an absolute virtue, he thereby opened it up to the most varied interpretations. If Agnon, so to speak, got stuck inside Judaism, this situation can also be seen as a virtue, for it created the possibility of a rich intertextual relationship between his works and the treasures of Jewish culture.

Thus Kafka entered the realm of world literature while Agnon has always been seen as an integral part of Jewish literature, the tradition that stretches from the Bible and the Talmud to this day.

VI

With Hebrew translations of Kafka's works available since 1924, the younger, Israeli-born generation of authors read them (if at all) in Hebrew (or possibly English) translations. For such writers born in the 1920s, Kafka was an enigma. Some not only read him but also tried to imitate him, without success, however, since for them locale and history were always crucial. Furthermore, they were much more conscious of their Israeli existence than of the Jewish past in the Diaspora, toward which they were, at best, very ambivalent. They detested what they considered to be the typical characteristics of Diaspora Jewry: anxiety, paranoia, fear of authority, eternal wandering—an attitude that was fostered by the new Israeli education, which had set itself to the task of changing the Jewish mentality and revolutionizing Jewish life with the motto: "New people on an old land." In such a social milieu, the possibility of understanding Kafka was minimal.

This distance can also be seen from the themes of representative works of this period. The most important writers of this generation, S. Yizhar (b. 1916) and Moshe Shamir (b. 1921), wrote heroic novels. Shamir's *Melekh basar va-dam* (The King of Flesh and Blood) is a historical novel set in the time of the Hasmoneans. The novel's hero (I use this term quite consciously), the cruel king and conqueror Alexander Yannai, is treated quite critically, but he and his antagonists still remain romantic figures. Kafka's ironic anti-heroes are, of course, virtual antitheses of these characters. Whereas Kafka expressed the postnationalistic despair of the twentieth century, Shamir's works are permeated by a late romantic nationalism that can be found in other literatures of the early nineteenth century. Thus the sociological and psychological attitudes of the first generation of Israeli-born writers made it difficult for them to understand and assimilate Kafka. The absolute absence of his influence in their

works emphasizes the significance of his influence on later generations of Israeli authors.

Toward the end of the 1950s, Israel underwent a spiritual revolution that paved the way for a reappraisal of Kafka. Important social
factors changed the mood and attitudes not only of the elite but
also of a significant part of the youth. With a decline in romantic
idealism there emerged on the Israeli literary scene a new generation that included survivors of the Holocaust who had come to
Israel after World War II. These writers, scarred by their terrible
past, had a self-consciousness as well as an attitude toward Judaism and life in Israel that were completely different from those of
their predecessors, and their experiences influenced their Israeli-
born literary peers. Unlike the earlier generation their life no longer
rested on a given existential or ideological basis. They shattered the
naïve, collective belief in the state. History and territory—as well
as Judaism—were no longer clearly defined matters. This skep-
ticism and uncertainty was conducive to a fresh consideration of
Kafka.

The influence of the Holocaust on a new understanding of
Kafka is, of course, not restricted to Israeli literature. Visions of
persecution and accusation and unexplainable feelings of anxiety
no longer belonged to the realm of nightmares but had become
reality. History itself had endowed Kafka's works with concrete
meaning, turning their "surrealism" into "realism," almost as if the
gaps in his texts had been filled by this monstrous collective experience. For today's readers these works take on a prophetic quality:
Paradoxically, Kafka found his way back to history because reality
turned out to be more grotesque and more surrealistic than even
his fictional nightmares.

At this point I would like to mention two younger Israeli writers
who were particularly influenced by Kafka, one a survivor of the
Holocaust, the other Israeli-born—Aharon Appelfeld and A. B.
Yehoshua, both of whom acknowledge their debt to Kafka.

Appelfeld was born in 1932 in Tchernowitz, Bukovina. He experienced World War II as a child, surviving its atrocities in Eastern
Europe and coming to Israel in 1947. His first collection of short
stories—which, significantly, bears the title *Ashan* (Smoke)—was

published in 1962, followed by a number of short stories, novellas, and novels, some of them translated into various European languages. Appelfeld writes of being deeply influenced by Kafka;[11] nevertheless, despite his use of allegory (*Badenheim 1939*), his works, by contrast, are always inextricably bound up with locale and time. His characters, mostly survivors of the Holocaust, cannot extricate themselves from their traumatic past. Neither Europe nor Israel can provide a sense of security, for they are persecuted not by an authority but by their own past, which, regardless of where they settle, never allows them to find inner peace. The post-Holocaust world can offer these refugees neither safe shelter nor redemption.

The short story "To the Isle of St. George," the tale of a man who survived the death camps and has been on the run ever since, may serve as an example. The very character traits that helped him survive the camps make it impossible for him to manage in a normal world. Constantly involved in black market affairs, fleeing from one country to another to save his skin, he moves to Germany, Italy, and Palestine; but the same cyclic plot repeats itself time and again to determine his fate. This cyclic syndrome is very close to Kafka's notion of repetitious fate conveyed by the plots of his works. Finally, Appelfeld's hero travels by small boat to the Mediterranean island, St. George, whose only inhabitant is a Christian monk preparing for a pilgrimage to the Holy Land. On this island, the restless man hopes to escape his fate.

The cyclic plot, the paranoia of the anti-hero, and the allegorical hints are reminiscent of Kafka (and Agnon). But Appelfeld restores his characters to history because he is acutely aware of living within history and believes that the quintessence of history can be portrayed by concrete components rather than by means of the abstractions that Kafka employed to reach this aim. In Appelfeld's works Hebrew literature becomes Jewish again, depicting *Jews* as persecuted victims; the Israeli romantic heroism only serves as an antithetical background. From the vantage point of literary history, Appelfeld's importance lies in the fact that his works are the very antithesis of those of his precursors, Shamir and Yizhar. The conscious choice of Kakfa and Agnon[12] as literary models helped Appelfeld to formulate his new anti-heroic approach in which Jews are the victims of history.

A. B. Yehoshua, born in Jerusalem in 1936, has also been influenced by both Kafka and Agnon. He published his first book, a collection of stories entitled *Mot ha-zaken* (The Death of the Old Man) in 1963. Since then he has published a few collections of short stories, novels, and dramas, almost all of which have been translated into various European languages. His relationship to Kafka may be even more conscious than Appelfeld's;[13] certainly it is more "literary" and technical. Yehoshua also uses the model of Kafka to overcome the heroic narratives of his predecessors, which he considers common and trivial. The surrealistic technique serves him to come to grips with the complexities of his environment and his self. Yehoshua was one of the first young authors to point to the dark side of Israeli heroism and Zionist idealism; that is, the "old man on the new land" is the dark shadow of the "new man on the old land," as he suggests in his early stories. Yehoshua felt that the Jewish past had stood far too long in the background of Israel's artistic and social concerns when it should actually be the center of attention. His characters are scared, lazy, hysterical, passive, and at the same time aggressive, which makes them very different from those of his precursors. His plots tend toward the absurd and the bizarre, his style, a strange mixture of lyrical and grotesque elements.

One of Yehoshua's earliest short stories, "The Flood of the Sea," is so Kafkaesque that it does not even constitute what literary theory calls "artistic treason." It tells the story of a prison warden on an island that is flooded by torrential rains. The warden finally releases all the prisoners while he and his dogs stay behind in the prison. As the flood waters rise, the warden reads the "Book of Rules." This story, in which time and space are not defined, is reminiscent of Kafka's *Penal Colony*. Some critics have even interpreted it as a political allegory of Israeli life. What is especially remarkable, however, is the strong death wish expressed in this story, which stands in contrast to the exuberant will to live of the first generation. This contrast is a recurring theme in Yehoshua's short stories and in his novels, *The Lover* (1977) and *A Late Divorce* (1982). However, to the extent that Yehoshua concerns himself with Israeli social life, he commits "artistic treason" in adapting Kafka's tradition to the contemporary scene. In his second collection of novellas,

Facing the Forests (1968), he portrays the immediate environment much more concretely than he had in his previous works, although the structure is still influenced by Kafka and Agnon, tending toward the absurd and the grotesque. One character, for example, an aging bachelor and eternal student, becomes a forester to escape the city, only to witness a huge forest fire kindled by an Arab. Other figures are an impotent engineer suffering from cancer, an aging poet and his retarded son, and yet another bachelor who looks after the son of his former lover. The plots of these stories always end in catastrophe. Fear of dying bound up with a wish to die are, as mentioned above, their main theme, but these stories also carry a social message.

Accordingly, Yehoshua's works, which utilize Kafka's basic themes of anxiety and persecution, also often commit "artistic treason" against Kafka's methods by employing the social realities of Israel as the material and the background of his stories. Yehoshua openly opposes his predecessors by portraying the darker aspects of the "old Jewish man in a new land."

Kafka, the cosmopolitan whose works are classics of world literature, bore the Hebrew name Amschel, after his maternal grandfather. Thus the two sides of the man. His deep influence on Hebrew literature reunited him with his tradition, which moved and appealed to him and with which he conducted a continuous and intense dialogue until his very last days. Even in one of his last diary entries, in June 1922, he dealt with Blüher's anti-Semitism.[14] Earlier, in September 1917, he had summed up his urge for faith and religious return: "I would put myself in death's hands, though, Remnant of a faith. Great Day of Atonement."[15]

NOTES

1. Franz Kafka, *The Diaries of Franz Kafka*, ed. Max Brod, trans. Martin Greenberg, vol. 1 (New York: Schocken Books, 1948), 25 Dec. 1911; *Tagebücher 1910–1923*, ed. Max Brod (New York: Schocken Books, 1948–1949), 197.

2. Franz Kafka, *Dearest Father*, trans. Ernst Kaiser and Eithne Wilkins (New York: Schocken Books, 1954), 171–172.

3. Kafka, *Diaries*, 8 Jan. 1914; *Tagebücher*, 11.
4. Franz Kafka, *Letters to Friends, Family, and Editors*, ed. Max Brod (New York: Schocken Books, 1977), June 1921; *Briefe 1902–1924*, ed. Max Brod (Frankfurt a. M.: Fischer, 1958), 337.
5. Max Brod, *Franz Kafkas Glauben und Lehre* (Winterthur: Mondial-verlag, 1948), 81–82.
6. Walter H. Sokel, "Franz Kafka as a Jew," *Leo Baeck Institute Year Book* 18 (1973): 238.
7. Lucien Goldmann, *Towards a Sociology of the Novel* (London: Tavistock Publications, 1975), 159.
8. Walter Jens, "Ein Jude Namens Kafka," in *Statt einer Literaturgeschichte*, 7th ed. (Pfullingen: Neske, 1978), 299.
9. Hermann Pongs, *Franz Kafka: Dichter des Labyrinths* (Heidelberg: Rothe, 1960), 83. See also Max Brod, *Franz Kafka: A Biography* (New York: Schocken Books, 1960), especially 187–191.
10. S. Y. Agnon, *Ad henna* (Unto Here) (Tel Aviv: Schocken, 1952), 76.
11. Aharon Appelfeld, *Masot be-guf rishon* (Essays in First Person Singular) (Jerusalem: The Jewish Agency, 1979), 15–18.
12. Ibid., 101–107.
13. Gershon Shaked, "Yair ve-etsim: S. Y. Agnon ke-'maaviv' mercazi be-toldot ha-siporet ha-ivrit" (The Forest and the Tree: S. Y. Agnon as the Major Literary Transformator in Modern Hebrew Literature). *Ha-universitah* 25 (Spring 1981): 12–18. A. B. Yehoshua has published a critical interpretation of one of Kafka's stories, "An Attempt to Describe the Insect: A Psychoanalytic Interpretation of 'Metamorphosis' by F. Kafka" (in Hebrew), *Moznayim* 58 (1984–1985): 9–13.
14. Kafka, *Diaries*, 16 June 1922; *Tagebücher*, 23.
15. Kafka, *Diaries*, 28 Sept. 1917; *Tagebücher*, 187.

the Wassermann case

I

Der Fall Maurizius (*The Maurizius Case*) by Jakob Wassermann, first published in 1928, made its Jewish author famous in its day and is currently being reread widely in the German-speaking world.[1]

Wassermann called himself a "German Jew," in contradistinction to a "Jewish Jew,"[2] although his lifelong wish—never to be realized—was to belong to the latter category. Today the work of this assimilated German Jew, who died in 1934 before the destruction of German Jewry, invites investigation of the specifically Jewish dimension of his experience. He and his contemporaries—Franz Kafka and Arthur Schnitzler, Karl Kraus and Stefan Zweig, Franz Werfel and Max Brod—have of course not changed. But we, the potential readers, have. And it is in terms of our changing perspectives, our cumulative store of personal and group experiences, that literary works maintain an ongoing existence. The story of the character Waremme-Warschauer or, if you will, that of Wassermann, is now being filtered through the experience of our own, post-Holocaust generation.

II

Let us first consider Wassermann's spiritual autobiography, *Mein Weg als Deutscher und Jude* (*My Life as German and Jew*), first published in 1921, and a collection of essays and autobiographical sketches, called *Lebensdienst* (Life of Service), published in 1928.

These two personal documents reveal the tragic figure of a de-racinated Jew, out of touch with his Jewishness, portrayed with a vehemence beside which other descriptions of uprootedness found in Hebrew and Yiddish literature appear mild in tone. His writings interweave intense self-hatred and equally intense self-love, a burning desire to belong to the Jewish people and a burning desire to cut that Gordian knot. Wassermann is cruel in his criticism of Heine the Jew, who sold his Judaism for a mess of pottage and then poured his venomous bitterness out upon Germany. But his hatred for Heine betrays a secret bond between the two (*My Life*, pp. 95–101). Like Heine, he both loved and hated the German nation, and, like him, he was a foreigner in its midst. Repulsed by the idea of conversion, he suffered unwillingly the heritage of his father. His conscious relation to his national and spiritual foundations, the components of his psychic world, is infinitely ambivalent. As he wrote to Martin Buber in the 1920s:

We know them, my dear friend, we know them very well, and we suffer on account of them, and because of the thousands who are called "modern Jews," who chip away at all the foundations, since they themselves have no foundations, discarding everything they achieved yesterday and fouling to-day what they loved the day before; they, who take pleasure in treachery, who make a kind of ornament of baseness, and for whom negation is an aim (*Lebensdienst*, p. 176).

On the other hand, he admired that manifestation of Judaism that he called "Jewish Judaism," as opposed to what he called "German Judaism." A letter to Buber describes a figure that contrasts with the modern Jew, and he sings the praises of those Eastern Jews who were also the cynosure of Buber's eyes:

The Jew, in contrast, whom I call Oriental—is naturally a symbolic figure; I might even have called him the fulfilled or the legitimate heir . . . since a noble consciousness, a blood consciousness links him with the past, and an enormous responsibility obligates him to the future; and he cannot betray himself for he is a revealed essence. . . . He knows his sources, and he lives with the matriarchs, he reposes and he creates; they are the ever wandering people who cannot be changed (*Lebensdienst*, p. 177).

These words are not merely a paean to the Jew from the other side of the dark mountains to the east (Does he mean Eastern Europe? the Middle East?) but also an analysis of the "Jewish condition." Cosmopolitan Jewry—detached and unconnected, empty and profane—is ashamed of its Jewishness; it is the external Judaism of the Wassermanns. On the other hand, the Judaism that dwells with the matriarchs—that retains all its enormous, irrational power—is the inner Judaism of the Wassermanns. Judaism bereft of obligations and responsibilities, with no homeland, is contrasted with a Judaism whose past obligates it, proudly, toward its existence and its future.

Thus, Wassermann is contemptuous of his own mask, the camouflage of the "German Jew" who vacillates between these extremes, who is nothing but an uprooted, tainted cosmopolitan. He idealizes the hidden self that connects him with the source of his visions and the wellspring of his creative activity—the world of the Jewish matriarchs.[3] That the vacillation pained him is made clear in the memoirs: "Why, then, were we still Jews, and what did it mean? This question became ever more urgent for me; and no one could answer it" (*Mein Weg*, p. 15; *My Life*, p. 17). Perhaps that very puzzlement was the source of his admiration for those Jews who were not self-conscious about their identity but lived their own essence as something self-evident. He envied their confident pride. Like Moses and the promised land, he saw authentic Jewry before him but could not enter. He was enthralled by Jewish pride because of the humiliation he suffered at being rejected by cultured German society, the very society that he longed to penetrate. "Emancipation," says his hero Waremme-Warschauer, "is a cunning invention to deprive the repressed of any pretext for complaining (*Maurizius*, p. 310). He was well aware that Jewish emancipation in Germany was illusory, that he was merely a tolerated presence (*My Life*, p. 11). All his life he sought acceptance as a true German, but he remained an outsider. As much as he sought the sacred vestments of a German author did he suffer from the knowledge that he was always regarded as an interloper by his broad readership:

They would not concede that I too bore the color and stamp of German life; they would not let the kindred principle approach them. Its unconscious, inherent elements they considered deliberately thought out, born of Jewish ingenuity, Jewish shrewdness in pose and misrepresentation, the dangerous Jewish power to delude and ensnare (*My Life*, pp. 146–147).

Wassermann never found consolation for his ostracism among his own people. His loneliness never became a source of pride but remained a source of suffering. While he complained about the Jewish mentality, in which feelings of superiority and persecution are intermingled, that mentality actually characterized Wassermann himself. Disgust (or perhaps fear) toward the gentile was typical of the group mentality of deeply rooted Jews; petty self-denigration that admired a rabbi more, as Wassermann testifies of himself, for having a *blond* beard than for his virtues typified the assimilationists (*My Life*, p. 14).[4] However, not even his attitude toward blondness is unequivocal. His fiercely negative remarks about the German people bespeak the frustration of the unrequited lover.

The remarks with which, in 1921, he summed up his attitude toward the German and Jewish peoples express not only deep personal hurt at the way the Germans related to him but also what today sounds like a nightmarish prophecy of doom: "Vain to adjure the nation of poets and thinkers in the name of its poets and thinkers. Every prejudice one thinks disposed of breeds a thousand others, as carrion breeds maggots" (*My Life*, p. 226). He concludes: "Vain to live for them and die for them. They say: He is a Jew" (*Mein Weg*, pp. 125–126; *My Life*, p. 227). Wassermann has no illusions. Knowing that there is no way to bridge his Jewishness and his Germanness, he remains like a bone stuck in the throat of history, a bone that can be neither spat out nor swallowed.

III

In comparison with the alienation of Wassermann, the deracination of the Hebrew writers Berdyczewski, Brenner, Gnessin, Shofman, Agnon, and Berkowitz seems profoundly rooted. Wassermann is torn between a Jewish consciousness with a stigma attached to his ethnic origin and the fact that German is his one and only language of expression, an unbridgeable gap that brought him to his fundamental experience of the Jewish heritage as an ugly, debilitating hump on his back. To a degree, the Hebrew writers of the day share his fascination with the forces of evil, spiritual and national; his feeling of isolation; his sense of the dreadful injustice in the situation of the Jew, in particular the German Jew. Disgust with the Jewish heritage can be found in Brenner; longings for "the other side of the river" are far from uncommon in Berdyczewski's work; and the feeling of isolation is not absent from Shofman's army stories. But all these problems are far more intense in Wassermann's writings since, in contrast to the Hebrew (or Yiddish) writers, he has no linguistic matrix, no means of expression save that of the culture that repudiates him. Unlike them, he has no means to vindicate his Jewish existence, as the Hebrew and Yiddish authors could do simply by virtue of their language. Wassermann rebels against this forced inclusion in the community of Job. Condemned to serve a sentence despite his innocence, he cries out for vindication as a human being.

IV

Wassermann perceived his life as a kind of punishment for the sin (that he never committed) of being a Jew, and he felt that he personally had to pay for the collective guilt of his origins by experiencing the tortures of the Jewish question.[5] It is therefore illuminating to look for the roots of his literary works in this personal anguish.

I shall begin by commenting on the general structure of *Maurizius*, which was to be the first part of a trilogy describing the development of a young German, Etzel Andergast. The two following parts were *Etzel Andergast* (1930; English, 1932) and *Joseph Kerkhovens dritte Existenz* (Joseph Kerkhoven's Third Existence, 1934). All three of the novels were commercially quite successful: Wassermann was highly skilled at constructing plots that would appeal to the common reader. But the professional literati accused him of pandering to the vulgar horde.[6] Predictably, Wassermann himself was uneasy on this score, seeking to distinguish himself as a "true author" rather than a mere "scribbler" and thus, because of his defensive position, casting redoubled suspicion upon his artistic sincerity (*Lebensdienst*, pp. 314–315, 502ff.).

The Maurizius Case was what one might call a second-rate suspense plot, in which the young Andergast reexamines the verdict obtained by his father, the state prosecutor, in the Maurizius case some eighteen years previously. Maurizius had been convicted of murdering his wife. Young Andergast, suspecting that there had been a miscarriage of justice, runs away from home to find and interrogate the state's witness, Waremme-Warschauer. Approaching him anonymously, Andergast ultimately makes him admit that he lied on the witness stand—the murder was not committed by the accused but, rather, by the accused's mistress, his wife's sister. Moreover, it happens that the murderer was also the mistress of the state's witness.

The son is motivated in his quest by a desire to loosen the grip of his father's authority; indeed, it becomes progressively weaker as the son draws closer to the truth. The father, in response to the son's flight, comes to grapple with the case anew and realizes that he was responsible for condemning an innocent man. After the victim has served eighteen years in prison, the former prosecutor obtains a pardon for him, though without exculpating him. But when the son returns bearing proof of Maurizius's complete innocence, he is too late: Maurizius, finding that he has no chance of being reabsorbed into the life of society, has committed suicide. Etzel's efforts were in vain; but the father, whose authority has been totally undermined, collapses in the face of his son's accusations.

The novel is framed by the story of the struggle between father and son. In addition, two subplots throw light on the affair. The accused and the witness, in their two confessions, assume the roles of primary protagonists, to the extent that we no longer know whether the main burden of the plot concerns the conflict between the generations or the revelation of the world of the "accused." Each element makes its own contribution to the whole structure.

The different units of the novel evidence many parallels in plot and theme. There is, for example, an underlying similarity in the relations between fathers and sons—in the relations between Andergast and his son, between Maurizius and his father, and between Andergast and Waremme-Warschauer, who regards young Mohl (the name that Etzel uses in his contacts with him) as his spiritual offspring. In a second instance, the somewhat cruel attitude taken by the elder Andergast to his divorced wife and her lover is paralleled by his relation to the entire Maurizius affair. Also conspicuous is the inner parallel between the various seekers of justice: Etzel; the prison warden, Klakusch, who commits suicide after he becomes convinced that Maurizius was convicted despite his innocence; and the girl Melitta, who also does battle with her strict employers for the sake of social justice. These correspondences emerge in the smallest details; for example, both Maurizius and Waremme-Warschauer have daughters whom they have never seen.

The narrative structure of the novel, based on interchanges between the advancing plot and the various digressions that impede its progress toward its tragic climax, creates an outer tension. At the same time, the structure of parallels creates an inner pattern, suggesting that the world of the novel is governed by a single law. The characters similarly play dual roles and thereby shed light on the German Jewish agony. They are individuals who set the overt suspense plot in motion and lay it bare; and they are also significant (mythic) elements whose relations with each other provide the hidden meaning of the novel.

v

The deep structure—which gives the narrative its inner meaning and is revealed by means of the outer plot—is unconscious. Wassermann, the "German Jew," dressed most of his writings in the cloak of universality (with the exception, perhaps, of the early *Die Juden von Zirndorf*), and in this he was generally highly successful. Jewish problems, therefore, are only implicit in his works.

He himself claimed in "A Remark on *The Maurizius Case*," that the idea of justice was at the center of his work and had always been, in his opinion, the nexus of his world view.[7] Moreover, in the concluding dramatic dialogue between the father and his son, which precipitates the climax and determines it, the son declares that nothing in the world is more important than justice (*Maurizius*, p. 540): Justice, not authority, is the measure of all things. Nevertheless, although the problem of justice is clearly a central theme in Wassermann's work, it does not stand on its own.

Wassermann observes the human condition from four vantage points in the novel: (1) man as an accuser, an official prosecutor; (2) man as a prosecutor in the name of absolute justice; (3) man as an innocent victim of circumstances that find reinforcement and justification in the principles of official justice (Maurizius); and (4) man as the accused and persecuted, standing before the tribunal of absolute justice (Waremme-Warschauer, the Jew, and to a certain extent the father himself).

The mythical system that is only barely concealed behind that tissue of relationships has been the recurrent nightmare of Jewish life for generations: the injustice committed against "the son of God," the father of Christianity, who bore the sufferings of the world and was crucified because of the "betrayal" of the Jews—and the repercussions of that act. Waremme-Warschauer is without doubt an incarnation of Judas Iscariot, the eternal Jew, and an eternal wanderer, upon whose forehead the mark of Cain is visible. Waremme-Warschauer did not sell his friend for thirty pieces of silver, but his betrayal is an expression of the struggle between the Jew and the gentile. Maurizius is a present-day servant of God, who suffered because he loved and loved because he suffered. Andergast the elder is a kind of Pontius Pilate. He sets himself up in judgment over human fate only to find that the principle of formal, official justice cannot withstand the test of criticism: He is left with blood on his hands. His son Etzel, a spokesman for justice, attempts to bring light to the mythical darkness, to tear off the mask of lies (which is a tangle of evil instincts), and to restore justice to its pristine purity. The problem of justice is anchored in Wassermann's own feelings of guilt and his sense that he was being punished for his Jewish identity: "Sometimes I felt as if I were paying off my share of the guilt and odium attached to Jewry."[8] That experience determines to a considerable extent the two categories of experience in this novel: that of the victim and that of the man who demands justice.

If the accusation is baseless, then the accused—the victim—must seek out justice and truth. Etzel's search for truth, his failure and his success, can be understood in that light. He realizes that the judicial struggle had not been waged over moral issues of good and evil, justice and injustice. Rather, the trial revealed a conflict of instinctual desires. Waremme-Warschauer had fought for his life; Maurizius, for his love; the father, for his authority. Etzel Andergast's error, perhaps also the source of his power, lay in his innocent seeking to elevate the principle of absolute justice above the drives and instincts that motivate human beings. The dialectic of conflict between the spiritual principle of pure justice and the dark instincts that threaten it can be seen as an analogue of conflict between father and son. As in Kafka, its roots lie in the tension and conflicts that characterize the Jewish condition.[9]

Tension between fathers and sons is a typical feature of Jewish literature in German. It is no coincidence that it was Freud who found the dramatic conflict between the generations to be at the center of the human psyche, just as it is no coincidence that in Kafka's works the relation of the son to the father, which is central to his work, manifests itself in the form of *the law*. The attempt to rebel against the world of the father (see his famous *Letter to His Father*) is a fitting expression of the Jewish situation at the beginning of the twentieth century. The fathers in the world of Freud, Kafka, and Wassermann are secularizations of the Jewish conception of God, an angry and jealous God who is revealed through the law and who demands absolute obedience of his children. The incarnation of divine authority in the figure of the father, or the attribution of divine powers to the human incarnation of the God figure, issued from Kafka's portrayal of K., a man who is subjugated by an authority he can neither understand nor investigate. While Kafka had no positive feeling for the heritage inherent in the acceptance of patriarchal authority, he could not free himself from its yoke.[10]

The Jewish divinity who shapes the fate of the Jewish individual was incomprehensible to Kafka; arbitrariness, in his view, destined the individual for ostracism and exile. His own father, who determined his son's fate as a Jew and an outcast, and the divine father of the universe, who destined the Jewish nation to exile among seventy fierce wolves, were identical. Kafka demanded of both that they deal justly and that the judgment leveled against him—for no other reason but sheer biological chance—be rescinded. He demanded that his suffering be given meaning and that his soul, which committed no transgression, receive justice; but his demand went unanswered, leaving his heroes frustrated in their quest, crushed in their struggle. The Jewish condition, that of the innocent man who is condemned, persecuted and sentenced without a trial, is an extreme expression of the modern human condition. Kafka's works, therefore, speak to contemporary readers.

Wassermann does not raise issues to the high metaphysical plane so characteristic of Kafka. His works anchor the human condition in the social situation—at once their strength and their weakness. Etzel Andergast frees himself from (or rebels against) his father's authority and reveals its nakedness. Authority and righteousness are not identical; authority unaccompanied by justice is vacuous. Once the son reaches this understanding the father must inevitably collapse. In its belief in an authority beyond authority, Wassermann's outlook is more naïve than Kafka's. Yet Wassermann recognizes that the discovery of the principle of justice is not likely to bring redemption to the world. Justice came to light, as the Jew Waremme-Warschauer had prophesied (*Maurizius*, pp. 488–489) only after the righteous victim, Maurizius, had already taken his own life. Spiritual vindication is one thing; physical redemption another.

A significant indication of the Jewish and personal source of the novel's theme is to be found in the analogous story that preceded the Maurizius case in the life of Etzel Andergast: A Jewish boy was ostracized by his gentile friends who uncovered in him an apparent moral flaw. Etzel, convinced of his friend's innocence, sets out to find the truth and discovers that the real guilty party (one of the other boys) had sneaked his own pornographic pictures into the Jewish boy's desk at school in order to accuse him falsely. That incident, which derives from Wassermann's own personal experience (*My Life*, pp. 59–60), is a small-scale blood libel. Etzel has laid bare its essential nature: The blind hatred that preceded the act was given a legal basis by falsely staining the Jew's name (*Maurizius*, pp. 132–136). The analogy casts light upon the main plot, the story of a "blood libel" in which Etzel Andergast discovers the true guilty parties, but in vain! The German girl who murdered her sister continues her calm, bourgeois life; Maurizius kills himself. The realm of dark instincts is exposed, but nothing changes in the essential structure of the world. The blood libel can be repeated as if it had never before happened.

VI

In the character of Waremme-Warschauer the Jewish problem appears, painfully undisguised. Wassermann writes that he conceived the figure in the gloomy environment of Chicago (*Lebensdienst,* pp. 61–70), and, indeed, Waremme-Warschauer's description of American life is one of the best passages in the novel (*Maurizius,* pp. 333–342). But his remarks about Judaism and the Jews are far more excoriating, echoing as they do Wassermann's own confessions in *Mein Weg* (*My Life,* pp. 87–92). Waremme-Warschauer must be the Jewish "shadow" that pursued Wassermann all his life. It is Wassermann himself whom Waremme-Warschauer describes when he tells his own story to young Mohl (i.e., Etzel):

I was the child of Jewish parents who were living in the second generation of bourgeois freedom. My father had not yet arrived at the consciousness that the condition of apparent equality was actually only one of toleration. People like my father, otherwise a splendid man, were religiously and socially up in the air. They no longer had the old faith, they refused to accept a new one, that is to say Christianity, partly for good reasons, partly for bad. The Jew wants to be a Jew. What is a Jew? No one can explain this with complete satisfaction. My father was proud of being emancipated. Emancipation is a cunning device, it removes the pretext for complaint from the suppressed. Society excludes him; the State excludes him; the physical ghetto has become a mental and moral one; one sticks out one's chest and calls it emancipation (*Maurizius,* pp. 309–310).

Waremme-Warschauer sprang out of the dreadful darkness of his Jewishness as a kind of enormous, volatile golem, the embodiment of all the vital powers of the nation. Like Wassermann his creator, he tries to make his way to the German world, while severing the roots that bind him to his childhood. He fantasizes a gentile childhood and gentile parents for himself and wears the mask of the ultra-German. As the spokesman for militant Germanness, he wins a respectable place for himself in the alien society. He employs any means and is prepared to pay any price. To prove himself is the highest aim, justifying everything; but the more he tries to distance himself from Jewish existence, the more he returns and wallows in its depths. He is never reconciled to his Jewishness; it dominates him against his will. Finally, the man who had been the herald of pure Germanness ends his life a lonely old Jew, seeking comfort in Hasidic literature (*Maurizius*, p. 351). He is a Judas Iscariot, an Ahasuerus wandering among distant nations and lands (America!). His single hope lies in the East, where a daughter whom he never knew awaits him and where he will find rest for his weary head and solace for his tempest-tossed soul (*Maurizius*, p. 499).

Waremme-Warschauer pours out his heart to Etzel Andergast, confessing his perjury and identifying the true guilty party, Anna Jahn. But his self-defense ultimately outweighs his self-accusation: He is an impressive figure, who, we discover, suffered hardly less than his victim, having been dogged by persecution both before the Maurizius affair and after it. In contrast to the accused, however, suffering is for him a source of strength and endurance. Whereas Maurizius commits suicide on account of his lost daughter, Waremme-Warschauer heads East in search of his daughter. Revealed, too, is that the woman over whom the two fight, Anna Jahn, is merely a petite bourgeoise, unworthy of their sacrifices. The archetypical struggle for the German "soul" was, in other words, vacuous because that soul itself was empty. Waremme-Warschauer's American adventure story, in the person of its central protagonist, sheds further light upon his own existential state. Joshua Cooper, a black man, reveals the other side of his world—the world of a man who is persecuted though he has done no wrong, who is the object of blind racist hatred. Waremme-Warschauer's description of the lynching he witnessed reveals his deep identification with the victim:

There was nothing of the human being left about them—beasts? Why, every beast has the soul of a Quaker compared to theirs. They were people to whom robbing and murder was a business, they were people who silence you by a blow in the face and think less of it than others of breaking a window, Acherontic figures, the two-legged beasts of the suburbs; we haven't that kind in this country, the most depraved here reminds one still that a mother has borne him; their most infamous trick consists in devising crimes which they then ascribe to the negroes; this, of course, proceeds from some intellectual centre—as formerly in Russia, when the Jews were massacred—and is called lynch law. No, not if I get to be as old as Methuselah, shall I ever forget my Joshua fleeing before those howling brutes, with the swiftness of a ghost, the stream of blood running over his innocent black face and his arms stretched out in front of him. I never saw him again, I never heard of him again. God knows where his carcass is rotting (*Maurizius*, p. 342).

The link between the blood libel in Russia and the lynching in America is significant. Waremme-Warschauer is Joshua Cooper's alter ego. In other words, Judas Iscariot is the alter ego of Jesus (Joshua). In the figure of Waremme-Warschauer, the "eternal Jew," these contraries are unified. Though in the course of the novel he is described as a monster, he emerges as a human being more sinned against than sinning; as Judas Iscariot (or Ahasuerus) he is perhaps more righteous even than the innocent Jesus because he knows sin, knows boundless suffering, and is purified by his confession.[14] Maurizius—the figure of the condemned innocent who brings misfortune upon himself because he is simply unable to live in this world—has many parallels in Wassermann's other works (principally the figure of Caspar Hauser from the novel of that name [1908]). Wassermann presents in Maurizius a non-Jewish victim figure against whom a Jew has sinned—an incarnation of Jesus who bears the suffering of this world. The accusation against Waremme-Warschauer is the accusation of Christianity against his people, with Maurizius as a kind of living emblem of the Christian victim of the Jewish demon.[15] However, a closer examination of the figure reveals that the gap between Waremme-Warschauer and Maurizius is not wide and is bridged by the black man, Joshua Cooper. The three men are thus all various aspects of a single Jewish experience: as the victim of dark urges and hostile circumstances, of instincts and laws beyond his control. The two figures of Maurizius and Waremme-Warschauer are not antagonists but analogies. The one confesses to the elder Andergast; the other, to Andergast's son. And both, in the final analysis, are more sinned against than sinning.[16]

In *Maurizius*, Wassermann sought justice through the figure of Etzel, laid arbitrary power bare in the figure of the elder Andergast, pardoned sin in the figure of Warschauer, and embodied the aggrieved resignation of the victim in Maurizius. But it is his Jewish obsession with the tortuous experience of the innocent victim that animates and unifies the complex web of the novel.

NOTES

The Maurizius Case was translated into English by Caroline Newton and published in 1929 by Horace. It was republished by Liveright in 1957 and in 1985 by Carrol and Graf. All translations and references here are from the last edition.

1. See the "Nachwort" by Fritz Martini in Jakob Wassermann, *Der Fall Maurizius* (Frankfurt a. M. and Hamburg: Fischer, repr. 1964), 441–465.

2. *Mein Weg als Deutscher und Jude* (Berlin: Fischer, 1921, repr. 1927), 108. Cf. *Lebensdienst* (Leipzig, Zürich: Grethlein and Co., 1928). All citations are from these editions. Most translations from *Mein Weg* in the text are taken from Jakob Wassermann, *My Life as German and Jew*, trans. S. N. Brainin (New York: Coward and McCann, 1933). Other translations from German are by the translator of this essay, Jeffrey Green.

3. The concept of the matriarchs, *die Mütter*, is taken from *Faust* II.A.6162 et seq., and it has special significance in the German language. The matriarchs are the source of creative power, a sign of a man's unconscious bonds with the treasury of his culture (the collective unconscious). The concept has, therefore, a decidedly archetypical character.

4. Wassermann exhibits many of the negative traits that Max Nordau attributed to assimilated Jews. A Zionist reaction to Wassermann's confession can be found in Siegmund Kaznelson's essay, "Um jüdisches Volkstum (zu Jakob Wassermanns *Bekenntnisbuch*)," *Der Jude* 4 (1921): 49–52.

5. See *My Life*, pp. 151–154. Also cf. examples from American Jewish literature: Bruce J. Friedman, *Stern: A Novel* (New York: Simon and Schuster, 1962), and Saul Bellow, *The Victim* (New York: Vanguard Press, 1947).

6. Martini, in the article cited in note 1 above, discusses Wassermann's difficulties with the German critics. I have chosen to discuss *Der Fall Maurizius*, in which the Jewish aspects are latent and concealed, rather than *Die Juden von Zirndorf* (1897), which discusses the question of Jews and Judaism openly, because it seems to me that the later novel is more revealing of "the Wassermann case" than the earlier, explicitly "Jewish" novel. A scathing review of this novel is to be found in Wolfgang von Einsiedel, "Nur ein Roman (zu Wassermanns 'Fall Maurizius')," *Die Schöne Literatur* 10 (Oct. 1928): 478–481.

7. Einige Bemerkungen über den "Fall Maurizius," in *Lebensdienst*, pp. 336–338. The theme of justice has been the main point of departure for most interpreters. See, for example, John C. Blankennagel, "Jakob Wassermann's View on Justice," *Monatshefte für deutschen Unterricht* 35 (1943): esp. 170–171.

8. *My Life*, p. 112. Cf. the treatment of a Jew's hatred for his origins in Bernard Malamud, *The Fixer* (New York: Farrar, Straus, and Giroux, 1966), and Friedman, *Stern*.

9. See the article by Walter Jens "Ein Jude namens Kafka," in *Statt einer Literaturgeschichte* (Pfullingen: Neske, 1957), 259ff. Jens attempts, in very interesting fashion, to point out the Jewish aspects of Kafka's work. That

attempt is extremely important, especially in a period that attempted to ignore that author's Judaism and treat him as an existentialist, removing him from any actual social setting. See the essay "Kafka, Jewish Heritage, and Hebrew Literature" in this volume.

10. In contrast to the Hebrew writer, Y. H. Brenner, for example, for whom the collapse of the father is also a central theme. Brenner too never succeeded in freeing himself from the shadow of the authoritarian father, but the collapse of the father in his world is not an utter catastrophe, since there remains the possibility of action within the national boundaries, beyond the circle of the father's authority. Rebellion against the father is central in the works of another Hebrew writer, M. J. Berdyczewski. The portrayal of the father is central in the works of another nineteenth-century Hebrew writer, M. Z. Feierberg. An examination of the work of Bialik, Berkowitz, and other Hebrew authors for their treatment of this question would be fruitful but must be left for another occasion. Cf. the essay of Itshak Akabiahu, *Demuto shel ha-av ba-shirah ha-tseirah* (The Father Figure in the Poetry of the Young) (Tel Aviv: Eked, 1969). It is possible, too, to see the father in Philip Roth's *Portnoy's Complaint* (New York: Random House, 1969) as a kind of undermined authority whose place is taken by the mother.

11. Self-hatred of that kind is also conspicuous in Friedman's novel, *Stern*. For discussion of Waremme-Warschauer as a transformation of the mythical archetype of the eternally wandering Jew, Ahasuerus, see Rudolf Fürst, "Ahasver Dichtungen," *Das literarische Echo* 4 (August 1904): 1467–1477, 1539–1549. See also P. V. Brady, "Ahasver: On a Problem of Identity," *German Life and Letters* 22 (1968–1969): 3–11.

12. I do not know whether the choice of the name "Jahn" was coincidental. In Germany it has a clear connotation. M. Jahn was one of the most outspoken advocates of German nationalism during the 1920s, and afterwards a Nazi court poet. The transfer of the racial struggle to the arena of eros is perhaps a typical means of artistic expression for oppressed races. The novels of Philip Roth and James Baldwin provide clear examples.

13. Wassermann traveled to America and told the story of his experience with American blacks in an interview: "Jakob Wassermann: Erzählt von seiner Amerikareise," *Die literarische Welt* 3 (May 20, 1927): 1.

14. Cf. an incarnation of the Judas Iscariot archetype in American Jewish literature, the protagonist of Bellow's *The Victim*, pp. 57–58.

15. For guilt as a central motive in his work, see G. V. Jones, "Some Unpublished Letters of Jakob Wassermann," *German Life and Letters*, 3 (Oct. 1949): 27–28. A correspondence with Thomas Mann followed his biographical confession in which the two men discussed Wassermann's Jewish origins. See also M. Karlweis (Wassermann's second wife—G.S.), *Jakob Wassermann: Gestalt, Kampf und Werk* (Amsterdam: Querido, 1935), 332–338; and *My Life*, pp. 151–152.

16. The Jew as victim continues to be a central figure in American Jewish literature: see particularly Bernard Malamud's *The Assistant* (New York: Farrar, 1957) and his short stories.

You are clever. I am not. But I see what you cannot see because your cleverness exempts you from seeing. You have the grace of reason, I, the grace of misery.

(Joseph Roth to Stefan Zweig, Nice, 13 July 1934)[1]

the grace of reason and the grace of misery
on the Zweig-Roth correspondence

I

This study seeks to gain an understanding of the complex relationship between two major literary figures on the Middle European German Jewish scene: Stefan Zweig and Joseph Roth. Each can be seen to represent a different side of the complex Jewish psyche. Zweig, born 1881, son of a wealthy, Jewish, upper-middle-class Viennese family, committed suicide in 1942 in Petropolis, Brazil; Joseph Roth, born 1894, in Brody, son of a lower-middle-class Jewish Galician family, lived most of his life in Western Europe and died in Paris in 1939.[2] The interaction between these men is revealed in their correspondence—some two hundred letters—published in the collection of Joseph Roth's letters, 1911–1939. The volume includes most of Roth's letters to Zweig from 1927 to 1938 as well as a considerable number of Zweig's letters to Roth.

Epistolary exchange is a very common phenomenon in relationships between literary personalities—the correspondence between Schiller and Goethe in the nineteenth century and between Kafka and Brod in the twentieth being probably the best known. The main interest of the Roth-Zweig correspondence lies in its setting in one of the crucial decades of the century and in the intensity of

Library of
Davidson College

Roth's attachment to his correspondent. There were weeks when Roth wrote every other day, or even daily. Indeed, the relationship tended to be one-sided: Roth courted Zweig aggressively; the latter responded passively. Although Zweig replied to Roth's letters with some degree of warmth, he nonetheless never mentioned him in his memoirs, *Die Welt von Gestern* (*The World of Yesterday*).[3] Indeed, for all the intensity of Roth's letters, his actual relationship with Zweig was much more ambivalent, even negative, as David Bronsen, Roth's biographer, concluded after interviewing a number of the authors' mutual friends.[4] Nevertheless, although it is almost impossible to determine the precise nature of this, or perhaps any, human relationship, we can attempt to understand, through the written evidence we possess, the pattern of interaction between these two Jewish types.

II

Any exchange of letters between two personalities may be considered a kind of pseudoepistolary novel, provided that the quantity of literary material produced by the two parties (or even by only one) is sufficient to allow for narrative interpretation. Given such a "narrativity," the correspondents become the main characters of the "novel," and other persons mentioned become the minor characters. A communication that is prolonged in time (nearly eleven years, 1927–1938) and that includes various locales (Nice, Amsterdam, Paris, etc.), can create the effect of dialogue (even if only one part of the dialogue has been preserved, as in Kafka's letters to Felice and Milena), and a plot pattern can emerge. The Zweig-Roth correspondence, which meets all of these criteria, offers an excellent case study.

Each author assumed a certain role in the correspondence. Moreover, Roth "built up" his image of Zweig according to his own psychological needs, as is made clear by the fact that he adopted very different personae with other addressees, such as Blanche Gidon, his French translator, or Hermann Kesten, a personal friend.[5] Each of the minor characters in this ongoing communication (Roth's

Library of
Davidson College

wife, his mistress Manga Bell, the editors Victor Gollancz and Herbert Reichner) was assigned a role in the emerging drama.

Progressing through the correspondence, the reader finds that the images of the two major participants lose their documentary value as signifiers of external referents and gradually become figures in a fictional world in which each assumes functions accorded him by the other. In addition, the very act of publication has added a third party, an implied reader, to a relationship that originally consisted of the two intimate correspondents only. This individual then fills in gaps and infers connections.[6] In just this way, the publication of Kafka's letters and diaries transformed that "documentary" material into an integral part of the Kafka literary corpus and endowed it with semifictional, or even fully fictional, status.[7]

Much has been written about the thin line between fact and fiction, "real" character and image, identity and role playing, and the interaction between biographical material as document and as projection. The fictive status of nonfictional material is determined by the decision of an unimplied reader to read the text as if he were implied. As such he will interpolate the role playing of the correspondents, interpret the images they project, and educe the plot implicit in the sequence of letters—despite its own quite arbitrary beginning, middle, and end. In the present discussion, I shall assume the role of an unimplied "implied" reader of the Roth-Zweig correspondence.

III

Beginning with an analysis of the two major characters in this "epistolary" novel, I shall then proceed to a delineation of their relationship, the "plot" created by their prolonged contacts, and the basic myth that underlay this *Wahlverwandtschaft* (kinship by choice).

Roth perceived Zweig to be a major figure in the inner circle of the European intellectual establishment, one who could obtain for him entrée to every important literary institution—publishing houses, critics, and periodicals—and thereby open the gates of

THE SHADOWS WITHIN   42

fame. This image projected by Roth is accepted and confirmed in Zweig's responses. Although most of Roth's requests were for patronage and connections, he also, from time to time (especially from 1932 on), asked for money. In radical contrast to Zweig, who owned a castle on Salzburg's Kaputzinerberg where he hosted some of the outstanding European writers of his time, Roth never lived within his means and never established himself in the bourgeois world. He never possessed a place of his own and spent most of his life in rooms in the Hotel Foyot in Paris or the Eden Hotel in Amsterdam.[8] But despite his rejection, even abuse, of the bourgeois way of life, he longed for the security and stability enjoyed by its devotees. To Zweig he wrote, "Liberate me from uncertainty" (p. 432, Oct. 1935).

In this regard, Zweig represented for Roth more than a symbol of capitalistic success and a *thesaurus gratia*, a source of all the benefits of the good life—security, stability, fame, and achievement. He was also a symbol of Apollonian tranquillity and peace of mind: "How cheerful is even the saddest [story] you tell" (p. 158, Apr. 1930). And "I don't want you to be less cheerful because of me. You are subject to different laws than I am" (p. 230, Sept. 1932).

To the gloomy, melancholic Roth, Zweig was a spiritual opposite, the angel of mirth, whose sad stories, even, were always enjoyable. Yet, it seems that this projection sometimes had an ironic undertone; the role fitted very well into Roth's *Weltanschauung*. Zweig was the literary representative of the bourgeois mirth that characterized the secure world of the Habsburgian past, in stark contrast to the gloomy and depressing world of Weimar and Hitler or Dollfuss.

Zweig also appears in Roth's letters in the roles of father confessor, prosecutor, judge, and superego. Roth often identifies him with human reason (*Vernunft*); and Zweig accepts this role in Roth's morality play. He preaches in the name of *Vernunft*—"Clarity, please! Reason, please!" (p. 358, July 1934)—against all kinds of excess and prodigality, especially alcoholism—the root of Roth's misfortunes. Roth, attracted to and repelled by his own projection of rationality, often rebelled against it: "I feel there a kind of didacticism that does not fully grip me and attempts to affect me in a way that is all too logical and consequential" (p. 438, Nov. 1935). Whereas he longed for logical consistency, such an attribute was completely contrary to his own nature. In a sense, then, he requested pedagogic advice, yet hated it when it was forthcoming. Zweig in turn assumed and reinforced the role of the humanist as elderly pedagogue that Roth had fashioned for him by bestowing the blessings of good advice and good will. Time and again he inveighed against Roth's alcoholism,[9] which he considered a symbol of immorality, a violation of the bourgeois "golden rules." He preached against his excesses like a Christian "Seelsorger": "You should not (not to speak of your health) spend more than a certain sum of money on alcohol if only because it is immoral to spend more on booze than a normal family needs" (p. 446, Jan. 1936). Directives like "you must" and "you should" occur very frequently in Zweig's letters: "You must give up this self-destruction, this self-aggravation" (p. 359, July 1934). "You must recover. Nothing is more important than preserving yourself" (p. 359, July 1934). Played out in these letters is the struggle of a balanced, well-meaning Viennese bourgeois superego against the volcanic and chaotic eruptions of a Dionysus unbound.

The material of this correspondence is rather unbalanced. Roth's letters predominate; Zweig's replies are relatively few. But the latter played more or less the same role in his letters that he enacted in his autobiography, *Die Welt von Gestern*, an impersonal document in which he discloses only his social and literary persona. He scarcely mentions his marriage and divorce but stresses (for instance) his collection of autographs and the social contacts of "Zweig the collector." He presents himself as typifying a generation rather than as an individual. As such it is the apologia of a conventional son of a middle class Habsburgian family who, despite his grievances against the "world of yesterday," prefers it nevertheless to the world of today. His family, like most of the Jewish middle class, accepted the liberal-traditional norms of the *fin-de-siècle* Austrian monarchy: Whatever was old and well established was ideal and worthy of imitation.

The young Zweig had longed for more freedom and open-mindedness, but when the postwar rebellion of the young succeeded in achieving some of its social and artistic goals, he took fright. The arrogant and exhibitionistic younger generation seemed to him repulsive, he says in his autobiography (p. 218); and he insisted that he had achieved his literary success in spite of the new trends. In the late twenties, at the peak of his career, he felt that he had returned to the security of his childhood, a golden age that had been shattered by the upheavals of the war and its aftermath: "I could be satisfied. I liked my work and therefore I liked life. I didn't have to worry about my livelihood; even if I never write another line, my books would have taken care of me. It seemed as if I had achieved everything; destiny had been tamed. The security I had known in my childhood at my parents' house, and which was lost in the war, had been regained through my own efforts. What more could I ask for?" (p. 256).

When he wrote this passage he had already lost the paradise regained. And even in his imagined paradise there was no place for a turbulent, instable neurotic like Roth, who was clearly an outsider, if not an outcast. Perhaps for this reason Zweig *never* mentioned Roth in his memoirs.

Zweig longed for the fading glory of a world of which he was a real representative. Roth, on the other hand, longed for a world of yesterday that he had never actually been a part of. Zweig tried very hard to be true to himself to the very end. He warned Roth of the dangers of trying to adapt oneself mentally and emotionally to unappealing changing circumstances. The individual should refuse absolutely to compromise; he should refuse to accommodate himself to the disgusting facts of life: "No, Roth, to become hard with the hardness of the times means to accept and to reinforce it. Do not become bellicose and intransigent, for the intransigent triumph on account of their brutality" (p. 513, Sept. 1937).

Man's task, Zweig insisted, is to confront the hardships of circumstance and remain true to the ideals of humanism. He wished to be considered the heir and reincarnation of his own great idol, Erasmus, in defense of the one and only ideal: "the absolute untouchability of individual freedom" (p. 514, fall 1937). But, according to this correspondence, he did not live up to the standards of either his idol or the persona he attempted to project: His courage failed him in his confrontations with the Germans. In his correspondence with Roth he claimed to be taking an apolitical stance in the midst of the surrounding political chaos.[10] But his actual attempts to enter the intellectual-political arena were in fact quite ridiculous, such as when he masterminded letters of protest against the Nazis.

Thus, the illustrious addressee was far more a character in Roth's own inner drama than a real person. Yet, in his own way, Roth had profound insight regarding Zweig: He perceived that the Apollonian spirit was fascinated by the demonic forces of darkness.[11] Roth knew very well that Zweig was as drawn to his chaotic nature as he, Roth, was drawn to Zweig's clarity and rationality. He realized that Zweig was cognizant of the shadowy side of life but could not come to terms with it. When Zweig lost hope and felt himself betrayed by Romain Rolland's defection to the Communists, Roth wrote to him: "Because you see twilight breaking in, you stand confused before the phenomenon of night, which will come very soon, and you think, in addition, that it only comes to spite you" (p. 496, July 1937). Roth made the acute observation that Zweig, the angel of mirth confronting twilight, was as helpless and impotent as Roth in the grip of his own turbulent soul. The remainder of Zweig's tragic life proved the truth of this insight.

IV

The protagonist correspondent must be seen to be Joseph Roth himself. Most of his dialogue with Zweig was taken up by complaints about his women—the "millstones around his neck"[12]—his health, and, to be sure, his financial situation. He was the underdog in the relationship because he needed Zweig as provider, father confessor, and consoler. His letters may be understood as letters to a surrogate or adopted father, and the complicated ambivalences that they express are the understandable consequence of this basic attitude.

Roth hated himself for being a "schnorrer" (a beggar), unable to change: "I run around parched with thirst, a schnorrer, with a hanging tongue and a wagging tail" (p. 450, Feb. 1936). The image of the hungry and panting little dog was only one of various self-deprecating portrayals of himself. He also appears frequently as a hypochondriac: "Every day I am humiliated, and the contempt I feel for myself is transformed into all kinds of physical illnesses"

(p. 443, Dec. 1935). He was aware of the psychosomatic aspects of his troubles—that his sense of inferiority and self-hatred was a factor in his physical condition. In applying to himself the Yiddish expressions "schnorrer" and "nebbuch" (p. 502, Aug. 1937), which connote helplessness, dependency, and misery, he underlined his membership in the Jewish community and his participation in its collective self-condemnation. In fact, the problem and meaning of Jewish identity was a recurring theme in Roth's letters to Zweig, and with no other correspondent did he treat the question with such intensity. Their dialogue turned increasingly to a discussion of Jewish destiny, and it was in this context that Roth played his self-abasing role.

In Zweig, he encountered an assimilated Jew who (at least in his correspondence) seemed to be untroubled by his identity and to suffer no guilt over it. Zweig stressed his innocence and his inability to understand the reason for persecution. In his contacts with Nazis during the Richard Strauss affair (when he lived under the illusion that his libretto to a Strauss opera would be performed) he emphasized that he was *Stefan* and not *Arnold* Zweig, implying that the persecution of the latter was justified because of his leftist political views, whereas he himself was as innocent as a child (p. 261, Apr. 1933). He could not grasp, or would not accept, the fact that he was victimized simply because of his Jewish origins. Roth envied Zweig his inability to comprehend his fate; by contrast he himself internalized it. He felt that his agony and doom, caused primarily by his Jewish origins and identity, were deserved. Nonetheless, he was offended and humiliated when Zweig called him "a poor little Jew" (p. 464, Mar. 1936), like the millions of others who had to adapt to the uncomfortable facts. Roth responded defensively with the assertion that he was proud of his "low" Jewish origins: "What a poor little Jew is you don't have to tell me, of all people. I've been one since 1894 and am proud of it. I am a believing Eastern Jew from Radziwillow. Leave it alone. I've been poor and little for thirty years. I am poor" (p. 465, Apr. 1936).

Generally, however (in this correspondence and in other areas of his life), Roth strenuously denied his Jewish origins, even to the point of fabricating a myth that he was the illegitimate son of a non-Jewish father.[13] He proclaimed that he reacted to Nazism—as to any other political or existential challenge—as a human being and not as a Jew (pp. 417–418, July 1935). Yet these protestations did not prevent the transformation of his own self-hatred, with its very personal and psychological causes,[14] into Jewish *Selbsthass*. The personal self-hatred had various expressions. He saw himself as a nuisance to Zweig[15] and as a son of the forces of hell and darkness, trapped by the phantoms of his chaotic soul: "How surrounded I am by darkness!" (p. 349, July 1934). And he claimed to be haunted by the fear that he would become insane like his father. All of these feelings, however, were transmuted into Jewish self-hatred that assumed the familiar form of flamboyant repudiation. Roth insisted that his "Jewishness" had always seemed an insignificant factor in the definition of his self,[16] "a merely accidental characteristic, more or less like my blond moustache" (p. 417, July 1935). He attempted to give the impression that he had been an Austrian officer; and in the late 1930s he played the part of a Catholic monarchist.[17] His intense self-hatred took him so far, indeed, as to equate Zionism with Nazism: "A Zionist is a National Socialist, a Nazi is a Zionist" (p. 420, Aug. 1935), this on the occasion of his repudiation of Zweig's plan to invite the Zionist leader Chaim Weizmann to sign an anti-Nazi manifesto.

In the thirties Roth longed for the kind of universalism and internationalism that Zweig had effortlessly achieved long before (but that he eventually lost as a result of changing historical circumstances). Roth too pined for the Habsburg monarchy, which he well knew was gone forever, out of a realization that only in such a utopian never-never land could he come to terms with his hated identity. This was the main thrust of his dialogue with Zweig. Although he expressed entirely different views in *Juden auf Wanderschaft* (1927),[18] in which he depicted Jews very sympathetically[19] as victims rather than victimizers, in his correspondence with Zweig he goes out of his way to make vicious anti-Semitic slurs, such as: "a beaten up (on the outside) and spoilt (at home) Jewboy" (p. 148, Feb. 1929); "Jews are very foolish. Only the even more foolish anti-Semites can believe that Jews are dangerously clever" (p. 243, Dec. 1932); "I can't stand little Jews with this kind of hair and haircut" (p. 399, Jan. 1934).

Zweig admitted to his Jewish identity, but his Jewish roots were very shallow; Roth's were much deeper, but he found them hateful.[20] And this ambivalence was exacerbated by the shameful self-image of the little Eastern European Jew being fed by his big Western brother and trying to express his shame by besmirching their common identity. At the same time he would not let Zweig deceive himself that Jews were persecuted on an individual basis because of the commission of any specific sins. When Zweig proposed to write an article on the situation of fathers who have eaten sour grapes and set the children's teeth on edge, Roth responded ironically: "You are wrong in the assumptions you attribute to the Hitler-monsters. Jews are persecuted not because they have sinned but because they are Jews. From this point of view, children are as 'guilty' as their fathers" (p. 264, May 1933). For all this self-hatred, Roth understood the Jewish question existentially much better than the assimilated Zweig.

Such were the characters of the participants in this correspondence between opposites. Roth himself formulated their relationship in terms of binary oppositions that dramatize and intensify the differences between the two men: Zweig possessed the grace of reason that he lacked (p. 353). Zweig was a natural *Weltbürger* (p. 213) or *Weltkind* (p. 511); Roth, in his own opinion, was not. Zweig had been born into happiness, whereas he had been thrust into misery by sheer force of circumstance (p. 353). The contrast between them was essentially that between the uprooted Eastern and the assimilated Western Jew, an opposition that Roth employed frequently in his novels.[21] Their correspondence highlighted the contrast between a Jew in permanent flight (*Flucht ohne Ende*, one of Roth's novels) and a Jew expelled from his cultural and actual homeland. Roth left the shtetl but never struck roots anywhere else. Zweig took with him into exile the world of yesterday as a coherent paradise lost.

Roth projected himself as a kind of Ahriman, the god of darkness and author of all evil, or alternately as a version of Ahasuerus the wandering Jew, yet also as the victim of the overwhelming demons of Pan. (He uses the word *Panik* frequently.)[22] Zweig, by contrast, was projected as a kind of Ormuzd, the god of light and source of all good. Like Milton's Satan, the incarnation of darkness longed for "holy light," whereas the angel of mirth was fascinated by the forces of agony and desolation.

V

The range of topics comprised in this epistolary dialogue was wide (although surprisingly, the subject of literature was of only secondary importance).[23] With the rise of National Socialism in Germany politics became a prominent item, as the prevailing atmosphere forced most intellectuals to take a position vis-à-vis the regime. In the dialogue between the two correspondents each expressed a totally different attitude toward the "new Germany." Zweig, perhaps because of his far more numerous vested interests in Germany, held (wishfully) that Nazism was a passing episode[24] and tried to maintain connections with the Insel publishing house up to the last possible minute.[25] Roth, totally without illusions from the very beginning,[26] detested Zweig's naïve attempts to approach the Nazis as if they were rational human beings.

Disillusion would become one of the major motifs in the correspondence, the heart of a dramatic dialogue between the realistically skeptical "wandering Jew" from Eastern Europe and the naïve, assimilated, liberal Middle European Jew, who believed in the basic goodness of man. Roth doubted that mere words could alter historical trends; Zweig believed that they might (pp. 286–290). But beneath the surface of the ideological discourse lies the fictive enactment of the relation between a dependent son and an adopted father or father confessor. Ostensibly, Zweig was Roth's literary mentor and financial resource, but in reality Roth was begging for attention and love. Time and again, in a kind of emotional blackmail, he told Zweig that he was starving on his deathbed and would expire if abandoned by his protector: "I misuse you, this is certain. But I need you and I can't go on living without you"—literally, "can't go on living" (p. 430, Oct. 1935). At times Roth appealed to Zweig as if he were God, calling upon him *de profundis:* "Whom shall I call if not you? You know that God answers too late, mostly after death. I don't want to die, though I'm not afraid of death"

(p. 443, Dec. 1935; also p. 447). At times he appealed to Zweig like a helpless creature begging for grace and protection; other times he spoke like a "lost son," confessing his love and loyalty to his father: "I don't have to say anything now except the last words that one says on one's deathbed. I love you and I don't want to lose you, this I say to you" (p. 463, Mar. 1936; cf. pp. 467, 506, 509).

Whether or not we take these sentences at face value, it is nonetheless the imagined role of the sender and the internalized function of the addressee in his life that shape the rhetoric of this pathetic confession. In this "letter to an adopted father" from an abandoned child, the real external referent, Zweig, becomes less and less important. For this reason, the letters express the constant demands and complaints of a grumbling, melancholic, always defensive child. They display scarcely any sign of the marvelous sense of humor that Roth revealed in his numerous feuilletons and in the novels *Die Büste des Kaisers* (in French, 1934) and *Die Geschichte von der 1002 Nacht* (1939).

VI

Roth realized his own life as a character in an as yet unfinished pseudonovel, and he recognized that his correspondence with Zweig revealed one of the major lines of its plot. As he wrote to Zweig: "Fate presses upon me in a terrible, too cheaply symbolic way, as if it wants to imitate a stupid novelist" (p. 460, Mar. 1936).

He had the presentiment that his life was doomed to end tragically, being keenly aware of his own self-destructive drive (p. 248, Dec. 1933). Overwhelmed as he was by the force of the demon Alcohol—at once an escape and a self-punishment—he clung to Zweig as to a guardian whose purpose and mission was to delay the hour of execution. Zweig's gifts, personal favors, and benevolent letters were the last barricades that in any way checked Roth's panic-stricken suicidal drive,[27] as he gradually poisoned himself with alcohol.

The unfolding of this drama has formal correlatives in the sequence of the correspondence itself. The structure of this epistolary pseudonovel is of course not regulated from within; the rhythm of the exchange of letters was not determined by an "implied author" but was dependent upon extrinsic, nonliterary factors. But changes and turns in the relationship are reflected in the rhythm of the letters, in variations of style, tone, and manner. As begun in September 1927, the correspondence was quite formal. Roth sent his first letter in response to Zweig's complimentary remarks about his "Judenbuch" *Juden auf Wanderschaft* published in 1927 (p. 108). Thus their first contact was over a matter of Jewish interest, as was its continuation for the most part.

For two years Roth addressed Zweig according to the customary and quite official formula in German letter writing: "Sehr veehrter Herr Stefan Zweig" (To the very honorable Mr. Stefan Zweig). During the next years, however, their contact became less "literary" and official and more personal, as expressed in the opening formula: "Sehr veehrter und lieber Herr Stefan Zweig" (The very honorable and dear Mr. Stefan Zweig), which appears from 1 April 1930 (p. 157). More than a mere formal variant, the addition reflected a growing intimacy. In the middle of the same year Zweig took the initiative and asked Roth not to address him as "Herr" any more; and Roth subsequently used the address "honorable and dear Stefan Zweig" (p. 178). During the week they decided upon this formal informality (22 Sept.) the frequency of their letters increased. Roth wrote to Zweig three times (pp. 178–179, 180, 181–183).

After 1930, there were several periods in which the correspondence intensified: March 1933; July 1933; September and November 1933; June and July 1934; August, October, and November 1935; January and March 1936; and August and September 1937. Each of these periods had its own dominant subject, usually external events, such as the rise of Hitler; but the mutual need to sum up the existential meaning of their *condition humaine* (July 1937) also played its part.

In October 1932 there was another shift to a more cordial intimacy. Roth and Zweig stopped addressing each other by their private and family names, using instead the formula "Lieber teurer Freund" (Dear, dear friend), and from then on Roth's attitude became more and more ambiguous, tormented, and complex, whereas Zweig's reaction became more apologetic and defensive.

The correspondence that had started as a social contact ended in a personal clash. Roth, in one of his last letters to Zweig, cries out in the accents of grief, of one abandoned and offended: "Between the two of us there are so many links, which would make indifference or animosity seem abstruse. My silence is only a chronic dumb reproach" (p. 522, 13 July 1938).

Zweig's was the last word in this dialogue (Dec. 1938), an apology for a sin he never consciously committed; his uneasy conscience suspects that Roth harbors a grudge against him: "Dear Joseph Roth, I have written to you three or four times without getting a reply, and I think that because of our old friendship I have the right to ask you what you are trying to say through this stubborn and hopefully not malevolent silence" (p. 525).

Indeed, the rest was to be silence. The two friends neither corresponded nor met again; their "plots" developed independently in life, not in letters. The relationship came to an end in the last year of Roth's life, when the younger man was, in effect, committing suicide with alcohol. The adopted son-father relationship had ended in disappointment and despair because the "father" was unable to meet the "son's" expectations. Not many years later, the "father" followed suit, a world away, in Brazil.

Thus our two characters in fact both come to a tragic end, as Roth had put it, in a terrible but cheaply symbolic manner, as if destiny were imitating a foolish novelist. And if we, in our reading and interpretation of this pseudoepistolary novel are conditioned by our knowledge of the end of the affair, with its double suicide, is not the act of reading inevitably conditioned beyond the pages of the fiction by that historical present that is the life of the reader?

NOTES

1. Joseph Roth, *Briefe 1911–1939*, ed. Hermann Kesten (Cologne: Kiepenheuer and Witsch, 1970), 353. All translations are mine. This paper was read at the Zweig Centennial Conference held at the Ben-Gurion University of the Negev in Beersheba, 30 November–2 December 1981.

2. For Joseph Roth's biography, see David Bronsen, *Joseph Roth: Eine Biographie* (Munich: D.T.V., repr. 1981). Stefan Zweig wrote his autobiogra-

phy, *Die Welt von Gestern: Erinnerungen eines Europäers* (Frankfurt a. M.: Fischer, 1944, repr. 1980). Page references in parentheses refer to these editions.

3. Here he mentioned most of his literary friends including Asch, Bahr, Beer-Hofmann, Dehmel, Duhamel, Freud, von Hofmannsthal, Romain Rolland, Verhaeren, Schnitzler, Wassermann, Werfel, and many others. Other sources bearing on their relationship are Zweig's.

4. Bronsen, *Biographie,* pp. 305, 367–368. According to Bronsen's sources, Roth despised Zweig as a writer (pp. 367ff.)

5. His main correspondents were Blanche Gidon, Hermann Kesten, Gustav Kiepenheuer, Klaus Mann, Benno Reifenberg, Bernard von Brentano, Felix Berteaux, and his family.

6. In Wolfgang Iser's sense, *The Act of Reading: A Theory of Aesthetic Response* (Baltimore: Johns Hopkins University Press, 1978).

7. Kafka's letter for instance was addressed to his father only, but has become the subject of various literary interpretations. See H. Binder, *Kafka: Kommentar zu den Romanen* (Munich: Winkler, 1976), 422–445.

8. Roth, *Briefe,* p. 145, Feb. 1929.

9. Ibid., pp. 354, 359, 454.

10. "Given three months ago on one condition: Not a word of politics and revision [of the interview before publication], and it was published without a word of politics. Anything else that was foisted upon me was just untrue" (pp. 321–322, Mar. 1934).

11. Zweig wrote a number of books on masters of demonic art, *Drei Meister* (1920, about Balzac, Dickens, Dostoevsky); *Der Kampf mit dem Dämon* (1925, about Hölderlin, Kleist, Nietzsche); *Die Heilung durch den Geist* (1931, about Mesmer, M. Baker Eddy, Freud).

12. Pp. 144, 154, 180, 195. Later he wrote a great deal about Manga Bell (the woman with whom he lived) and her two children.

13. Bronsen, *Biographie,* p. 35. The ambivalence of his approach to the reality and historic meaning of being Jewish in the new age of anxiety appears in very concentrated form in a letter to Zweig (pp. 258–261, Mar. 1933) in lines such as the following: "As to the Jewish element in us, I agree with you: We should not create the impression that we care for Jews only and for nobody else"; "I have never overrated the tragedy of being Jewish, especially now, when it is tragic enough to be just a human being"; "As a soldier and officer I was not a Jew. As a German writer I am not a Jew either (in the sense we are speaking of now)"; and "I am afraid that there are moments when Jewish restraint is nothing more than the reaction of tactful Jews against the chutzpah of the tactless" (p. 26).

14. A reasonable interpretation of Roth's attitude to his Jewish forefathers is given by David Bronsen, "Austrian versus Jew: The Torn Identity of Joseph Roth," *Leo Baeck Institute Year Book* 18 (1973): 220–226.

15. For instance, "You are tired, I know, and I am disconsolate because I make you even more tired" (p. 450, Feb. 1936).

16. "You could not deny the 6,000 years of Jewish heritage, but by the same token you can't deny 2,000 years of the non-Jewish one. We descend more from 'emancipation,' from humanity, from the 'human' in general, than from Egypt" (p. 257, 22 Mar. 1933); and "One is—as I have told you—committed to Voltaire, Herder, Goethe, and Nietzsche no less than to Moses and one's Jewish forefathers" (p. 260, 26 Mar. 1933).

17. See Bronsen, "Austrian versus Jew." On Roth's monarchism, see p. 264 (May 1933), p. 282 (Oct. 1933). He had some great illusions about Austria: "In Austria the situation seems absolutely secure. You are not to be afraid of National Socialism at all." Roth's monarchism is also discussed by H. Scheible, "Joseph Roths Flucht aus der Geschichte," in *Text und Kritik: Joseph Roth*, ed. H. L. Arnold (Munich: Edition Text und Kritik, 1974), 56–66: "The turn to old Austria was characteristic of the later Roth. It happened when Roth felt that the future was lost."

18. He always preferred inhabitants of the *shtetl* to their Western relatives. In this respect he resembles other German Jewish writers such as Wassermann, who expressed the same view in a letter to Buber. See Jakob Wassermann, *Lebensdienst* (Leipzig and Zürich: Grethlein and Co., 1928), 177.

19. He wrote the greatest homage to the decline, fall, and possible resurrection of Eastern Jewry in *Hiob: Roman eines einfachen Mannes* (Berlin: G. Kiepenheuer, 1932); and an essay on Jewry after the rise of Hitler is included in his prophetic work *Der Antichrist* (1934) in *Werke*, vol. 3, ed. Hermann Kesten (Cologne and Berlin: Kiepenheuer and Witsch, 1975–1976), 448–455.

20. C. Magris, *Weit von Wo: Verlorene Welt des Ostjudentums* (Vienna: Europaverlag, 1974) offers a very interesting analysis of Roth's Eastern Jewish roots and his problematic existence as an Eastern Jew in the Western world.

21. Gabriel Dan, L. Bloomfield, and Phöbus Böhlaug in *Hotel Savoy*; Baranowicz and Tunda's family (in the West) in *Die Flucht ohne Ende*; Brandeis and the Bernheims in *Rechts und Links*; and Mendel Singer and his sons Shemariah and Jonas in *Hiob*.

22. "I can't live in permanent panic. But I have lived in panic for years. So long as I live in this panic I can't see the truth of any advice at all" (p. 439, Nov. 1935).

23. Roth criticized Zweig's style in the biographies of Fouché (p. 155), Mesmer (p. 181), Erasmus (p. 300), and Castellio (pp. 474–478). His touchstones were clarity and simplicity, even austerity; he found Zweig's style too pompous. He was very cautious in his remarks, but even his most positive comments had a critical undertone (p. 181, Sept. 1930). Whatever negative opinions he held of Zweig's literary works he revealed (according to Bronsen) in his table talk; in his letters he played the role of an admirer. Zweig on the other hand took Roth's talent for granted and served far more as his agent than his critic, encouraging him to complete his novels and

helping him to find publishers and translators. Only at the beginning did their relationship seem to be based on mutual artistic interests.

24. The Richard Strauss affair (stirred up when Strauss used Zweig's libretto in one of his operas) had many repercussions (pp. 375 [1934 letter to Marcuse] and 404).

25. P. 263, May 1933. Roth prophesied that the Inselverlag would betray Zweig. Roth was critical about a letter Zweig had written to the Inselverlag (p. 288, Nov. 1933). Zweig defended himself and his dealings with the Germans by saying, "You can't erase seventy million Germans by protesting them out of the world" (p. 291, Nov. 1933).

26. "Germany is dead. For us it is dead. You can't reckon with it any more. Neither with its baseness nor with its nobleness. It has been a dream. Do see this at last, please" (p. 294, Nov. 1934).

27. Bronsen, *Biographie*, pp. 559–561, deals with various aspects of the "death wish" of his characters. Carl Sanger, "The Figure of the Non-hero in the Austrian Novels of Joseph Roth," *Austrian Literature* 2, 4 (Winter 1969): "Finally in his knowledge of being the last of his line, the non-hero unable to master life, frequently entertains a death wish."

shadows of identity
a comparative study of German Jewish and American Jewish literature

I

What is Jewish literature in non-Jewish languages? Is it any literature written by Europeans, Americans, or other nationals who
happen to be of Jewish origin? Until what generation? Shall we define these writers according to Jewish law, or the racial laws of various nations, or is the genetic definition valueless and meaningless?
Can a person of any religious or ethnic origin whatsoever be cate-
gorized according to the language of his literary loyalty?

Another approach to the questions is to define Jewish thematics
and then ascertain whether, and to what degree, these themes are
manifest or implied by the works under discussion. Accordingly,
those who best represent these themes are Jewish writers, and
those whose works are most distant from it must live, die, and be
buried outside the walls.

Yet another alternative, a semiotic definition, is rather easy to
adduce, claiming that Jewish literature is any literature in which a
portion of the existential rites to which it refers are connected to
forms of behavior derived from the Jewish social group.

I would argue that these definitions and their refutations are of
little practical import, for the answer lies in an empirical realm:
Jewish literature in non-Jewish languages is, most fundamentally,
that written by individuals who define themselves as having a dual

identity. They write for publications that have dual identities; and their work employs subjects and forms that respond to the national and the Jewish needs of their addressees in all the areas mentioned above: origins, thematics, and semiotics. A sampling of those binational publications that embody the contrast between (non-Jewish) linguistic identity and (Jewish) social identity reveals the implicit self-consciousness of both the contributors and their audiences.

The German Jewish periodical *Sulamith,* published in German between 1806 and 1833, was the heir, as it were, of the Hebrew journal *Ha-meassef* (1783–1811) and a contemporary of *Bikkurei ha-ittim* (1821–1831). After *Sulamith,* many other German Jewish periodicals appeared, from the *Allgemeine Zeitung des Judentums* (1837–1888) to the Zionist *Der Jude* (1916–1924), edited by Martin Buber. Alongside the vast number of Hebrew and Yiddish periodicals in Russia, there were Jewish Russian-language publications, such as *Razsvet* (1860–1861) and the *Voskhod* (1881–1906).

In the United States, Jewish magazines were published in English from the mid-nineteenth century. The *Asmonean* first appeared in New York in 1849, and *The Hebrew Leader* lasted from 1856 to 1882. Since then a large number of American Jewish magazines have been published, the best known of them being *Commentary* and *Midstream.* Today, these periodicals are of course far better known and more widely distributed than Hebrew magazines in America, such as *Hadoar* and *Bitzaron* (which have led a precarious existence since their establishment) and than Yiddish newspapers, of which the *Jewish Daily Forward* (1897–) is the only one still in existence.[2]

What emerges from even this superficial survey is that a culture with a dual identity is not simply a theoretical creation of historians of literature[3] but, rather, an empirical entity. Its literature is a highly complex embodiment of both identities.

II

Critics have long recognized the existence of a dual-identity literature created by Jews who wrote in German. As early as 1922, Gustav

Krojanker published a collection of articles in which Jewish literary critics discuss such writers as Franz Werfel, Franz Kafka, Albert Ehrenstein, Jakob Wassermann, Otto Weininger, Martin Buber, Else Lasker-Schüler, Peter Altenberg, Arnold Zweig, Arthur Schnitzler, Carl Sternheim, Max Brod, and others.[4] Since then many others have written about this body of literature. Harry Zohn, for example, has researched the Viennese writers,[5] and Hans Tramer has dealt with selected poets.[6]

In the United States, a number of Jews—American by birth or choice—have tried to define Jewish literature for themselves. Some have tried to free themselves from the stigma of dual identity; others have approached the problem sarcastically and critically;[7] yet others have provided us with literary meditations. The efforts at definition are often provocative, and the examples of Ludwig Lewisohn, Max Schulz, and Cynthia Ozick indicate the dimensions of the problem.[8]

Lewisohn, one of the "founding fathers" of American Jewish literature, answers the question head on: A Jewish book is one written by someone who is well aware that he is Jewish. Jewish literature, therefore, consists of all the works—written in every age and language—whose creators knew they were Jewish. To paraphrase the sixteenth-century English poet Sir Philip Sidney: They looked in their hearts and wrote. Taking a different approach, Schulz writes of the Jewish imagination that it "has been stirred by the aesthetic possibilities of a radical sophistication, which simultaneously entertains contrary intellectual systems: the secular view of man alienated in an absurd universe and the religious view of man enthroned by divine fiat in God's earthly kingdom" (p. 26). Whether or not this definition fits the Jewish paradox and correctly characterizes American Jewish literature, Schulz's remarks certainly indicate the concern of writers and scholars with the nature and function of that literature.

Ozick, our third example, takes an original approach to this issue. She seeks to justify both the author's identity and that of other American Jews in the golden exile. Again, although a number of the arguments are questionable, they are indisputable evidence of a deep need to come to grips with the realities of a dual identity.

"Gentile readers," Ozick writes, "may or may not be surprised at this self-portrait of a third-generation American Jew (though the first to have been native-born) perfectly at home and yet perfectly insecure, perfectly acculturated and yet perfectly marginal" (p. 156).

Ozick argues that American Jewry, a latter-day Yavneh, will create a new exilic Jewish culture that is the heir of the rabbis of the Talmud and of the authors of the Golden Age of Spain. It will do so because the aesthetics of the Jewish novel is different from the aesthetics of many contemporary American novels: Whereas the latter worships the idols of art, the former, as always, "passionately wallow[s] in human reality" (p. 165). Taking her argument yet further, she contends that only those who wrote as Jews are remembered as Jews by Jews. Those who attempted to be universalistic are quickly forgotten. "The fact is that nothing thought or written in the Diaspora has ever been able to last unless it has been centrally Jewish. If it is centrally Jewish it will last for Jews" (p. 172). To ensure its survival, then, American Jewry must create a culture and language of its own (English as a new Yiddish), a sort of new Yavneh, with imaginative literature assuming the role once played by Talmud. Ozick concludes with the challenge: "From being envious apes we can become masters of our own civilization—and let those who want to call this 're-ghettoization,' or similar pejoratives, look to their own destiny" (pp. 180–181).

Ozick's hope for a "new Yavneh," however, seems to be more wishful thinking than reality. I am not persuaded by her basic assumption that Jewish literature "passionately wallows in human reality" whereas non-Jewish literature is coldly aesthetic. Surely, it is belied by exceptions: the gentile whose work is "Jewish" in spirit, and the converse. Nevertheless, a convincing message does emerge from her essay. By making "feeling" into a doctrine, she turns a shortcoming into an advantage, an undefinable situation into a defined one. Many of the Jewish writers in Germany and America (the two non-Jewish cultures with which I am most familiar) have grappled with that experience. Indeed, one may say of their work that the issue of identity itself is its most important characteristic.

III

Although this essay deals with the problem of identity in Jewish literature written in non-Jewish languages, the same problem challenged Hebrew and Yiddish writers as well. It is appropriate, then, to bring into our analysis the very intense and pointed words of M. J. Berdyczewski's Hebrew story "The Stranger" (1908): "He left his people! What did he leave? Shattered bodies, shadows, just shadows. What do you see in the Jews except shadows? But those shadows dwell in his spirit, in his essence, and in everything within him. They say, 'The seed of Abraham has passed away,' but they have not passed away. The individual is finished, but they are stronger than the individual. You and your thoughts will wither away in inactivity, and they will not die out. They will mock and deride you."[9] There is a pervasive sense that the protagonist wishes to rid himself of his Jewish heritage but understands very well that he is pursued by it. Thus the powerful, irrational powers of the shadows within overcome the rational forces of light in the souls of his characters.

For all that this formulation expresses the consciousness of the authors and the heroes in Hebrew literature, and often in Yiddish literature, as well as in the literature of Jews writing in other languages—the actual existential situation of the authors was in fact different. Those writing in a Jewish language *identified* with the shadow powers. The language itself spread over them like a shadow, providing refuge from one Jewish culture but at the same time offering itself as a substitute. Those who wrote in Hebrew (and to some extent in Yiddish) *chose* their identity. They may have struggled against it, criticized it, and resented it, but they did so from within. They expanded and deepened it with every expression of love, envy, and hatred.

That is not the case with writers who chose another language. Although a writer may have opted for the path of "spirit and light" (to use Bialik's phrase), the shadow is always a present, if latent, antagonist. We may ask: What character did that struggle between the shadow and (what appears to be) the linguistic "powers of light" assume? In what ways was the struggle modified when it passed from the hostile cultural environment of Germany to the welcoming pluralistic cultural environment of America?

IV

In addressing these questions, I shall begin with an author who occupied an intermediary place between linguistic cultures and ideological positions: Ludwig Lewisohn (1882–1955). Born in Berlin, he emigrated to the United States with his parents in 1890. After a rather thorough assimilation, Lewisohn returned to Judaism (in the national sense), so much so that in the 1920s he became an avowed Zionist.

The Island Within (Als eine Insel), first published in 1928, is a kind of novel of repentance, in which an assimilated Jew (Arthur) has a relationship with a gentile woman (and with the world she represents) but ultimately returns to his Jewish roots. This book by a Jew from Germany, written in English in the United States, is quite typical of much of German Jewish fiction as well as of some American Jewish fiction. In these works the problem of identity (for both the characters and their creators) derives mainly from the struggle against an outside world that is unwilling to accept the Jews as completely German or American. One copes in one of two ways: by bearing Jewish identity as a tragic destiny or by turning this disadvantage into an advantage.

Jewish literature in Germany sought to accommodate itself to the tension between a minority with a dual identity and a majority with a single one. The majority stigmatizes the minority. Worse, in general, the minority internalizes that stigma by frequently accepting those assumptions[10]—believing that it lives in the foreign, alienating environment by sufferance, not by right. That internalization frequently took on pathological proportions, as in the case of Otto Weininger, whose theoretical work Sex and Character (1903) presented the most extreme expression of the existential condition of persecution: someone pursued from all sides who has internalized the rationale of the pursuers and thereby justified his own fate as the victim.[11] That condition often influences the literary form of the works. Many, for example, are similar in plot to The

Island Within, in which the protagonist confronts his identity after encountering barriers to erotic (or other) self-realization in the foreign world that both attracts him with its charms and repels him with its hatred. In many of the writers of that generation (1900–1940) the problem of identity was repressed, only to reappear in metamorphosed guise.

From a literary standpoint, the weaker examples tend to be those offering an overt treatment of the problem of Jewish identity, with manifest use of Jewish, generally Eastern European, semiotics. This category would include not only Lewisohn's novel but also Max Brod's *Rëubeni, Fürst der Juden* (Rëubeni, Prince of the Jews, 1925), which depicts a Jew's path from assimilation to Zionism. This rather trivial work recounts the life of David Lemel of Prague who, assisted by an assimilated Jew named Hirschel, rebels against his father, falls in love with a gentile woman, and runs away with her. After she leaves him, he returns, repentant, to his people, as David Rëubeni, a "false" Messiah—"false" in the eyes of the people, who are unable to recognize the truths he imparts.[12] The message is unambiguous: The Jews must become a nation like all others by returning to their ancient homeland; but they refuse to be redeemed. Much of the book is a conventional piece of German Jewish literature, the erotic attractions of the alien world providing the ideological justification for the abandonment of family, tribe, and religion and Lemel-Rëubeni's rejection by the alien world ultimately leading him to repent. Brod distinguishes himself from most of his contemporaries in his presentation of a messianic Zionist ideology that seeks to liberate the Jews from dependence on that alien world.

Such a simplistic and rather overt approach to the topic of identity also characterizes the "Jewish" works of Arthur Schnitzler, *Professor Bernhardi* (1912) and *Der Weg ins Freie* (1908). The former is an apologetic play about a Jew who seeks to defend himself against intolerance, prejudice, and the irrational hatred of the anti-Semites (a kind of response to a small-scale blood libel); the latter, a novel about two Jews, one assimilated Jew who struggles with the problem of identity and another who seeks a Zionist solution to an otherwise hopeless problem. Such rather simplistic ideological works fail to penetrate the problem of existence very deeply.

v

Much more significant are the works of writers who tackle the problem of identity on a subtler, implicit level. It is moreover often the case that such writers display a gap between their direct expressions of Jewish consciousness in journals, essays, and letters and the absence of such explicit expressions in their fiction. We find implicit and profound depiction of the problem in the works of three very different German Jewish writers: Joseph Roth, Franz Kafka, and Jakob Wassermann.

Roth was born into an Eastern European family.[13] But, after leaving his hometown, he assimilated to such a degree that he fabricated a fictional identity for himself as the son of an Austrian officer with whom his mother had had an illicit romance. In the late 1920s, he became a Habsburg monarchist, idealizing the empire as the model of an international, pluralistic paradise in which Jews, too, could find a safe haven, unencumbered by their identity. Roth lavished praise on his subjective utopia (which, of course, had never existed) both in his imaginative works, such as *Die Büste des Kaisers* (1935)[14] and in his essays and travel writing, *Juden auf Wanderschaft* (1927), in which he described various centers of Jewish life. There he comments on the situation of the Jews: "They have no fatherland, the Jews, but every country where they dwell and pay taxes demands patriotism and a heroic death from them and reproaches them for not being pleased to die. In that situation Zionism is really the only way out: as long as there must be patriotism, it might as well be for one's own country."[15] But one must not conclude on the basis of that passage that Roth was a Zionist. He was not. Indeed, he was, to my knowledge, the first to compare Zionism with Nazism—that in 1935 in a letter to Stefan Zweig.[16] He rejected all nationalism as narrow and believed in deracinated supranationalism, universalistic and free from all national obligations. He tried to give a political dimension to "positive deracination"—an idealized incarnation of the defunct Habsburg empire.

That issue concerned Roth throughout his life. But his works are less an expression of the *joy* of the universalist existential situation than they are, if one may say so, the dreadful misery of one resigned to it. His novella *Die Flucht ohne Ende* (1927) gives voice to this sentiment. Tunda, a half Jew, fights in World War I and, following his imprisonment by the Russians, wanders across various landscapes and ideologies. He leaves his cosseted, bourgeois Viennese home (and his conventional fiancée) to travel through Soviet Russia (with his Communist mistress), to postwar bourgeois Germany, and from there on to cosmopolitan Paris. The deracinated hero, it seems, is at home everywhere and nowhere, always marginal, exceptional, and expelled. Wherever he finds himself, the pattern repeats itself, and so the novel finishes with the following description:

It was 27 August 1926, 4:00 P.M.: The shops were full, in the department stores women shoved, in high fashion boutiques models spun about, in the patisseries idlers chattered, in the factories wheels whirled, on the banks of the Seine beggars picked at their lice, in the Bois de Boulogne couples kissed each other, in the parks children rode on the carousel. It was at this hour. There stood my friend Tunda, thirty-two years old, healthy and chipper, a strong young man with all sorts of talents, in the Place de la Madeleine, in the middle of the capital of the world, and he didn't know what to do. He had no profession, no love, no desire, no hope, no ambition, and not even any egotism. No one on earth was more superfluous than he.[17]

This marvelous description emphasizes the impossibility of living in the abstract: without place, without time, without defined identity. The primary, unconscious psychological processes of fiction, in other words, admit what the lips otherwise never dare to utter—that the universal, pluralistic ideal is empty, that living without a shadow exacts a dreadful price. The flight from identity leads into a cul-de-sac of dismal despair.

Kafka imbued the problem with metaphysical and metapsychological significance. It is not by chance that although his protagonists have appellations similar to that of their creator (K. or Joseph K., for example), most of them lack an identity. Letters stand for humans, who are mere ciphers symbolizing universal, utterly deracinated man. Born into emptiness, they occupy neither historic time nor geographic space. (Only *Amerika* of all the novels is still populated with characters from the Austro-Hungarian empire.) Kafka's works are the most complex internalization in "foreign-language" Jewish fiction of the feelings experienced by characters whose identity is determined by persecution and ambiguity: accused of a sin they did not commit and yet justifying the verdict (*The Trial*); expelled from their society, which does not recognize their identity (*The Castle*). As marginal subtenants, they are exposed to false accusations.

Kafka's protagonists are not pursued by external forces or accused by courts that hold real jurisdiction. Rather, they embody the psychological and existential dimension of their social predicament. The universal Jew—persecuted and having no identity or place in space and time—typifies the modern "human condition"; the Jewish plot, in other words, is actually a universal human metaplot.

Our final example in German is the work of Jakob Wassermann. His *Die Juden von Zirndorf* (1897) is a *Bildungsroman* like many Hebrew novels of the Haskalah (Jewish Enlightenment) period, such as Brod's *Rëubeni*. The metamorphoses of the topic of identity, persecution, and guilt are given splendid expression in *Der Fall Maurizius* (1928), which actually does not treat a specifically Jewish topic. Like Roth and Kafka, however, Wassermann frequently dealt with the tension between his Jewishness and his Germanness in his journalistic and documentary writing, and like them he preferred the authentic Jew, whom he called "Oriental" (referring to Eastern Europe), to the assimilated Jew.

It should come as no surprise that these three assimilated Jews, who were ashamed of their identity or viewed their dual identity as tragic, admired those Jews who, rather than concealing their identity, exhibited it conspicuously. Wassermann relates to them in terms taken from the lexicon of German romantic nationalism as "a noble consciousness, a blood consciousness" that "lives with the matriarchs."[18] They, it seems, are the true *nation*. Those authentic Jews are to be admired because they are almost "non-Jewish" in that they have a nationality—in total contrast to the Wassermanns, Kafkas, and Roths, who have none. In fact Wassermann vehemently rejects German Jews such as himself. He vacillates between these two identities, most poignantly expressed in his work *My Life as German and Jew* (1921), a kind of dismal monologue by a jilted lover who blames his rejection upon his identity: "You may try in vain to die and live for them [the Germans], they will always say, 'He's a Jew.'"

This, in essence, is Wassermann's predicament: All his life he tried to be completely German and failed abjectly. Like Roth's Tunda, he stands at a spiritual crossroads, with no idea which way to turn. Toward the end of his life Wassermann had planned a novel to be called *Ahasuer*—its protagonist, the wandering Jew.[19] And in *Der Fall Maurizius* he had taken up that theme. Waremme-Warschauer, one of the central characters, is reminiscent of Judas Iscariot and Ahasuerus. By his perjurious testimony he brings about the unjust condemnation of his friend Maurizius and from that time is doomed to wander throughout Europe and the United States, like Ahasuerus. Waremme-Warschauer tries to hide his past by pretending to be a German nationalist. But by the end of his life he acknowledges that the attempt to mask his identity had failed. With the destruction of all his Germanic illusions and hopes, only his miserable Jewish identity remains. He wishes to convert his handicap into an advantage and travel to Eastern Europe, to his daughter and the Hasidim, as a positive response that emphasizes one-half of his dual identity.

It can be said of all the writers considered here that the attempt to return to Jewish identity provided a spark of hope, although none of them realized that hope on either the fictional or biographical level. Roth opened various gates to repentance for his Eastern European protagonists. In *Job* (1930), the main character emigrates to America. He despairs after the death of his wife and children but finally emerges into a new life. Roth's novella *Der Leviathan* (1940) tells the story of Nissen Piczenik, a coral merchant who sinned by selling artificial corals. He repents by plunging into the sea to seek the Leviathan, the father of all corals; and there, in the ocean, he finds his own death. At the end of his own life in Paris, Roth formed deep bonds of friendship with a rabbinical scholar, Joseph Gottfarstein, and in attendance at his funeral was a grotesque mélange of characters: a rabbinical scholar, a rabbi, a Catholic priest, and a deputation of the Habsburg royalist party.[20]

In Kafka's work one finds, in my opinion, no optimistic Jewish message at all. That was not so in his life, for throughout it he sought to form a bond with the Jewish world. He studied Hebrew, he was in sympathy with Zionism, he contemplated a visit to Palestine, and at the end of his life a Jewish woman, a Zionist named Dora Diamant, cared for him.

Wassermann, of the three, was the most personally ambivalent, although he remained a member of the Jewish community of Gratz until his death.[21] In his later years he became extremely sensitive to the fate of the Jews, and he planned, as noted, to write a novel about the fate of the wandering Jew, Ahasuerus. According to one of Wassermann's letters to his publisher, that work was to encompass the turning points in the history of the Jewish people over two thousand years, to be presented in the form of tableaux and dialogues, some of which he had already written.[22] There would be conversations with St. Paul, Julian the Apostate, Charlemagne, Pope Innocent III, Isabella of Spain, Spinoza, Richelieu, Cromwell, Catherine II of Russia, Frederick the Great, Maria Theresa, Napoleon, Karl Marx, Bismarck, Lenin, and Hitler. He promised, in addition, scenes of persecution and expulsion, of yeshivot and the formation of religious sects. Thus we see that (before his premature death) he wished to write what he thought was *the* Jewish book of his generation. That project is a convincing expression of the trauma of the wandering Jew: In the wake of events in Germany, Wassermann had to take up *his* own wanderer's staff.

Generally speaking, then, German Jewish literature was a literature of flight from identity, a burdensome identity that was imposed on the victims as a stigma and then internalized by them. The conflict between identities, as well as the experience of lacking an identity, was negative and destructive, to such a degree that it could not be resolved by our authors' literary plots.

VI

Although American Jewish literature and German Jewish literature have similar origins, it must be emphasized that American Jewish literature today is prouder of its dual identity than any other "foreign" Jewish literature has ever been. Daniel Walden's anthology, *On Being Jewish*, documents three stages in the literary embodiment of the American Jewish experience: (1) immigration, (2) Americanization, and, finally, (3) Jewish Americans and American Jews.[23] Among the books belonging to the first stage (though in fact Walden places it in the second) is Henry Roth's novel *Call It Sleep* (1934), doubtless the most interesting of them all.[24]

Still permeated by the world of Eastern Europe, this work describes shtetl life as it is transplanted from Eastern Europe to the United States. Roth details the inner disintegration of the community in America—the collapse of paternal, divine, and communal authority. In its wake there arise problems of the individual's identity and his relations with the non-Jewish world. The author successfully gives his characters authentic linguistic and behaviorial identities by conveying Yiddish conversation within the family in correct English and conversation outside the family in broken English. *Call It Sleep* is close in its materials, semiotics, and thematics to Hebrew and Yiddish literature of Eastern Europe, in many respects closer to Sholem Aleichem's *Motl peyse dem khazns* (the story of the emigration to America of an Eastern European Jewish family told from the child's point of view) than to many American and Jewish American novels of its generation.

Roth's tale focuses on young David, who discovers his human identity through unraveling a dark family secret, the roots of which reach down deep into its country of origin. Genya, his mother, had been seduced by a gentile lover and married her Jewish husband as a last resort. Having committed the original sin, the shaken family tumbles from the shtetl in Europe to its crumbling reincarnation in New York, where Genya's past overshadows her present, determining her fate and that of her son. Because of her deep feelings of guilt, she submits to all her husband's caprices; and the boy feels rejected by the father. Roth's themes—the loss of paternal authority and the oedipal tension between fathers and sons; the opposition between erotic sin (the hidden secret underlying the family relations) and the norms of family existence; the opposition between the house as a shelter and the external world as a primal forest arousing fears—are all subjects and motifs typical of Hebrew literature (M. J. Berdyczewski, Y. H. Brenner, I. D. Berkowitz) and Yiddish writing (Chaim Grade, Isaac Bashevis Singer). In this sense, *Call It Sleep* is a Hebrew or Yiddish novel written in English that tries to imitate Yiddish. Like Joseph Roth's *Hiob*, it is a Yiddish novel in its use of language, in its behavioral norms, and in the Jewish identification of the protagonists. Similarly, the Yiddish and Hebrew works set in America attempt to find an equivalent for English.[25] This phenomenon is in evidence elsewhere as well. Hebrew novels such as *Ḥayyei nissuim* (Married Life, 1929–1930) by David

Vogel or *Shaul ve-yohannah* (1956–1967) by Naomi Frankel are, in that sense, German novels written in Hebrew. *Vengeance of the Fathers* (1928) by Yitzhak Shami is an Arabic novella written in Hebrew. And Isaac Bashevis Singer's *Enemies, a Love Story* (1972) is a novel originally in Yiddish whose linguistic materials are Yiddish, Polish, and American. In all of these works, even though the characters explicitly identify as Jews, one can already discern the first stages of the collapse of identity that would lead to the works of "American Jewish" writers.

Chaim Potok's *The Chosen* (1967), written thirty years after Henry Roth's novel, is close to it in several respects.[26] It too is based on the language and semiotics of the American Jewish shtetl society. In the American context, it raises the very issues of the conflicts among Enlightened Jews, Hasidim, and Zionists that had been familiar to Hebrew and Yiddish readers decades earlier. Both of Potok's protagonists, different as they are, have their roots in their Jewish heritage. Danny Saunders, the son of a Hasidic rebbe, yearns for secular education; Reuven Malter, the son of a traditionalist Zionist intellectual, seeks the light within Judaism. Yet despite their conflicting ambitions, neither has doubts about his identity as a Jew—which places this work closer to the Hebrew and Yiddish literature of the turn of our century than to German or American Jewish literature of this century. The characters' Jewishness per se is not in question, despite its yearnings for spirit and light.

For *assimilated* American Jews, however, as for their European fathers and brethren, the problem of identity arises with its full gravity—surprisingly, since America as a host society differs in its pluralistic character from European societies in general and from German society in particular. Yet subjects, motifs, and conflicts that had been common in German Jewish literature appear in American Jewish literature, albeit in rather strange guise. American Jewish literature also features the paranoid who flees from himself and from his environment because of external pressures; but some of the works, unlike their German predecessors, hint that the pressure is merely superficial and that the situation being described is actually a parody of the former one, which had inner justification.

Such a parody of the experience of anxiety and flight is found in

Bruce J. Friedman's novella *Stern* (1962), the story of the existential fear of a Jewish anti-hero who cannot stand his own identity and tries to escape from it and from people who seek to impose this burden upon him. Stern, drafted into the Air Force, blames his Jewishness for his not being a pilot: "Somehow Stern connected his nonflying status with his Jewishness, as though flying were a golden, crew-cut, Gentile thing while Jewishness was a cautious and scholarly quality that crept into engines and prevented planes from lurching off the ground with recklessness."[27] He hates his Jewish identity, which contrasts with his positive image of the true American. (And, according to Friedman, the true Israeli is the Jew who embodies that same positive image.)

Apparently Friedman, in parodying self-hatred, has himself internalized an anti-Semitic doctrine: the Jew as anti-warrior. Friedman's protagonist flees because one of his neighbors insulted his family with the word "kike." That flight (like the stigma), arising out of persistent European anxiety, in Friedman's view, lacks any objective justification in the American context. Paranoia has become empty, a psychosis with no empirical basis.[28]

We can see from this example that American Jewish literature partakes of the legacy of German Jewish literature. The state of having a dual identity is unaltered—although the outer pressure has abated, at first slightly, then much more so. There are works by Bernard Malamud, Philip Roth, and Saul Bellow that are far closer to their German Jewish kinsmen than one might first imagine. One striking example is Roth's "Eli the Fanatic." It concerns Eli, who has been asked by his community to prevent recently arrived European Jewish refugees from flaunting their identity, which has been an embarrassment to their American brethren. Instead, to the astonishment of the community, Eli dons the traditional Jewish garb. The refugees, it seems, are more authentic to him than the people he represents. Thus, Philip Roth, like Joseph Roth and Jakob Wassermann, uses the image of Eastern European ultra-Orthodox Jews—their language, costumes, and customs—as a model of authentic Judaism that is opposed to the assimilated, shallow version of the American suburbs, which he vigorously rejects. This strange nostalgia for a foreign world that no longer exists grows out of the perception that the world that has replaced it is far worse.[29] In this respect, then, Philip Roth evidences his affinity with the German writers who consciously and unconsciously chose the Jewish world of yesterday, with its single identity, over their contemporary world of dual identity.

About this point Cynthia Ozick offers an ambivalent and ironic thesis. We have noted that she calls for the creation of a "new Yiddish," claiming that the world of American Jewry, with its dual identity and single language, can exist as an autonomous cultural realm. Its drawbacks must be converted into advantages, since its duality is inherent, a fact of life. For one thing, even Hebrew and Yiddish culture has lost its singleness of identity today. An emphasis on the opposite and complementary aspect of a Jewish dual identity can be found in Ozick's story "Envy; or, Yiddish in America."[30]

It tells of the envy felt by the Yiddish poets Edelshtein and Baumzweig toward the Yiddish novelist Ostrover. They write poems in Yiddish and remain within the pathetic, moribund confines of a backward language; he writes stories that are translated into English to become treasures of American literature. It is no startling revelation that the prototype for Ostrover seems to be Isaac Bashevis Singer. What is important in this story is not so much the acute description of the writer or the sarcastic portrayal of the wretched poets but, rather, the implication that shtetl culture has no future in America: Anyone seeking to create a secular culture cannot do it with a dead language, and anyone writing in that language comes to life only if he is translated from the idiom of the shtetl into that of the city and suburb.

In this work of fiction, Ozick, who attacked "universalism" with such vehemence, comes out against the wretched "localism" of the representatives of Yiddish culture who seek to break through the walls of the ghetto. In other words, Yiddish "culture," if it is not to be embalmed as a living cadaver, must cross the border and put on local, American clothing. And, in fact, the refugees themselves know they must assimilate in order to survive; they are as eager to fit in as the culture is open to accommodate them. It is only through translations—that is, the readership of strangers who are also relatives—that Isaac Bashevis Singer, for instance, achieves any sort of literary identity. Ozick senses the depths of the conflict of the cultural refugees—the writers, who, in contrast to physical refugees, are liable to swear themselves to silence because they have lost their natural environment—unless they succeed in passing from their original language to that of their potential readership. Ozick makes it clear that there is no room for nostalgia: The one and only possible identity in the American Jewish world is a dual identity. Her work implies that the best the Jews can hope for is that their authors not ignore the duality in their deep desire to abandon their Jewishness and become uniquely American in identity.

The relation between the original identity and the target identity is, as noted, a subject that has preoccupied American Jewish literature, although it has apparently been freed of external pressure, far more than one might first suspect. Still, it could almost be said that, as with German Jewish literature, that topic of identity defines the Jewishness of the literature.[31]

The more traditional issue of an identity forced upon a person against his will is the main theme of Bernard Malamud's *The Fixer* (1966), which recounts the case of Yakov Bok. (This book, which purports to be a historical novel, is a reflection of the Beilis affair, one of the most notorious blood libels in Czarist Russia. To the post-Holocaust American Jewish audience, the Russian blood libel seems like a harbinger of the horrifying spectacle to come.) Bok relates to his Jewish identity as a cruel fate: "From birth a black horse had followed him, a Jewish nightmare. What was being a Jew but an everlasting curse? He was sick of their history, destiny, blood guilt."[32]

In Malamud's "Last Mohican," one of a volume of stories about Fidelman, the artist with a dual identity, the protagonist tries to escape the curse of Zusskind, an "authentic" Jew who appears as a miserable "schnorrer" (leech), arousing guilt in Fidelman's heart.[33] The two figures—ego and alter ego—are bound to each other like Siamese twins and no man can sunder them. In other stories by Malamud, and particularly in "The German Refugee" or the pathetic, allegorical tale, "The Jewbird," Jewish identity is conceived as something imposed on a person like the sword of Damocles.[34] As with their counterparts in much of German Jewish literature, these characters would prefer to separate the ego from the alter ego, the image of American light from the Jewish shadow.

The nature of Jewish identity and the status of Jews in America is one of the major issues in Saul Bellow's novel *The Victim* (1947). Leventhal, the main Jewish character, assumes indirect responsibility for the firing of his friend, Albee, and for his nephew's death, although he is guilty of neither. What we have is the metaphysical and existential experience of guilt and persecution that typified the work of Kafka, here reduced in dimension (almost parodically) to fit the narrower, concrete scale of human society. It is astonishing that the subjective experience of the protagonist or, implicitly, that of the author who resented that character, has been transferred, unaltered, from a closed non-Jewish society to one that is open and pluralistic. Leventhal's antagonist, Albee, makes anti-Semitic statements that are reminiscent of Germany: The Jews pollute the culture; they are children of Caliban; they seek to destroy the foundations of the American upper class.

In fact, this anti-Semitism is a domesticated version of the ingrained European anti-Semitism of the past. The model for persecution has independent existence as a suprapersonal entity embodied in various trivial events, and it is not connected with the changes that took place in the host country.

VII

Although several German Jewish literary models—in terms of character, plot, and subject—recur in strange fashion in American Jewish literature, without doubt great changes have taken place in the depiction of Jewish dual identity. Philip Roth formulated the difficulty of depicting the new Jew.

Jews are people who are not what anti-Semites say they are. That was once a statement out of which a man might begin to construct an identity for himself; now it does not work so well, for it is difficult to act counter to the ways people expect you to act when fewer and fewer people define you by such expectations. The success of the struggle against the defamation of

Jewish character in this country has itself made more pressing the need for a Jewish self-consciousness that is relevant to this time and place.[35]

Roth argues, further, that it is ridiculous to pretend to be a victim in a country where no one forces you to be one if you choose to live otherwise.

Three major writers of American Jewish literature, Bellow, Malamud, and (Philip) Roth, struggled with the problems of identity. Implicitly, they ask time and again: What is the "Jewish identity" of one who is not persecuted yet feels persecuted?—in Malamud's *The Assistant* (1957); in Bellow's *Herzog* (1964) and also in *The Adventures of Augie March* (1953) and *Mr. Sammler's Planet* (1970); and, of course, in Roth's *Portnoy's Complaint* as well as his other books. In *The Assistant* the question is asked outright by the rabbi who eulogizes Morris Bober: Who is a Jew and in what way was Morris Bober Jewish? His (not particularly convincing) answer, essentially, is that a Jew is a good person. For Malamud, a "Jew" is someone—who need not be Jewish—for whom achievement is not the ultimate value. The novel's protagonists do not flee from their Jewish identity; in fact, the Jew and even the gentile (Frank Alpine) embrace it. Malamud respects this identity, in contrast to the typical American Jewish, achievement-oriented way of life. The individual who fails by those standards gains in the spiritual realm what he loses in the material world.[36]

Thus Malamud converts defeat into moral victory and translates the historical failure of the Jews as a persecuted minority into the economic failure of a ne'er-do-well minority. Bober remains an authentic Jew because he does not wish to leave the confines of the local shtetl; as a consequence, he does not fit like the majority of his brethren into the American way of life economically or socially. But by virtue of his economic failure, the character preserves his identity (and integrity); conversely, economic success entails losing it. Malamud seems to suggest a connection between economic upward mobility and cultural assimilation. One infers from the overall structure of the work that the author values the existence of some kind of Jewish identity in pluralistic American society, this in contrast to German Jewish writers, whose characters wished to rid themselves of their identity.

Bellow approaches this issue in more complex fashion, removing the problematics from the area of relations between Jews and non-Jews. The structure of relations he describes in *Herzog* is mainly intra-Jewish. The two main characters of the novel are both Jews: Herzog, the refined, aristocratic intellectual, on the one hand; the plebeian, vulgar Gersbach, on the other—two faces of a new generation of Jews. They vie, as creators and purveyors of the spirit, for influence in American society; and their competition for the same woman represents a kind of struggle for the "world."

Much has been written about the persona of the "schlemiel" in Jewish literature. But Herzog is certainly *not* this type: Women are fond of him, and he has a position in the academic establishment. Still, he takes Madeleine's betrayal as a kind of absolute treachery, isolating him and making all his activities in the world seem unreal. Instead of taking action to influence the realities of human life, he composes political and philosophical epistles. He lives in a fictional world of his own creation, enjoying his role as a tortured romantic, whereas his friend and his divorced wife take pleasure in this-worldly vanities.

Bellow's view of the romantic in a mass society is very ambivalent.[38] Herzog struggles for his identity against a society that blurs identities but, to a great extent, he enjoys his plight of weakness and isolation. He has been separated from the one social group that might have protected him: the Jewish family. Having left its protective embrace, he is exposed to the ravages of American society and to the intellectual battles that mark the quest for achievement in the cultural sphere. This uprooted Jew endures the struggle as best he can until he becomes overwhelmed and his brother and sister come to the rescue.

So Bellow, like Malamud, feels nostalgia for the identity of the primary matrix, the family, which welcomes the hero unconditionally and does not demand that he prove himself in an erotic and pseudointellectual war in which the talented but vulgar survive. In other words, "modern" society splits his uprooted identity, and he must constantly prove himself anew. Only in the world of his parents, the world of yesterday, does his identity exist as an unshakable wholeness.

In *Portnoy's Complaint*, Roth presents the Jew whose identity is not defined with the "assistance" of outside pressure but who nonetheless struggles with it. (Similarly in the work of Roth's followers and imitators, such as Alan Lelchuk and Erica Jong.) The protagonist, like his German Jewish counterparts, gets no pleasure from his Jewish identity and, along with his father, is smothered by the embrace of his mother, who demands complete identification with the tribe. He is expected to remain an infant all his life and yet to serve as a substitute for his impotent father. Moreover, on the one hand, he is called upon to open the gates to the non-Jewish world that were closed to his father, whereas on the other he is expected to remain loyal to his mother and the family.

Lying on his psychoanalyst's couch, Portnoy recognizes his predicament. This awareness, however, does not alter the experience. Indeed he seems to enjoy it: fleeing from his mother to the bosom of strange women (although he never takes the decisive step and marries one), both hating the mother's tribal Jewish identity and experiencing revulsion for the gentile women and their families. Whereas that ambivalence is certainly a source of pain, the hero nevertheless revels in his use of psychoanalytic rhetoric. His story amuses him, filled as it is with jokes and puns and memories. Recounting his experiences, he relishes every relived moment; indeed, the analyst's couch itself seems to be the source of his greatest pleasure.

The tale finishes without offering a solution. Rather, its conclusion is its beginning: In response to the protagonist's monologue, the analyst proposes that they begin! Thus the author signals that this is a circular process that has no termination: Portnoy's "complaint" will go on and on forever. Just as the hero has enjoyed his own cleverness up to now, so the enjoyment will endure; just as he enjoyed reviling his mother and father, so he will also continue to make ironic fun of the WASPs. As he is revolted by his family's weakness, so he is revolted by the qualities of his gentile "hosts," who stand for the good, the marvelous, and the enlightened everywhere and at all times. Roth's *Portnoy's Complaint* sings the praises of abnormality. Rather than "Lucky me, I'm an orphan" (as Sholem Aleichem wrote), he says, "Lucky me, I'm neurotic; lucky me, I suffer from a dual identity." When he encounters a Jewish woman with a healthy, integrated personality in Israel, he loses his bearings and becomes impotent because he is not equipped to deal with normality.

There is a pathology in Malamud's and Bellow's characters, who take pleasure in their peculiar identity as self-persecutors. Roth's Portnoy enjoys his neurosis and derives his satisfaction from being psychoanalyzed, not from the possibility that he may find fulfillment outside the analyst's office.

VIII

The German Jewish authors I have discussed took their identity as imposed and absolute, a cruel fate against which they all rebelled. Nonetheless, they viewed those who rejected it with contempt, as miserable anti-heroes, hopeless and pitiful. American Jewish writers place less emphasis on pressure from the outside and emphasize the positive-negative bond between the characters and their identity. They choose it even though all gates seem to be open before them in their pluralistic country: Frank Alpine converts; Moses Herzog flees to the bosom of his family in his hour of need; Alex Portnoy does not marry a gentile woman. How can we explain the pleasure that the characters take in ambivalent situations and in pain and suffering? It is, of course, possible to offer universal (psychological and philosophical) interpretations. But American Jewish literature of the 1960s formulated its explanations in openly tribal and ethnic terms, whereas in the German Jewish literature of the 1920s (but before then and afterwards too), the tribal and ethnic terms were implicit.

European Jewish culture was almost completely destroyed during the Holocaust, including both the society that had produced German Jewish authors and the authors themselves, who left no local heirs. Thus, the postwar period has seen no comparable "European" Jewish literature. If European Jewish literature in general, and German Jewish writing in particular, have any heirs, they are on the other side of the Atlantic. The culture with its dual identity has passed, in modified form, from one place of exile to another. The identity of its Jewish readership has changed, as have the authors. Yet the problem of Jewish identity plagues Jewish writers, their characters, and their readers as much as ever.

NOTES

1. For a very sensitive example of conspicuous concern for the definition of Jews and Judaism in literature, see Hans Mayer, "Comrade Shylock" and "Jewish Figures in the Bourgeois Novel," in *Outsider: A Study in Life and Letters*, trans. Denis M. Sweet (Cambridge, Mass.: MIT Press, 1982).
2. See *Encyclopaedia Judaica* (1972), s.v. "Press."
3. Dov Sadan, Introductory essay (in Hebrew), in *Avnei-bedek* (Tel Aviv: Ha-Kibbutz ha-Meuḥad, 1962), especially 16–25.
4. Gustav Krojanker, ed., *Juden in der deutschen Literatur* (Berlin: Welt-verlag, 1922). Arnold Zweig, *Bilanz der deutschen Judenheit* (1933; repr. Cologne: J. Melzer, 1961), is a particularly interesting book, mentioning all the varied achievements of German Jewry and discussing their literary activities with enthusiasm (pp. 238–263).
5. Harry Zohn, *Wiener Juden in der deutschen Literatur* (Tel Aviv: Editions "Olamenu," 1964).
6. Hans Tramer dealt with the problem of identity in the poetry of Karl Wolfskehl, in particular, and also discussed several other poets in "Über deutsch-jüdisches Dichtertum: Zur Morphologie des jüdischen Bekenntnisses," *Bulletin des Leo Baeck Instituts* 2 (1957): 88–103.
7. For example, see the essays by Philip Roth, "Some New Jewish Stereotypes," "Writing about Jews," and "Imagining Jews," in *Reading Myself and Others* (New York: Farrar, Straus and Giroux, 1975).
8. Ludwig Lewisohn, *What is this Jewish Heritage?* (New York: B'nai B'rith Hillel Foundation, 1954), 81–83; Max F. Schulz, *Radical Sophistication: Studies in Contemporary Jewish American Novelists* (Athens, Ohio: Ohio University Press, 1969); Cynthia Ozick, "Toward a New Yiddish," in *Art and Ardor: Essays* (New York: Knopf, 1983), 155–177, first presented as a lecture at the Weizmann Institute in Rehovoth, Israel, in 1970. Page citations in the text are taken from these editions.
9. M. J. Berdyczewski, "The Stranger" (in Hebrew), in *Kol kitvei ber-dishevski* (Collected Stories) (Tel Aviv: Devir, 1951), 67. First published: "Re-vivim" 1 (1908).
10. The term "self-hatred," coined by Theodor Lessing in *Der jüdische Selbsthass* (Berlin: Zionistischer Bücher-Bund, 1930), is appropriate here. Mayer, *Outsider*, gives a brilliant account of the connection between self-hatred and Jewish identity: "Jewish integration in Europe proceeded from the assumption that Jewish language and history were to be sacrificed, just

as Moses Mendelssohn taught; that there would be no Jewish nation. Everything was to be 'adopted' from the host country and people: language, culture, region. That failed" (p. 363).

11. See Hans Kohn, *Karl Kraus, Arthur Schnitzler, Otto Weininger: Aus dem jüdischen Wien der Jahrhundertwende* (Tübingen: Mohr, 1962), especially 34–37. Some of Kohn's remarks contrasting Weininger's relations with his father to those of Kafka (p. 36) are not always persuasive. A Hebrew author, David Vogel, wrote a novel (*Ḥayyei nissuim,* 1929–1930) based on Weininger's doctrine.

12. Max Brod, *Rëubeni, Fürst der Juden: Ein Renaissanceroman* (Munich: K. Wolff, 1925). Brod's presentation of Rëubeni resembles Haim Hazaz's depiction of Yuzpa in *The End of Days,* trans. Dalia Bilu (Tel Aviv: Institute for the Translation of Hebrew Literature, 1982). See Gershon Shaked, "*The End of Days* and the Expressionist Play," in Hazaz, *The End of Days,* pp. 131–158.

13. David Bronsen, *Joseph Roth: Eine Biographie* (Cologne: Kiepenheuer and Witsch, 1974).

14. Joseph Roth, *Die Büste des Kaisers* in *Werke,* vol. 3, ed. Hermann Kesten (Cologne: Kiepenheuer and Witsch, 1975–1976), 192.

15. Joseph Roth, *Juden auf Wanderschaft,* in *Werke,* vol. 3, p. 304. Translations from German are by J. Green.

16. Joseph Roth, *Briefe 1911–1939,* ed. Hermann Kesten (Cologne: Kiepenheuer and Witsch, 1970), 419–422. I refer to the letter dated 8 Aug. 1935, in which he makes rather harsh remarks about Zionism, such as: "A Zionist is a National Socialist; a Nazi is a Zionist" (p. 420). And he continues: "Therefore I cannot fathom how it is that you wish to start the fight against Hitler, who is merely an imbecilic brother of the Zionist, using a brother of the National Socialist, i.e., a Zionist, even the most ingenious of them. Perhaps you can protect Jewry in that way. But I wish to protect both Europe and mankind from Nazis *and also* from Hitler-Zionists. I don't wish to protect the Jews, except as the most endangered vanguard of all mankind." In these remarks, addressed to another assimilated Jew, Stefan Zweig, pathological universalism reaches its apogee.

17. Joseph Roth, *Die Flucht ohne Ende,* in *Werke,* vol. 1, p. 421.

18. Jakob Wassermann, *Lebensdienst* (Leipzig: Grethlein and Co., 1928), 177.

19. I have seen Wassermann's handwritten notes on Heinrich Graetz's *History of the Jews* and on other sources, made in preparation for this novel. The manuscripts are in the Schiller German National Archive for German Literature in Marbach am Neckar. I am grateful to that archive for allowing me to examine those materials.

20. Bronsen, *Biographie,* pp. 598–608.

21. Two of Wassermann's letters are highly instructive about his ambivalent attitude toward his dual identity. One, to the Jewish community of Gratz dated 15 May 1933, informs them that he cannot pay the amount demanded of him for membership in the community because his books are

no longer sold in Germany (on the one hand he is bound to the community, but on the other hand he slips away from it). The second, rather pathetic letter, dated 1 Aug. 1933, is addressed to the Association of German Writers. He retracts his letter of resignation from that organization, claiming that he had left the organization after seeing an announcement in the press stating that any non-Aryan author would be expelled; not wishing to be expelled, he submitted his resignation first. In the meanwhile, he says, he has learned from his German friends that the announcement was in error and that only new non-Aryan members would be rejected. Therefore, he withdraws his resignation and encloses his membership dues. That letter is in the Schiller German National Archive in Marbach am Neckar. It shows the humiliating self-abnegation to which Wassermann brought himself in order to belong to the institutions of the German people.

22. The précis is given in a letter, dated 25 Aug. 1933, to Klement, apparently the intended American publisher of the proposed book. That letter is also in the archive at Marbach.

23. Daniel Walden, ed., *On Being Jewish: American Jewish Writers from Cahan to Bellow* (Greenwich, Conn.: Fawcett Publications, 1974).

24. Henry Roth, *Call It Sleep* (1934; repr. New York: Avon, 1969).

25. I refer to the novels and stories about Jewish migration to America written in Hebrew by writers such as Reuben Wallenrod, *Ki fanah yom* (1946), *Be-ein dor* (1945); Simon Halkin, *Yeḥiel ha-hagri* (1928), *Ad mashber* (1945); Samuel Leib Blank, *Mr. Kunis* (1934), *Al admat amerikah* (1958); and the Yiddish novels of Joseph Opatoshu, *Lost People* (1922), *Die tentserin* (1929), and others.

26. Chaim Potok, *The Chosen* (New York: Simon and Schuster, 1967).

27. Bruce J. Friedman, *Stern: A Novel* (New York: Simon and Schuster, 1962), 54.

28. It appears to me that the interpretations of Friedman's novel and of Edward Wallant's *The Pawnbroker* (New York: Harcourt, Brace, and World, 1961) offered by Schulz are no less symptomatic than the works themselves. Schulz ignores the problem I have raised almost completely and even disregards the fact that Friedman intended to parody Jewish fears. See Schulz, *Radical Sophistication*, pp. 186–194.

29. Roth himself discusses a series of letters to the editor that protest the "anti-Semitic" character of his works (the writers refer to stories such as "Defender of the Faith"). Philip Roth, *Reading Myself and Others*, pp. 149–169.

30. Cynthia Ozick, "Envy; or, Yiddish in America," in *The Pagan Rabbi and Other Stories* (New York: Knopf, 1971).

31. I believe that the struggle for identity and doubts about it are part of that desperate striving for historical continuity that is typical of contemporary secular Jewish culture. Here is Robert Alter's formulation: "I would suggest that Jewish life since the entrance of the Jews into modern culture

may be usefully viewed as a precarious, though stubborn, experiment in the possibilities of historical continuity, when most of the grounds for continuity have been cut away." Robert Alter, *After the Tradition: Essays on Modern Jewish Writing* (New York: E. P. Dutton and Co., 1969), 10–11.

32. Bernard Malamud, *The Fixer* (New York: Farrar, Straus and Giroux, 1966), 187.

33. Bernard Malamud, *Pictures of Fidelman: An Exhibition* (New York: Farrar, Straus and Giroux, 1969).

34. Bernard Malamud, *Idiots First* (New York: Farrar, Straus and Co., 1962).

35. Philip Roth, *Reading Myself and Others*, p. 165.

36. Robert Alter links the figure of Bober to the schlemiel (as does Ruth Wisse in her book on the schlemiel as a modern hero). In Alter's opinion the main image in *The Assistant* is that of the prison: "The prison, like the *shlemiel* who is usually its chief inmate, is Malamud's way of suggesting that to be fully a man is to accept the most painful limitations; those who escape these limitations achieve only an illusory, self-negating kind of freedom, for they become less than responsible human beings" (*After the Tradition*, p. 122). Cf. Ruth Wisse, "Requiem in Several Voices," in *The Schlemiel as Modern Hero* (Chicago: University of Chicago Press, 1971), 108–124.

37. Wisse describes Moses E. Herzog as the spoiled child of a Jewish mother, trying to attain some great marvel, although he progresses toward it in ironic fashion, like a schlemiel, and, regarding the desire to advance in life, as he knows, childhood is decisive. I agree with Wisse's remarks about the central role of the Jewish family in the hero's life. Wisse, "The Schlemiel as Liberal Humanist," in *The Schlemiel as Modern Hero*, pp. 92–107.

38. That view of Herzog as a romantic in mass society is common among the critics. See Malcolm Bradbury, *Saul Bellow* (London and New York: Methuen, 1982), 71.

Jewish tradition and Western impact in modern Hebrew literature

I

Just as Jewish philosophy grew out of the ongoing struggle between its internal development and outside influences, so Hebrew literature came into its own during the Golden Age in medieval Spain and, even before, as a result of the constant tension between internal and external literary and linguistic traditions. Later, in the eighteenth century, the work of Moses Hayyim Luzzatto stood at the crossroads of Hebrew literature; while its roots were in Hebraic mystic literature, it was also influenced externally by the Italian pastoral plays, especially those of Guarini.[1] In general, this tension between ancient Jewish tradition and contemporary European cultures characterizes the new Hebrew literature that began to blossom in the late eighteenth century.

This applies especially to Hebrew fiction and drama, which were very open to outside influence, having been only modestly developed in the premodern Hebrew literary tradition. Although the Bible and the talmudic fable, various kinds of folk tales, and *maqama* literature (in rhymed prose) all had their own literary norms in their own time, they did not together constitute a consecutive, diachronic tradition of narrative. Moreover, the novel, short story, and novella, which are characteristic of the new Hebrew fiction, are strikingly Western forms, born in the European literature of the Renaissance. (Modern Hebrew poetry, by contrast, has a very rich ancient literary tradition that began with the Bible, continued with the ancient *piyyut* [liturgical poetry in Palestine under Roman and Byzantine rule], and flourished again in medieval Spain and in Renaissance Italy.)

Just as the Hebrew language assimilated external forms into a written tradition, so Hebrew belles lettres combined native patterns with external forms and traditions. In order to comprehend this dialectical process, we will examine, firstly, the traditional elements that appear in Hebrew fiction and the roles they play in the structures of particular works; and, secondly, the possible traditional forms that have reemerged in the new Hebrew literature, transformed by their contacts with the West.

Hebrew literary traditions occur principally as symbolic motifs rather than as entire forms or models. For instance, in Jewish (as in Christian) tradition, the biblical Song of Songs was usually interpreted allegorically. In modern Hebrew literature, this type of allegorical exegesis eventually reaches parody, as in *My Mare* by Mendele Mokher Seforim. Entire talmudic tales (aggadot) or their main motifs reappear in Bialik's fables (such as in *Agadat sheloshah ve-arbaah*, The Legend of the Three and the Four). Other such motifs—for example, tales about King Solomon and Asmodeus—appear in I. L. Peretz's story "Shalosh ḥuppot" (Three Weddings). Many of David Frischmann's stories, such as "Ba-midbar" (In the Desert), are based on biblical sources; others, on reinterpretations of the legend of the golem and the Maharal of Prague (*The Golem*). Haim Hazaz's story "Ḥatan ha-damim" (A Bridegroom of Blood) is based on biblical material (the birth of Moses' first-born); so are stories by Asher Barash ("Shaul ve-ha-atonot," [Saul and the Asses]) and Yitzhak Shenhar ("Geḥazi"). Historical traditions ("The Tribes of Judah") may be found in the book *Or zaruah* (The Light that Emanated) by Yaakov Horowitz; and even contemporary younger writers such as Moshe Shamir (*The King of Flesh and Blood* and *Al suso be-shabbat* [On Horseback on the Sabbath]) and Nissim Aloni (*Aliyat elishah* [Elishah's Ascension]) resort to biblical and midrashic material in their short stories and novels. In most of these works, one exception being Bialik's *Agadat sheloshah ve-arbaah*,[2] the traditional element is used in a superficial manner and does not always affect the inner structure of the work.

In some works traditional elements transform the immediate narrative context of the novels as well as motifs and main characters, infusing them with symbolical significance. This happens in some of the major stories by M. J. Berdyczewski, such as "Parah adumah" (Red Cow) and "Be-seter raam" (Hidden Thunder), in which the characters are illuminated by a mythological aspect. By inference, the town's butchers appear as priests of Baal and the town's nabob as an ancient Israelite tribal chief, a reembodiment of Judah who took Tamar, Er's wife, under his protection. Ezekiel Hefetz, Brenner's hero in *Breakdown and Bereavement,* is a kind of reinterpretation of the biblical Job and the prophet Ezekiel, and Agnon's Yitzhak Kummer, in *Only Yesterday,* reembodies the archetypal Isaac and the sacrificial motif. Feierberg's novella *Whither?* is full of traditional elements,[3] and similar themes enrich the works of younger writers, such as Yehuda Amichai's *Not of This Time, Not of This Place* and Pinhas Sadeh's *Life as a Parable.* Jewish tradition is seen by these authors as a treasury of intertextual implications that impart symbolic or archetypal significance to the entire structure of the story or to specific characters.

Some Hebrew fiction also uses "simplistic," or "preartistic," forms such as fairy tales, riddles, jokes, and anecdotes. At times these forms are only superficial, as in the tales of I. L. Peretz and Judah Steinberg, which follow the patterns of Hasidic legend.[4] At other times the use of such forms is more significant. S. Y. Agnon's stories, for example, draw upon midrashic tradition, as in "Agunot" ("Living Widowhood") and upon Hasidic literature, as in "And the Crooked Shall Become Straight." Both Agnon and Hazaz make use of talmudic texts in their respective works *A Guest for the Night* and *Yaish,* to the extent that these become an integral part of the structure.

II

All these factors stamp the new literature with the qualities of the older tradition and prevent a total cultural assimilation. They are among the components that give it its originality. Moreover, the greater the tensions between these components and Western influence, the more interesting and complex this body of literature becomes.

At the beginning of the century, Ahad Ha-am (one of the major thinkers on the Jewish cultural revival) complained about the decline of Hebrew literature and the loss of its originality: "Since the beginning of our modern literature and until now, hardly any genuinely original books have appeared, books which we would feel reveal our national spirit in a particular way; everything is either a translation or an imitation, and even this is for the most part badly done: the translations fall far short of the originals, while the imitations are all too close . . . "[5] However, Ahad Ha-am overstated the case somewhat because he overlooked those tensions that, to a large extent, had also characterized our early literature. Tradition still flowed in the veins of the new literature, and its creators were contending with it. But the farther we move from the start of the century and the closer we come to the Hebrew literature of contemporary Israel, the fewer the symbols, themes, and patterns that have their source in tradition. Literature detached itself from the written tradition, with its historical roots, planted itself in the locale, and absorbed impressions from its surroundings. Space supplanted time: The "new man" came to reflect his native landscape rather than his past. The severance was not total, however, since the language itself was charged with traditional allusions. The process rather resembled that of the development that took place in the Hebrew language, marked as it was by ups and downs, advances and retreats. In sum, the vicissitudes of the new Hebrew literature reflect changes in ideas and in literary forms.

III

An additional factor that must be taken into account is what Ludwig Kahn called the sanctification process:[6] the absorption by the secular realm of religious concepts and experiences. Although some religious values were being secularized, as has been often noted, more often secular values were becoming sanctified.

This process is characteristic of a period of rebirth and the emergence of a national movement. As cultural patterns are transferred from the customary spheres, they carry their emotional content with them. In the narrative field, to a certain extent, Hebrew fiction was a substitute for the old didactic moral tales.[7] The various "narrative confessions" that characterized Hebrew fiction at the beginning of the century (for example, Feierberg's *Whither?* or Brenner's *In Winter*) were confessions of atheism rather than of belief; but the confessional need, the ardor and the yearning for deliverance and redemption that they expressed, had deep roots in religious writings. Thus the phrase "the sacred art" gained acceptance in Hebrew literature;[8] the sanctification of nature and labor became widespread;[9] a godlike man was postulated, whether as hero[10] or victim;[11] and the concept of the obsessively introspective man tormented by conscience was developed.[12] Love also substituted for the religious experience,[13] and the commitment to Zionist fulfillment replaced commitment to religion.[14] These are difficult intertextual processes to follow. It should be added that the dislocation from sacred to secular was not an exclusively internal Jewish affair. Certain fields that had become filled with religious content in European literature became similarly endowed in Hebrew literature; and the evidence suggests, even, that the altered world view was drawn directly from the European Christian tradition.[15]

IV

Here we arrive at the other pole of the dialectic process, namely, Western culture. From the start, the new Hebrew literature was decisively influenced by European literary sources and ideas, the setting in which it developed.

The literature of the Hebrew Enlightenment in Germany was influenced by German literature from Schiller to Goethe,[16] just as Hebrew literature in Italy had been influenced by its surroundings. In the latter part of the nineteenth century there was an awareness of the cultural challenge posed by Western influences, and for years the argument raged whether this influence was beneficial or destructive. As we saw, Ahad Ha-am was convinced that it endangered any original literary development. Other critics at the turn of the century, such as Reuben Brainin and David Frischmann, spoke out in favor of opening Jewish culture to external trends: "Our scholars and authors need to find an authentic compromise between general human development and that of our nation with its own particular qualities, in such a way that one will not damage the other but rather that the two worlds will strengthen and complement one another. Only thus can our literature be fertile and useful to our people."[17]

This problem was solved not in the pages of essays but, rather, through a lengthy and complex dialectical process. The debate was still alive in Israel as late as 1938, when Avraham Shlonsky, one of the major poets, defended the "opening up" of Hebrew literature with particular sharpness against those who preferred cultural isolation: "Even the great cultures, who for sheer quantity can supply all their own wants, throw their doors wide open and draw deeply from foreign sources; whereas a nation such as ours, whose literary culture is still in its infancy, prefers, out of some weird arrogance, to stew in its own juices."[18]

The influence of Western culture (literature, philosophy, and so forth) on Hebrew literature is not synchronous: There is no direct exchange of content from any European current to its Hebrew parallel. It is not even always affected by geographical propinquity.[19] Frischmann and Peretz, the most prominent prose Hebrew writers from Poland at the turn of the century, were influenced by Heinrich Heine and Ludwig Börne many years after the deaths of those two German Jews and, as well, by later French writers, such as France and Maurice Maeterlinck. Hebrew authors during the Second Aliyah (1904–1914), such as Agnon, Reuveni, and Kimhi, were influenced by the Scandinavian authors Jacobsen, Björnson, and Hamsun. Some of the first-generation native Hebrew authors who appeared on the Palestinian scene in the late 1930s were particularly influenced by Hebrew translations of Soviet Russian literature and by the American fiction from the 1920s to the 1940s, Hemingway in particular. These influences do not depend on time or place; they are not definitive literary schools. If on occasion a specific literary trend becomes noticeable in a certain writer's works, the impact is diffused and absorbed into the literature, which evolves according to its own rules.

A cultural influence shows itself in four principal aspects: translation, adaptation, imitation, and impact. Since the 1880s a great many seminal European books have been translated into Hebrew. The best Hebrew writers (including Frischmann, Peretz, Bialik, Brenner, Agnon, Gnessin, Barash, Shofman, Baron, Berkowitz, Kabak, Halkin, Horowitz, Shenhar, and Shamir) have all tried their hand at translating, and they have brought the Hebrew reader a spectrum of works by Russian authors (principally Dostoevsky, Tolstoy, Merzhekovsky, and Chekhov), French authors (Stendhal, Flaubert, France, and Maeterlinck), German (Schiller, Goethe, Spielhagen, Stifter, Zweig, Altenberg, Schnitzler, Wassermann, and Remarque), English (Shakespeare, Whitman, Wilde, and Beckett), and Scandinavian (Jacobsen, Björnson, and Hamsun). A number of writers have devoted most of their time to translation (Treivish, Wolfowski, Ben-Shaul, Levin, and Ginsburg) and the translations done by three major poets—Shlonsky, Alterman, and Lea Goldberg, from the 1930s to the 1950s, influenced the prose style of their successors: S. Yizhar, Moshe Shamir, Shlomo Nitzan, Nathan Shaham, Hanoch Bartov. The majority of this group, known as "the generation of the land," was born in Israel. The years of World War II made them very dependent on translations of modern American and Russian literature. And in the State of Israel, they would continue to absorb more and more English and American literary influences.

A history of adaptations and translations into Hebrew—as yet unwritten—would illuminate the development of the new Hebrew style. An examination of the main process is of course outside the scope of this discussion, although some remarks concerning it are relevant here. Farfetched adaptation was typical of both the Hebrew Enlightenment literature (1800–1880) and of early Yiddish literature (Meir Letteris's *Ben-Avuiah*, an adaptation of Goethe's *Faust*; Jacob Gordin's *Mirele ephros* [The Jewish Queen Lear], an adaptation of Shakespeare's *King Lear*). They became rarer during the first period of the Hebrew revival (1890–1920), although even then some translations read rather like adaptations. Moreover, some translations made an original contribution to Hebrew literature at times as important as some original works: Bialik's translation of Cervantes' *Don Quixote* (translated from the Russian), which is far from accurate but has literary merit of its own, is an epitome of

Bialik's poetic style. Berkowitz's Hebrew translations of Sholem Aleichem's Yiddish works attempt a transfer from a vernacular (Yiddish) that had become a literary language to a literary language
(Hebrew) that was trying to become a vernacular.[20] And Shlonsky's
translation of Romain Rolland's *Colas Breugnon* from the original
French is the zenith of all this linguistic innovation, mastery of the
neologism, and phrase wizardry.[21] In each of these three examples
the translator perpetrated, as it were, an "artistic treason." Bialik
"Judaizes" Cervantes; Berkowitz "stylizes" Sholem Aleichem; and
Shlonsky translates the French smith's argot into a "Hebrew dialect" of his own invention. It is a process of transplantation, a jux-
taposition of an original style to foreign material, by which the
translator is less a servant to the original work than a master who
shapes it according to his own creative drive.

Hebrew literature is not free from imitations. Its close affinity
with European fiction led it to borrow its patterns and forms, such
as the short story and the novel with their diverse narrative techniques, characterizations, and styles. Sometimes this proximity di-
minishes the imitator with respect to the author imitated, and sometimes the imitator breaks through on his own artistic merits. The
presence of Chekhovian influence in Hebrew fiction reveals the
possibilities and limitations of imitation, the fine line that separates
imitation from impact, where the source becomes a stimulus to
original creativity. The poet and literary historian Simon Halkin
rightly pointed out that many writers at the turn of the century
were influenced by Chekhov's stories and plays[22]—notably I. D.
Berkowitz, who translated *Boys;* Uri Nissan Gnessin, who translated *The Marsh; Talant,* and *A Woman Tells Tales in the Spring;* and
Gershon Shofman, who did *The Cherry Orchard* and *The Seagull.*
Berkowitz's and Shofman's own stories plainly reveal that they did
not stray from the conventions of the Chekhovian story, and some
of Berkowitz's stories are discernibly derivative.[23]

Gnessin is different. At the beginning of his literary career (*Shadows of Life*) he patterned his realistic stories on Chekhov, but in time
he paved his own way. His style, his methods of characterization,
and the relationship between the inner and outer structures de-
parted from those of his model. Committing "artistic treason" with
the Chekhovian rules, he elaborated what were secondary factors

in the original (an explicit stream-of-consciousness exposition of the mental state and detailed descriptions of landscape) and turned them into the principal feature of the "derivative" creation. In any case, a new organism that was no longer dependent on its antecedents had come into being.

Gnessin, however, is not a symptomatic example of the dialectical relationship between the internal and external traditions that together contributed to an original Hebrew literature. From the structural point of view, he could also have been a part of the evolution of Russian literature, for while he altered the contemporary Russian tradition of the long-short story, he did not juxtapose it to modern Hebrew literary tradition. Transplanting the Russian tradition with its conventions into Hebrew—whose spirit ill fits the Russian syntax imposed upon it—and into the Jewish social background has a certain novelty; but this "transfer" is less important than Gnessin's original modification of the conventions of the Russian long-short story.

v

At certain high points in Hebrew fiction Jewish and Western traditions actually combined, and the tension between the two traditions resulted in works of originality and artistic power. The outstanding examples of this phenomenon are the works of S. Y. Agnon and Haim Hazaz. (Bialik's poetry too, but it does not belong in the present context.)

Mendele's *The Travels and Adventures of Benjamin the Third* was based on Jewish travel tales and enriched by midrashic traditions, but it remained close to the conventions of European travel literature and the "Don Quixotiads."[24] In his *The Book of Beggars*, the Jewish tradition is represented by various aggadic themes and suggestions, but it is undoubtedly also related to the European tradition of the sentimental and satirical novel.[25] Both works belong to the literary tradition of the Enlightenment and its aftermath.

Agnon's *The Bridal Canopy* is a novel rich in traditional Jewish motifs.[26] Moreover, the plot itself is based on a custom of raising money to provide a dowry for a poor bride. The structure of the

THE SHADOWS WITHIN 92

book is drawn partly from the picaresque novel and partly from the
"banquet" novel. Again, the protagonists are close to the Don Quixote tradition. The combination of all these factors gives the work
its special character. In his *Only Yesterday,* the author unites the
structure of the historic "chronicle," common to European literature, with the Isaac myth of the sacrificed son—the main leitmotiv
in the book. Agnon's precise styling, based on the written tradition, endows all of his writings, like those of Hazaz, with their
uniquely Jewish quality. The strength of both writers is revealed in
their ability to unite Western models with their own particular style,
thus fusing traditional Jewish textures and Western structures.

The problem of adapting the Western literary tradition is one of
the basic problems of this fiction. Agnon's story "Tishre" (first published in *Ha-poel ha-tzair,* the Labor Movement weekly, in 1911)
serves as an outstanding example of both the problem and its solution. At that time Agnon was under the influence of the Scandinavian impressionists: His hero wishes to translate Jacobsen's *Niels
Lyhne;* Agnon himself translated Björnson's story "Dust" during the
years 1912–1913.[27] He was influenced by Hamsun as well: There is
a discernible parallel between Hamsun's *Pan* (which was translated
into German in 1895) and "Tishre." The love triangle in *Pan*—Lieu-
tenant Grann, Edvarda (the woman with whom Grann is infatu-
ated), and the Baron—is paralleled in "Tishre" by Hemdat (or
Naaman, as he is called in the first version), Yael Hayyut, and Sham-
mai. Hamsun's outcast stranger is the hunter who lives in the heart
of nature; Agnon's hero is a poet. In Hamsun's story pathos overcomes irony, and this is so in the first version of Agnon's story,
which was imperfectly styled. Both "Tishre" and *Pan* comprise a
story within a story. In "Tishre" this is the story about Salsivila
(which was deleted from later versions and for which a particular
place was set aside in the story "Leilot" [Nights]). In *Pan* there is
the legendary tale of the love between Diderick and Izerline. Although plot, structure (in Agnon, the omniscient narrator; in Hamsun, the narrator-hero), and relations between the sexes are handled
quite differently by the two authors, the young Agnon nevertheless stands too close to Hamsun; and the proximity does not serve
him well.

In a later version entitled "Giveat ha-hol" (Hill of Sand, 1920),

Agnon altered the story as a whole. He consolidated his style, broadened the epic scope, and heightened the irony. The previous lame imitation had evolved into an original work.[28] Although this may not at first appear to stem from the Jewish-Western dialectic, further examination reveals that Agnon's renewed connection with the Jewish cultural past through contact with major Jewish scholars in Germany (1913–1924) contributed richly to the evolution of his style. The origins of his tendency to do away with paragraphing, to unify sentences and balance them, which is so prominent in the final version, lie in traditional Jewish texture and techniques. What had been a sentimental impressionistic story becomes, in the stylized archaic diction of the sages, an ironic social tale.[29]

The dialectic between Jewish and Western culture is the scarlet thread that runs through Hebrew fiction of the revival period. At first, the Jewish tradition was manifest and the Western one implicit, as if, in response to Ahad Ha-am's demands, the authors were not writing novels and short stories after the Western fashion but, rather, were discussing problems of Jews and Judaism. Later these elements began to mingle. Berdyczewski's stories, rich in Jewish motifs, are close to the European Gothic novel; and Brenner's confessions adapt traditional archetypes to the pattern of the European psychological novel. Sometimes the literary-cultural tradition takes second place to the exigencies of life, and sometimes it is stronger. Gradually this literature became more explicitly Western, while the Jewish element became increasingly implicit (notably in the works of Gnessin, Shofman, Steinman, and Vogel).

Even Israeli writers, from the first generation to the present, who were no longer shaped by Jewish tradition, were not entirely westernized. Although their religious roots were severed, the traditions and conventions of an ancient culture still animate their works. One feels this tension in the poetry, fiction, and plays of Yehuda Amichai, who has a permanent intertextual relationship with Jewish tradition. Other notable examples are H. Levin, who has written a grotesque parodic dramatization called "The Sufferings of Job," and A. B. Yehoshua, whose novels at times have deep biblical substructures. The dialectical tension in modern Hebrew literature is sometimes expressed as the interaction between the recanonization of Jewish heritage and the translation of Western tradition. It is also a tug-of-war between a distant historical culture and one nearby, or between historical particularity and assimilation. It is, at any rate, one of the fundamental elements and motivating forces in the works of modern Hebrew writers.

NOTES

1. Fischel Lachower, *Toledot ha-sifrut ha-ivrit ha-ḥadashah* (A History of Hebrew Literature), vol. 1 (Tel Aviv: Devir, 1946–1948), 19–29; idem, "The Tower Gates: The Tower Fable" (in Hebrew), in *Al gevul ha-yashan veha-ḥadash* (On the Border Between Old and New) (Jerusalem: Mossad Bialik, 1951), 29–84.

2. Detailed treatment of these problems is not within the scope of this discussion. For Bialik's treatment of traditional sources see Gershon Shaked, "The Myth of Rebellion: An Interpretation of 'The Dead of the Desert' by H. N. Bialik," *Hebrew University Studies in Literature* 2 (Spring 1974): 92–116.

3. Specific research was done by Samuel Werses, "Legend in Feierberg's Works" (in Hebrew), in *Sipur ve-shorsho* (The Story and its Roots) (Tel Aviv: Massada Press, 1971), 88–103.

4. There are some writers who use the more sophisticated and artistic tradition of the medieval *maqama* (rhymed prose): Hayyim Nahman Bialik, *Aluf batslut ve-aluf shum* (Master of Onions and Master of Garlic); Yehuda Burla, *Shaul ve-linda* (Saul and Linda the Karaite) and in chapters from *ve-Eleh masei yehuda ha-levi* (And There Are the Voyages of Rabbi Yehuda Halevi).

5. Ahad Ha-am, "The Rebirth of the Spirit" (in Hebrew), in *Kol kitvei aḥad ha-am* (Complete Works) (Tel Aviv: Devir, 1947), 180, published in *Ha-shiloah* 6, nos. 5–6, (1903).

6. Ludwig W. Kahn, *Literatur und Glaubenskrise* (Stuttgart: Kohlhammer, 1964).

7. Dov Sadan claims that the decline of religion is a condition for the emergence of belles lettres, "In the Darkness of Contradiction" (in Hebrew), *Bein din le-ḥeshbon* (Report and Account) (Tel Aviv: Devir, 1963), 3.

8. Following are the names of the main writers in whose work these processes took place: Hayyim Nahman Bialik, I. L. Peretz, M. J. Berdyczewski, S. Y. Agnon.

9. Meyer Wilkansky, Shlomo Zemach, Dov Kimhi, Natan Bistritzky, Yosef Aricha.

10. Berdyczewski, Levi Arye Arieli-Orloff, Aaron Abraham Kabak.

11. Y. H. Brenner, Agnon, Haim Hazaz, Yaakov Horowitz.

12. Berdyczewski, M. Z. Feierberg, Brenner, Uri Nissan Gnessin, Amos Oz.

13. Bialik, Yaakov Steinberg.

14. Wilkensky, Zemach, Agnon, Aricha, S. Yizhar, Moshe Shamir.

15. Yonatan Ratosh found an affinity with the European Christian world view in the secular mythology, derived from religious sources, of Bialik's "Scroll of Fire." See Ratosh, *Bialik: yetsirato be-rei ha-bikoret, antologia* (Bialik: Critical Essays on his Works, an Anthology), ed. Gershon Shaked (Jerusalem: Mossad Bialik, 1974), 261–265, first published in *Haaretz*, 1951.

16. Important comparative work was done, for instance, by Fischel Lachower, "Goethe in Hebrew Literature" (in Hebrew), in *Al gevul*, pp. 123–136.

17. Reuben Brainin, "Our People and Our Literature" (in Hebrew), *Mi-mizrah umi-maarav* 1 (1896): 1–11. And since this mood continued, there is nothing to be gained by tracing all its stages (the *Shiloah* Manifesto). One of the more interesting articles on this issue is the one by I. E. Lubetzky, "On Hebrew Authors" (in Hebrew), *Ha-dor*, 30 Aug. 1904. Lubetzky announced: "The time has come for Hebrew writers to leave the European 'court' and to stand on their own feet. Not everything produced in the markets of Europe is sacred and exalted, and many things remain on which we, the Hebrew writers, can pride ourselves." (Strange words coming from a forum edited by David Frischmann, the most distinguished of the "translators" and the man who would open the doors to Europe.)

18. Avraham Shlonsky, "Original and Translation" (in Hebrew), in *Yalkut eshel* (The Eshel Anthology) (Tel Aviv: Sifriat Poalim, 1960), 143–145, first published in *Haaretz*, 15 June 1938.

19. The lack of synchronicity between the European schools and Hebrew literature had already been pointed out by I. L. Peretz in the periodical *Ha-hets* (Warsaw, 1894). And Simon Halkin rephrased the problem in *Mavo la-siporet ha-ivrit* (An Introduction to Hebrew Fiction) (Jerusalem: Mifal ha-Shikhpul, 1958), 422.

20. Dov Sadan, "On the Difficulties of Translating" (in Hebrew), in *Avnei-bedek* (Touchstones) (Tel Aviv: Ha-kibbutz ha-meuhad, 1962), 109–116.

21. Shlonsky developed a kind of "theory of translation" of his own: "one who produces something from something, as opposed to one who created something from nothing. See Shlonsky, "The Game Called Translation" (in Hebrew), in *Yalkut eshel*, pp. 148–150, first published in *Al ha-mishmar*, 19 Oct. 1956.

22. Halkin, *Mavo*, pp. 436–439.

23. Avraham Holtz, *Isaac Dov Berkowitz: Voice of the Uprooted* (Ithaca: Cornell University Press, 1973), 50, 55, 67–68, 70.

24. And for this see Meir Wiener, *Tsu der geshikhte fun der yidisher literatur in 19 jahrhundert* (Remarks on the History of Yiddish Literature in the Nineteenth Century), vol. 2 (New York: YKVF, 1946), 222–234.

25. Gershon Shaked, "Tales and their Transformations" (in Hebrew), in *Bein tsehok le-dema* (Laughter and Tears) (Tel Aviv: Massada Press, 1965), especially 102–103.

26. Werses, "Remarks on Behalf of the Sources in 'The Canopy' by S. Y. Agnon" (in Hebrew), in *Sipur ve-shorsho*, 183–200.

27. Arnold J. Band, *Nostalgia and Nightmare: A Study in the Fiction of S. Y. Agnon* (Berkeley: University of California Press, 1968), 10, 44, 60.

28. Gershon Shaked, "The Sleeping Prince" (in Hebrew), in *Omanut ha-sipur shel agnon* (The Narrative Art of S. Y. Agnon) (Tel Aviv: Sifriat Poalim, 1973), 151–153.

29. J. Zwiek, "The Germanic Period (1914–1924) in Agnon's Works" (diss., Jerusalem, 1968), 26–27, 34–36, 44–45.

Jewish heritage
revolt and transformation
in Israeli culture

I

Exilic culture, the culture of romantic grief and of passive hope, is doomed
to extinction. What shall we do until the dawn of our new culture, a culture of creativity and enterprise, emerges in the full light of day? Ghetto
strengths, the powers of preservation and of covering under protective
wings, no longer offer succor. Shall we find ample new strength both for
the effort of a gigantic creative leap and for sustaining the national soul
during the period of transition? Or, heaven forfend, are we the victims of
an abysmal tragedy: "to suffer labor pains but without the strength to give
birth"?

These words, written in 1919 by the Russian Jew Moshe Glickson, refer to a past that had but recently been annihilated and express grave doubts regarding the future. They are predicated on the
assumption that the culture of the ghetto was all but dead and that
the cardinal question facing the Jewish people was whether sufficient vigor remained to reestablish a new culture in a new land.
Glickson was not alone in his views. When Y. H. Brenner wrote his
essay about the works of Mendele Mokher Seforim he claimed that
Mendele had described a culture that richly deserved destruction.
In Brenner's uncompromising polemic, the internal logic of the process that European Jewry was then undergoing called for one thing
only: "settlements of Jewish workers in Eretz Israel." He also hoped
that a new secular culture would emerge from the cultural and economic revolution that would take place among the Jews. In contradistinction to Ahad Ha-am, however, Glickson did not hazard a

cultural forecast regarding the characteristics of the "cultural center" of the future; he merely expressed the hope that it would not resemble the doomed culture of the past. Perhaps it is enough to take Glickson's words on their own terms—as an expression of a deep-seated but inarticulate aspiration—without demanding more of them.

Zionist culture was born of the aspiration to expunge the culture of the ghetto and, for just as many, to take leave of Western culture. Some ideologists asserted that the Jews in Eretz Israel should adapt themselves to the regnant Middle Eastern culture. Accordingly, all elements that were imported from abroad would have to be transformed to suit the new environment, and only those that survived the interaction with the indigenous culture would leave their impress.

II

That Zionism sought to emancipate itself not only from the ghetto but also from the "decline of the West" is evident in the response of the majority of new immigrants to *Altneuland*, Theodor Herzl's liberal European vision. It did not appeal to those who envisioned Eretz Israel as a place of refuge from the cultural decadence of Europe. They aspired to a kind of cultural "October Revolution" that would transform the space and the spirit of a people.

Many short stories and poems of the period are imbued with this spirit, extolling the "blessings of the soil" and expressing contempt for European urban culture. The pioneering ideology (*halutsiut*) aimed its opposition primarily at the culture of the metropolis, at the process of accelerated urbanization that was then sweeping Europe. Avraham Shlonsky's poem "Metropolis" typifies such expressions:

METROPOLIS

Yet again I go a guiltless man

Sentenced to carry his soul to a far off crater
To see them the sons of Abbadon:[i]
Step-children both to Satan and to God.

i Hell

Here are they—sons of Moloch[ii]
And sons of Kemosh[iii]
To which granary shall they carry murder's crop?
Phosphorescence of rotting wood instead of tephilin[iv]
Do I see shining on every forehead.

Beautifully faithless city! Then and as today.
Looking like a mushroom sprouting, black like a phylactery
I am so confused in vanity of jubilation
Among metropolis' sparks cold as polar glow.

Then and today I am among allurements.
Seen and yet unseeing, a heedless spokesman
Wandering hurled thus your portraits, brothers,
I bound upon my right arm as an amulet.

I loved you, my brothers, between stabbing cacti
Trampled under hamsin's[v] claws and boulder's aridity.

Rebelling and in peace, we offer our necks:
Blessed is he whose yoke weighs down upon us.
Amen
Selah.

The polarity in this declarative poem—contrasting the "beautifully faithless city" with the "stabbing of cacti"—is also found, in various configurations, in the poetry of Uri Zvi Greenberg, Yitzhak Lamdan, and Shin Shalom as well as among most of that generation's storytellers. Some, in blessing the earth, left it to the reader to infer what they were rejecting. The "stabbing cacti" evoke more than the pioneering Zionist; they connote as well the world view of the populist Narodniks of Russia and its transformation in the philosophy of A. D. Gordon. But the existential experience was also a romantic one. Eretz Israel offered refuge from Western civilization and return to nature—return in the name of rebirth.

III

The pioneers who wanted to re-create Jewish culture in Eretz Israel faced a forlorn hope, for they rejected two basic factors that molded

ii *a deity to whom children were sacrificed*
iii *Moabite god*
iv *phylacteries*
v *dry desert wind*

contemporary Jewish history: both the traditional culture and, simultaneously—and this is a point that requires emphasis—the opposite tendency toward acculturation into the urban environment. What resources could they then marshal?

Indeed, their creativity was born of the very struggle between the polarities of tradition and assimilation. These Jews who were culturally and socially detached—"torn off"—like the "hero" of Jewish culture in the nineteenth century, had left the ghetto only to find Western society inhospitable or, upon closer observation, undesirable. The distress of this double disenchantment was transformed into a source of inspiration. The foundations for a new Zionist culture were laid, in other words, upon the dialectic of their twofold rejection: of the ghetto and of the West. Now, having chosen the Zionist solution, they needed to define its cultural expression: What would stimulate their artistic output in their new milieu? The position they had occupied while still in exile—between Judaism and assimilation, between the culture of the ghetto and that of the West—had yielded many notable literary and cultural achievements. The tension had been fruitful both when its resolution tended toward the West (as in the assimilationist works of Freud, Schnitzler, and Isaac Babel) and when its orientation still ostensibly tended toward the ghetto (as in the works of many Hebrew and Yiddish authors). This (creative) tension disappeared, or was muted, for some when they came to Eretz Israel. Indeed, one of the aims of *aliyah* (immigration, literally "ascent") was precisely to find release from that tension and to begin anew—what Shlonsky called "Another Genesis." But they realized full well that their *aliyah* was at once a social elevation and a cultural decline. Even granting that it offered a dimension unavailable in exile, Israel simply held out no promise of a cultural rose garden and could not compete with the cultural wealth available in the West.

In 1924, Yaakov Rabinowitz wrote about the development of Hebrew literature, clearly intending that his observations should be understood to subsume all the culture of modern Eretz Israel:

Literature will be different here, which is to say that it will not be Jewish in the conventional sense, but rather humanistic, comprising many genres and shades. Even its Jewishness will be *different*—as befits a Judaism adapting itself to the life here and deriving from it. There will be negative manifestations as well, so that here and there will be shrinkage and retreat. The base will broaden, the back will ache. Neither exultation nor embitterment are called for. One must merely observe and understand.

These words accurately reflect the outlook of such leading writers as A. D. Gordon, Gershon Hanokh, and David Horowitz, who generally held that the ordinary was preferable to pretension or unbridled ambition. They all joined in the double-edged rejection of the West and the ghetto. In practice, however, Western culture and literature continued to serve as models, even when this ran against the theory to which so many subscribed.

The majority of those who contributed to the new pioneering culture drew their inspiration from many different sources: not only from cultural tensions that characterized life in the new land but also from the traditions from their past that they had brought with them. They certainly did not create a culture *ex nihilo*. The love of the soil and labor inherited from the Russian Narodniks coupled with the strange dream of integration with the "Orient" were some of the elements that informed secular culture in Eretz Israel. European flavor (rejected in theory, but always a presence) combined with Jewish substance, remaining in constant tension.

The young pioneers who congregated at Beitaniya during the 1920s represented the best of the European intelligentsia. Even having come to Palestine to rebuild themselves in the process of building up the land, they testify that this achievement exacted a toll—there was a price to be paid for the new start. Occasionally they too remember the "onions and the leeks," the cultural flesh-pots of Warsaw, Vienna, and Paris: "I retied my spiritual bonds to Europe, antiquated Europe, disreputable excommunicated Europe. How great it is and how beautiful, how I long for it! For it is the breath in our nostrils and the marrow of our bones!" Thus wrote one of the members of Beitaniya in 1922 in their journal *Our Commune,* and he is echoed in that same publication by another who wrote: "Can you honestly forgo the thousands of cultural possibilities, give up the burning impressions of a European metropolis, the whole wide world churning with unknown wonders—and all that for the sake of realizing our ideas in this land?"

The response of the pioneers of Beitaniya to these vexing questions and aspirations—to their longing in the East for the horizons of the West—was ultimately that there was some existential significance to the new life they were creating, a significance that no European palace could possibly afford them. Some of these same longings are reflected today in the style and the content of some of our best recent writers, as in Yehuda Amichai's *Not of This Time, Not of This Place* and Amos Oz's *Elsewhere Perhaps*.

What, ultimately, were the hopes of these youngsters who relinquished both European culture and Jewish tradition? Repeatedly they asked whether the "inferior" culture that would evolve in Eretz Israel could compensate them, even if only slightly, for what they had forsaken. Would the new socioeconomic structure, their newfound independence, or even the future political asylum be able to indemnify them for cultural deprivation? Would they be able to withstand the pain of "two homelands," the one they had abandoned and the one they were creating? The principal reward lay in the creative experience of being cultural pioneers: They believed that they were the vanguard in a unique renaissance that would reconstruct a secular Jewish culture from the material of religious culture. To fail to perceive what is novel or remarkable in this is to fail to comprehend the great change that the Yishuv (pre-State Jewish society in Palestine) effected in the cultural sphere from the early years of this century until the 1940s.

The creation of a new language—spoken Hebrew—is today taken for granted. But the conversion of an ancient written tongue from a sacred language to a literary idiom, then to a spoken language again, and from a spoken contemporary language once more into the language of modern writers remains an amazing phenomenon. The language itself bears witness to the various social and cultural networks that constituted life in the new land. The vocabulary, syntax, and structure of modern Hebrew reflect the influence of Yiddish, the language of the Ashkenazi Diaspora. However, influenced by Jews from the East, a new pronunciation emerged, with the accent on the last syllable, and Arabic vocabulary also entered the language. Both the Ashkenazi and Sephardi Hebrew sources were affected by the vocabulary and syntax of European languages. This unusual combination of European syntax and Oriental phonetics in spoken and written Hebrew testifies to the ingathering and integration of exiles. (Further, this testimony to an organic development is far more credible than today's efforts at artificial resuscitation of ethnic folklore, the Moroccan festival of the Maimuna and some attempts to revive Kurdish Jewish and Persian Jewish pseudoreligious customs.)

Cultural integration took place in a variety of sectors of the evolving Israeli Jewish culture. Popular songs and folk dances, for example, are a strange concoction of dances and tunes brought from Poland, Russia, and Romania and current among the Jews of Yemen. Some of the "folk" dances that were choreographed—invented—by Gurit Kadman and Sarah Tannai Halevi were experiments in "semiotic" combinations that attempted to create a local culture by synthesizing East and West, a mixture fraught with tensions. Another example of this admixture was the fruitful collaboration between songwriter Nahum Nardi and Yemenite performers Brachah Zefira and Esther Gamlieli—an Eastern European composer striving to construct a musical style that would be compatible with the Oriental world.

This cultural "alchemy" was also attempted on the plane of "high culture": in Nahum Gutman's drawings, in the music of Paul Ben-Haim, Alexander Uri Boskovitz, and others, as well as in the poetry of Yonatan Ratosh. Even the culture of fashion undertook to find a "mediating language" between the Russian (rubashka) shirt and the Arabic (kaffiyeh) headdress. In fact, all the so-called marginal areas of culture witnessed an attempt to create something new out of extant materials from Russian, Eastern European, Yemenite, and Bedouin culture—both real and imagined.

This admixture became the new culture of the youth movements, seedbeds in which the new "languages" took root much more readily than in other sectors of society. The new configurations were then accepted as the norm because the youth movements, considered to be the elite of Israeli society, set the trends. Their adoption of new styles made them compellingly *au courant*. "Israeli" (synthetic) culture was employed to promote the absorption of new immigrants: Whoever sought acculturation had to accept the youth movements' rules for the game; and whoever eschewed these values perforce was barred from membership in the fashion-conscious group.

The attempts at integrating disparate cultural components were sometimes quite ludicrous. The Ohel theater, for example, staged a Russian play entitled *Jacob and Rachel*, translated into Hebrew by Shlonsky. The actors donned Bedouin costumes and mimicked Yemenite Hebrew accents, which had a strong undertone of Russian phonetics. Nevertheless, such efforts, indeed all of this experimentation, can be seen as a search for new forms of expression. The claim that it reflects a neo-Canaanite spirit, a yearning to strike roots in the new Middle Eastern landscape while severing the roots going back to the past, is an erroneous one. Genuine "Canaanites" did not seek to create new configurations by confronting or refashioning the old ingredients of Jewish culture; on the contrary, they wanted to rid themselves of tensions through the simple expedient of massive infusions of local color, the substitution of a new culture for the old. Authentic Israeli culture, however, is the *product* of cultural tensions rather than an escape from them, formed by blending and recasting the preexisting components into a new entity. The ideal of the cultural elite was to remove their *galut* finery and clothe themselves in the garments of the "homeland." Consequently, people took leave of their old names—preferring to be called Sadan rather than Stock, or Agnon rather than Czaczkes, Ratosh rather than Halperin, Zehavi not Goldberg, Mazor not Mizrahi.* To change one's name was a symbolic act signifying the adoption of a new identity and the abandonment of the old one.

IV

The ideal of fashioning a secular culture in Israel had deeper roots in Bialik's idea of "assembly" (Hebrew *kinus*), one of the most profound and important contributions to the nationalization of the religious tradition. The idea was to collect and choose, according to modern touchstones, relevant old Jewish texts and reestablish them in a new modern secular society. In effect, Bialik's concept of renewal was even more far-reaching than that of Ahad Ha-am. His ideological essays spoke in the name of secular *ideas* whose roots

* *Translations of European family names or inventions of new Hebrew names.*

extended back to religious society—as, for example, the idea of absolute justice. Bialik and Rawnitzki's *Sefer ha-aggadah* (1908–1911)
transmitted their old cultural tradition in modern dress both to
young people and to adults, including such budding authors as
Moshe Shamir. His major novel *The King of Flesh and Blood* remains a
prime example of the transformation of a religious tradition into a
secular cultural vehicle.

Jefim Hayyim Schirmann, in his *Ha-shirah ha-ivrit bi-sefarad uvi-
provence* (Anthology of Medieval Spanish and Provençal Poetry,
1954–1956), and Isaiah Tishby, in his *Teachings of the Zohar* (1969–
1972), both continued the task of compiling the traditional Jewish
materials according to the approach taken by Bialik. The latter had
removed legends and midrash from their original context and reor-
ganized them according to entirely secular principles: historically,
from Adam to the destruction of the Second Temple; morally, from
a man's proper relation to his fellow man to his proper relation to
his family. By contrast, in the original sources, such as the Talmud,
those stories were interwoven with discussions of the halakhah or
with interpretations of Scripture, or they were part of the traditional homiletics accompanying public prayer and ritual. Thus the
religious tradition was culled for its practical wisdom and edited to
meet the needs of a secular Jew—and in this way, in its new form,
became part of secular culture. The secular community, rejecting
the yoke of the commandments per se, was shaped nonetheless by
a transformed traditional literature; by a new selection of legends
from the halakhah and the midrash and, later on, by new selec-
tions from the poetry of the Middle Ages and the teachings of the
Zohar.

The basic ideological and practical premises behind these com-
pilations were brilliantly expressed by one of the spiritual fathers of
the reconstructed Israeli culture, Berl Katznelson. His oft quoted
remarks on the confrontation between the present and the tradition provided the theoretical foundation for many cultural enter-
prises in the evolving new Israeli culture: "An innovative and creative generation does not cast the legacy of past generations upon
the dungheap. It examines, probes, rejects, and accepts. At times it
seizes upon an existing tradition and adds to it, and sometimes it

digs about in the kitchen midden and uncovers something long forgotten, scrapes off the rust, and brings an ancient tradition to life,
if it can nourish the soul of the generation of seekers" (1934).

The influence of the Bible on the new national secular life is testimony to the process Katznelson described. The Bible has become
the cornerstone of Israeli education, even in the non-religious
schools, where it has undergone a thoroughgoing secular transformation. The "educational values of the Bible" were not necessarily "religious." For the secular Israeli, historical, archaeological,
and national approaches to Scripture have created a Bible whose
meanings are very different from those that the Bible held in the
culture of the ghetto (and, of course, continues to hold for religious
Jews). Secular biblical interpretation is, moreover, one of the major
sources of inspiration in modern Hebrew poetry and drama. Such
poets as Gilboa, Amichai, Gouri, Pagis, and Zach have reinterpreted
and parodied traditional characters and symbols, very often de-
heroizing the major figures of the biblical epic. Dramatists of the
Israeli generation, too, have tended to secularize and parody the
biblical source. Aharon Megged, in *Genesis*, uses the Adam and
Eve myth to create a stock type of comedy about man and woman.
Yehuda Amichai, in *Masa ninve* (The Vision of Nineveh), makes the
prophet Jonah a member of the lower middle class; Yaakov Shabtai,
in *Keter ba-rosh* (A Crowned Head), and Yisrael Eliraz, in *Ha-dov*
(The Bear), present an anti-heroic King David in house slippers.
This use of biblical metaphors to explode the myths of heroism in
Israeli society started in the 1920s but culminated in the sixties and
seventies. During this period, biblical figures and allusions became
a major intertextual frame of reference, the common cultural language. In the process, the "secularized" Bible has become one of
the major traditions of Hebrew literature; as such it has been preserved as the basic cultural treasure of the Jewish people.

A similar secular transformation has taken place with regard to
historical study in Israel, which has tended to deprecate the ghetto
and its culture and to emphasize the periods of independence that
preceded and followed it. So too, we find a reinterpreted religious
tradition, which is especially evident in the development of "Israeli" holidays from "Jewish" ones. Those that are essentially religious in nature, such as Rosh Hashanah and Yom Kippur, remain

central to the religious tradition. However, the new Israeli "tradition" took up holidays that had been marginal, such as Tu bi-Shevat (the festival of trees), whereas the major festivals of Pesach, Shavuot, and Sukkot were embraced as celebrations of nature and the earth. Moreover, some holidays took on nationalistic significance in the consciousness of secular Israelis. Thus, at the heart of Hanukkah it was no longer the miracle of the jar of oil but, rather, the courage and victory of the Maccabees. And at Pesach the theme that in every generation a person must regard himself as if he himself had left Egypt received a thoroughly Zionist interpretation.

Far from breaking completely with tradition, these transformations actually established a respectable link between the Jewish life of the past, which for many had lost much of its meaning, and Jewish life in the present. They restored the glory of the epoch that had preceded the antiquated culture of the ghetto yet did not entirely reject that culture. Instead, they attempted to transplant and rejuvenate it in the Land of Israel. We have, therefore, a sincere effort to adapt the tradition to pioneering and antiurban ideals, and in turn to link it to the new Israeli cultural elements, such as the dances and songs of the sowers and reapers. The Song of Songs became an Israeli love song, a song of courtship; the songs of Hanukkah took on patriotic significance; and the ceremonies of Pesach were given new agrarian form in the Haggadah of the kibbutz. These secular transformations were supported by the educational system, from the kindergartens to the youth movements, and by the social elite of the settlement movements, who had created a new Israeli.

v

But have masterpieces been created in literature, dance, music, and the plastic arts? As Yaakov Rabinowitz wrote: "There will be negative manifestations as well, so that here and there will be shrinkage and retreat. The base will broaden, and the back will ache."

The best modern Jewish culture was not created in a context that belonged entirely either to the ghetto or to Western assimilation. It was born of the dreadful tension between those two polarities, a tension that nourished the work of Bialik and Agnon, Bashevis Singer, Elias Canetti, and Itzik Manger—even Joseph Roth, Philip Roth, and Saul Bellow. Their works are products of the terrible fault that ran through Jewish life until the Jews decided to repair what had been damaged and to reconstitute themselves in new circumstances. By renouncing the limitless landscapes of the "malady," they found a "healthier" state that was at the same time more confining. In this new environment yearnings for a return to Europe and to Judaism coexisted with a sincere desire to sever those ties and integrate into the new surroundings. Both tendencies are present in Israeli literature.

The essential power of works like those of Yizhar lies in the attempt to become involved in the new domain, as expressed in detailed descriptions of the Israeli landscape; whereas the strength of other contemporaneous works is in their expressions of doubt that the Jews would be able to sink roots in the new land. The best literary works do not describe the processes of integration in a simple manner; they point at the gaps and vacuums, they ask questions and raise problems. Such are the literary achievements of A. B. Yehoshua, Amos Oz, and Aharon Appelfeld.

Thus literature is aware of the new problematics; but the power of the new cultural life, the creation of new cultural idioms, surpasses its artistic products. In any case, many works of literature, music, and the plastic arts show that a sincere effort has been made to create a new secular reality for the modern Israeli. With his roots planted in both past and present, he makes a new and independent *selection* from the Jewish cultural heritage—and in this regard he is actually no different from his forefathers. Their relation to the tradition also changed from generation to generation as they reinterpreted the past. Indeed, this state of flux is the source of the vitality of the tradition. The Zionist process involved not only selection but also rejection: rejection of the ghetto and of the West. The revolutionary experience of Zionism demanded that its partisans raze the old world to its foundations and build a new world on those foundations! "Abandon and demolish in order to build and be rebuilt," in the words of Berdyczewski, thus unwittingly following in the footsteps of Nietzsche as well.

VI

Modern Israeli literature since World War II has to be understood according to these assumptions. If American Jewish literature is a configuration of Jewish, American, and sometimes European elements and traditions, then modern Israeli literature is a configuration of the cultural elements we have described. The tensions between Middle Eastern and Western forms and between modernity and traditional Jewish symbols are the main features in the works of such diverse novelists as Yizhar, Shamir, Oz, Yehoshua, and Appelfeld, and of poets like Amichai, Zach, Pagis, and Wieseltier. We can even describe the differences between those authors according to the variety of configurations of those elements in their works. For example, in the works of Yizhar, the dean of modern Israeli literature, local elements and biblical allusions dominate. Yizhar's major novel *Yemei tsiklag* (The Days of Ziklag) is a tale of blood, soil, and war, deeply rooted in the Israeli landscape and alluding to the biblical locality of Ziklag.

From this point of view, the difference between the first generation of Israeli writers and the second is mostly a change in literary and cultural ingredients. Yehoshua, Oz, and Kahana-Karmon have become much more westernized, and their characters bespeak a transformation of the "old" uprooted Jewish anti-hero (from Kafka to Bellow) to one who is out of place even in his own homeland. The most radical transformation and "revival" of the old occurs in the novels of Appelfeld, who returns roughly to the point of departure of Agnon, Joseph Roth, and Saul Bellow, but from a different perspective. His uprooted post-Holocaust survivors had an opportunity to strike roots in Europe or Palestine but failed to reestablish themselves in either. Speaking of such a diverse group of writers, one finds that their language, their delineation of character, and their concept of plot are influenced by the most varied configuration of elements.

The paradox is, of course, that the great escape from the ghetto and the Western world, which was the major aim of the Zionist renaissance, did not succeed. According to the dialectics of cultural development, the new trend in modern Hebrew literature should be the antithesis of the earlier thesis of a "new beginning"; but, as

we have seen, even the literature and culture of the "new beginning" had its roots in the old traditions. It was only a matter of time
until some of them would come to the foreground again while the
new elements would recede into the background. We are now in
the middle of a revival of older traditions. In a way, Oz, Yehoshua,
and Appelfeld are much more akin in their *Weltanschauung* and
literary technique to their European Jewish forefathers and their
American Jewish cousins than to their older Israeli brothers. At the
same time, however, we should never forget that they are also the
product of the same cultural processes of secularization and transformation as their forerunners and contemporaries.

the great transition

The term "literary center" lends itself to various definitions. It describes a literary "school" or group of writers; it also refers to the social arena in which their literature is produced. The first meaning emphasizes particular literary conventions and traditions, whereas the second pertains to social and economic institutions related to production, including publishers, literary magazines, and even the audience of readers. The *sine qua non* of any literary center is a mutually recognized literary code and common frame of reference— the same synchronic linguistic structures (morphology, syntax, phonetics) and the same literary traditions—that are shared by the producers (the writers) and their addressees (their readers). Only when that condition is met can a new literary work be decoded.

According to that understanding, not every member of the producer's society is an addressee. For example, among the Jews of Odessa at the turn of the century, only the small Hebrew-reading minority was competent to receive and interpret Hebrew literary messages.[1] The consumers of Jewish literature in Eastern Europe were often competent in various codes—that is, in three or four literatures—and were, therefore, "target publics" for non-Jewish producers as well. The small number of readers of Hebrew literature were also part of the much larger group of readers of Yiddish literature (some writers, such as Mendele, Bialik, Peretz, and Berdyczewski, wrote in both languages); and for the majority of the potential Jewish reading public, Russian, too, was much more familiar than Hebrew. Nevertheless, the Hebrew readers in Odessa and also in other cities constituted the small but active intellectual mi-

nority that made Eastern Europe the Hebrew literary center of the
world from the late nineteenth century through World War I.

Their Hebrew code evolved out of the tension between yeshiva
education and the modern curriculum to which most of them were
exposed. The code, rich in biblical and talmudic allusions, produced a literature replete with the balanced rhythms of old Hebrew
syntax and the semantic mixture of revived modern Hebrew. More
complicated yet, it reflected the impact of European literary traditions and conventions.[2] Even after most Hebrew writers had left
the shtetl, it remained their primary frame of reference; having
abandoned or been banished from their former homes, these uprooted outsiders were often unable to strike roots in the alien environment of the large European city. This left the shtetl as the only
coherent social framework that had semiotic value for them. Consequently, its customs, morals, manners, and cultural codes continued to provide their referents. The antimodels of the big city
and its semiassimilated, "enlightened," intellectuals became the
antithesis of the shtetl model. Thus, although the frame of reference of the Hebrew writers' constituency was a fading social entity,
it was the only one to which they could refer.

II

This essay concerns the fate and vicissitudes of the Hebrew literary center. Although most means of literary production—literary
magazines, publishing houses, and critical establishments (critics, awards, writers' associations, literary cafés)—were dispersed
throughout Eastern Europe, the assumption that there were several
minor literary centers in Eastern Europe is questionable. While
there were minicenters of literary *production* in Warsaw, Odessa,
Vilna, and other cities of the Russian empire, the consumer market
for all was one and the same. Literary magazines published in
Odessa (such as *Ha-shiloah*, (1896–1926) were read in Warsaw, and
vice versa.[3] The literary establishment in Odessa reviewed the works
of authors who lived in other cities. But the story of Hebrew literature is not a "tale of two cities" as the critic Yaakov Fichman argued.[4] From the point of view of production and consumption,

Eastern Europe was a single cultural unit—albeit one of great diversity. This phenomenon is exemplified by the history of the quarterly *Ha-tekufah*. First published in Moscow (1918), it moved to Warsaw (1919–1925), then Berlin (1928–1929), Tel Aviv (1930–1936), and finally New York (1946–1950). *Ha-tekufah* was still being published when the Hebrew literary center in Eastern Europe was already in decline.

III

This center, which flourished between 1880 and 1920, began to lose its dominance in Hebrew life and letters after World War I. And since then the Diaspora has had no real Hebrew cultural and literary center.[5] After that time, the only country that had a balanced proportion of readers (per capita of writers) in its Hebrew literary constituency was Poland, with its independent Hebrew and Yiddish educational system. In addition, it had young Zionists, who trained themselves physically and spiritually for emigration to Palestine and used Hebrew as the language of their collective future. These addressees in Poland attempted to create their own literary organs (*Kolot*, 1923; *Ha-sneh*, 1929; *Ha-derekh*, 1932–1937; *Teḥumim*, 1937), but with only limited success. They too seemed to accept the fact that Poland—Eastern Europe—was no longer a "literary center."[6] The common code of producers and addressees no longer existed there. A number of Hebrew writers emigrated to the new center in Palestine, where most of them published their work.

Mattityahu Shoham (1893–1937), a major poet and playwright who remained in Poland, created his own artificial frame of reference, an imaginary Palestine. Visiting but never settling there, he neither grasped nor related to the realities of the country. Having no use for the "code" of the founding fathers of modern Hebrew literature and having lost contact with the established frame of reference of the shtetl, Shoham made a distorted attempt to revive Abraham Mapu's concept of a new biblical idiom. In his biblical plays and longer poems he also tried to create a high mimetic mode of heroic characters and an embellished scenery as a kind of fantastic visionary frame of reference.[7] In this respect, too, he followed

Mapu, who eighty years earlier had created a romantic landscape of Judaea and Samaria. Shoham's target public was the group of young Jewish Zionist pioneers who were still in Poland: They rejected the "old" frame of reference but did not yet face the realities of the new land. The new constituency of Hebrew readers in Palestine, by contrast, did not understand his "linguistic" code; and his highly esoteric plays were never performed. Theaters wanted them translated into a poetic idiom like Shlonsky's, which was accepted by the general target public.

Some poets and novelists lost any notion of target publics and wrote for imaginary readers; they failed to take into account the addressees' own frame of reference. David Vogel, for example, set his novels in *fin-de-siècle* Vienna; his book *Hayyei nissuim* (Married Life) reads like a Hebrew translation of an Austrian Jewish novel[8] and does not refer to any localities, customs, manners, or morals accepted and understood by most of the Hebrew-reading public in Palestine. Its Hebrew "code" is "spiced" with German calques (to use the critics' word for foreign idioms translated literally), and the frame of reference bears no relation whatever to any specific Jewish environment. Vogel's novels are as Jewish as those of Arthur Schnitzler, Joseph Roth, or Stefan Zweig—if not less so; his target public was (at best) the German Jewish Hebrew-reading community, if such a thing ever existed. Vogel remained on the fringes of the literary center in Palestine because, although he wrote in Hebrew, he used a foreign frame of reference. And as much as he wanted to be a member of the Austrian Jewish literary group, he was never an integral part of it either because he used a different linguistic code.[9]

IV

In the United States, Hebrew writers such as Ephraim Lisitsky, Simon Halkin, and Reuben Wallenrod were marginal to the Yiddish literature that flourished there at the beginning of the twentieth century. At first they tried to replicate the Eastern European center, continuing in their novels the story of the uprooted shtetl intellectual who migrated to the big city. These writers attempted to create their own literary establishments, but their target public was very small because most readers with the same frame of reference at first preferred the Yiddish code and later the English one.[10] Longing for critical reaction beyond the range of their close colleagues, they turned to the literary organs of Palestine, where they published most of their books.[11] Yet only a few ever attained acceptance in the major center that emerged after World War I in Palestine and flourished subsequently in the State of Israel. Halkin and Gabriel Preil were "accepted" there because their poetic idiom was understood by the young poets and critics of the 1960s and 1970s as foreshadowing their own poetics, which constituted a rebellion against the Shlonsky-Alterman symbolist tradition.[12] But the main topic of their novels (Lisitsky's *Eleh toledat adam* [This is the Story of a Man], Halkin's *Ad mashber* [Unto Breakdown], and Wallenrod's *Ki fanah yom* [Sunset]) was the decline and fall in the new country of the intellectuals from the old country.

The tragedy of these writers was that they lost their public. There was never a real revival of Hebrew in America; it never became a living "cultural" language there, and even less so, a vernacular. It became one more nostalgic reminiscence of the "old country," cherished by small social groups like the Brit Ivrit (Society for Hebrew). The agonizing fact is that there was no real Hebrew center in the Diaspora after World War I. Most Hebrew writers oriented themselves to the new center in Palestine, and the publishing houses eventually migrated there. Thus Palestine became the physical home for a wider spiritual center. There were of course quite a number of literary producers and consumers still in the Diaspora, but the producers contributed to the literary activity in Israel, while the consumers made the small production center financially viable. Subscribers from all over Europe and the United States supported the numerous literary organs in Palestine.

v

Although the Jewish population in Palestine in the 1920s and 1930s was small, the readers and writers of Hebrew literature in the Diaspora looked to this community for spiritual guidance. More and more, it became the spiritual center that Ahad Ha-am had envisioned, even though its intellectual and historical scope was more limited than he had expected. Its beginnings early in the century were very modest indeed, for it was actually no more than a small branch of the major Eastern European center. At that time the target public for writers like Smilansky, Brenner, and Agnon was mainly in the Diaspora. Smilansky wrote under the pseudonym of Hawaja Mussa in the literary journal *Ha-shiloah*, which was published in Odessa. The literary and social expectations of his audience very much conditioned his literary output. Smilansky shaped his figures to fit Eastern European Jewish taste; they wanted a "wild west" of their own, and he provided it. He depicted Arabs as noble savages or naïve victims of civilization, along the lines of the romantic models of James Fenimore Cooper's Indians; and his Jewish emigrants were the counterparts of the white pioneers.

The tension between the native and pioneer populations was not the only model to which the literature responded. The pioneers' struggle with soil and foe was another sentimental vision that the Zionist groups in the Diaspora needed for their spiritual and emotional nourishment. The target public preferred stories about an idealized Eretz Israel to stories about the hard realities of life there. Wilkansky, Zemach, and others (whom Brenner accused of falsifying the facts[13]) were actually responding to the wishful visions of their readers overseas. They did not deal in reality because their consumers demanded an embellished, romanticized picture of the promised land. At the beginning of the century most Palestinian magazines—such as *Ha-omer*, *Ha-poel ha-tzair*, and *Moledet*—were economically dependent for their very existence on writers and readers in the Diaspora. Until the end of the 1930s every Hebrew literary magazine in Palestine—*Hedim*, *Ketuvim*, *Moznayim*, *Gilyonot*, *Gazit*, and more—sought to obtain as many subscribers in the Diaspora as possible.

By the late twenties, Palestine was beginning to flourish as a literary production center: Hebrew had become a vernacular, and the necessary conditions for a new code and frame of reference had come into being. This reflected a development from the beginning of the century when neither Brenner nor Agnon had changed his basic code and still retained the shtetl frame of reference. Each had, however, created some configurational changes in style and material that brought about a definite shift in literary tradition. Brenner's local novels referred to the new vernacular, a mixture of Hebrew, Yiddish, and Arabic elements. His nonheroes from the shtetl faced an environment that was quite different from the conventional "big city" encountered by earlier escapees from the shtetl. The most fitting description of the situation is that of "traditional shtetl people confronting the challenge of a new world." The tensions between the diverse and variant elements of this configuration—character, landscape, plot, thematics, and style—created an altogether new frame of reference and also slowly modified the literary code.

There were writers in Palestine who consciously decided to innovate. In the twenties and thirties, a whole group of writers—Ever Hadani, Aricha, Hameiri, Zarchi, and many others in drama and poetry—presented an ideal Palestinian model of a new people on a new soil. These writers wanted to realize in their literary creativity what seemed to be a social revolution. The great transition in the physical locus of the literary center, they felt, ought to result in an absolute shift in literary traditions; but precisely because there was not yet a societal model on which to rely, and because the new language was still in its infancy, they were not very successful. They did not understand that sociological changes do not bring about total shifts in literary conventions; these develop in evolutionary steps and not in revolutionary upheavals. According to I. Even-Zohar, polysystems [14] never change totally; rather, change occurs as various elements come to the foreground or retreat to the background.

VI

Between the two world wars, Palestine became a literary center in both the sociological and historical senses. During those years many writers emigrated there and founded major literary institutions—writers' associations, publishing houses, and literary magazines—causing a definitive shift in the communication process. The Palestinian consumers became self-conscious and increasingly self-satisfied. The target public of most literary organs shifted and became mainly local; even though subscribers and contributors were dispersed throughout the Jewish world, by that time the majority of Hebrew readers and writers were in Israel. As mentioned above, this trend had a major influence on the thematics and style (reference and code) of the emerging tradition.

One can better understand the interaction between the Israeli center and the Diaspora by examining the list of those in the Diaspora who participated in and subscribed to one of the major literary organs, *Gilyonot*. This monthly, edited by Yitzhak Lamdan in Tel Aviv between 1933 and 1954, was one of the major links between Palestinian Jewry and Diaspora writers from Russia (Lenski, Freiman, Rodin, Freigerson, Kariv, and Hayyug), Poland (Shoham, Pomerantz, Stein, Tzessler, Rapoport, and Bunin) and the United States (Wallenrod, Twersky, Silberschlag, Bavli, Halkin, and Efros). The largest group of participants was of course from Palestine, among them I. Shenhar, A. Tabkai, Yaakov Har-Even, S. Shrira, B. Mordekhay, I. Ogen, Y. Rabinov, S. Kasher, J. Hanani, K. A. Bertini, and S. Yizhar. Most subscribers were local, but the magazine also had a remarkable circulation in the Diaspora. According to the journal's archives, it had 97 subscribers in the United States, 19 in Great Britain, 16 in Austria, 2 in South Africa, 2 in Canada, 3 in Argentina, 2 in Germany, 4 in Egypt, 20 in Lithuania, 23 in Poland, 1 in Hungary, and 1 in Cyprus.[15] There were, in other words, as many subscribers in any one of the European countries as in Haderah or Rishon Le-Zion. Moreover, the list of Diaspora subscribers and the list of literary contributors are sometimes almost identical. The statistical breakdown of the subscription lists confirms that there was a strong centripetal movement of Hebrew literature from the Diaspora to the Palestinian center during the 1930s. The Holocaust was then the physical disaster that followed a spiritual decline.

The big change, of course, was in the major shift in orientation of the Hebrew writers between the two world wars. All of them preferred to be published in the center rather than on the outskirts. Whoever did not publish there became obsolete and irrelevant, the tragic literary destiny of Arieli Orloff being only one of many examples.[16] The shtetl with its uprooted characters ceased to be the main frame of reference. There was an incongruity between the natural frame of reference of young Palestine-born or Palestine-nurtured consumers and the literary tradition that was still basically the literature of the Diaspora. Moreover, the modern Hebrew vernacular had become a different code and a new kind of diglossia developed: "written Hebrew, the language of literature, and spoken Hebrew ('our Hebrew'), the language of everyday life."[17]

As the traditional literature of the Diaspora became quite irrelevant and obsolete, literary criticism attempted to revive it and to create a meaningful rapport between the new center and the old tradition. Thus, the literary criticism from the 1930s to the 1960s can be understood as a collective effort of reinterpretation: the reinterpretation of Agnon by Sadan, Kurzweil, and others; the revival of Mendele by Shaked, Peri, and Miron; the revival of Gnessin and Brenner and the new understanding of Bialik by Zemach and Peri. A new choice of writers was made from the tradition, by Zach and others, brought to the foreground especially Steinberg, Vogel, and Preil, writers who had been in the background of conventional "reception." It was in a way also an intellectual campaign to reinterpret the literal frame of reference and to understand it metaphorically. The code was "opened," deconstructed, and reconstructed, with new emphasis on the symbolic and parodic functions of traditional allusions and idioms. The code itself was understood to be self-destructive. Rather than stressing its literal functions, literary criticism emphasized the parodic and metaphoric functions of its lingual signs.

VII

The Hebrew literary center of the Diaspora no longer exists. A long and gloomy process of spiritual decline, followed by the physical destruction of Eastern European Jewry, left behind a horrible vacuum that has never been filled. But in the interim Hebrew literature has been normalized in a new home, yielding a confluence of social and geographical place and spiritual locality. No more the spiritual nourishment of a wandering people, it has become the literature of the State of Israel. The only producers outside of the country are Gabriel Preil and émigrés such as Rachel Eytan and R. Lee. The small band of consumers of Hebrew literature outside Israel are mainly university students, along with Israeli émigrés. What began in the Diaspora as the living tradition of a minority within a minority group ended as "material" for the few in academic departments, and what was originally a minor branch of Eastern European Hebrew literature has become the one and the only Hebrew literary center.

NOTES

1. Steve Zipperstein, "Assimilation, Haskalah, and Odessa Jewry," *The Great Transition: The Recovery of Lost Centers of Modern Hebrew Literature,* ed. Glenda Abramson and Tudor Parfitt (Totowa, N.J.: Rowan & Allanheld, 1985), 91–98.

2. See the essay "Jewish Tradition and Western Impact in Modern Hebrew Literature" in this volume.

3. On *Ha-shiloah,* see Getzel Kressel, "The 'Storm' of the Young in *Ha-shiloah"* (in Hebrew), *Gilyonot* 26 (1952): 359–363.

4. Yaakov Fichman, *Ruhot menagnot: sofrei polin* (Singing Winds: Writers in Poland) (Jerusalem: Mossad Bialik, 1953), 9–14.

5. Gershon Shaked, "If Only They had the Spiritual Energy to Continue: Minor Centers in Hebrew Literature Between Two World Wars" (in Hebrew), *Tarbiz* 51 (1982): 479–490.

6. Ibid., pp. 488–490.

7. Gershon Shaked, *Ha-mahazeh ha-ivri ha-histori be-tekufat ha-tehiyah* (The Hebrew Historical Drama in the Twentieth Century) (Jerusalem: Mossad Bialik, 1970), especially 288–303.

8. Gershon Shaked, "David Vogel: A Secular Writer" (in Hebrew), *Haaretz,* 5 Oct. 1973.

9. Dan Pagis, introduction to David Vogel, *Kol ha-shirim* (Collected Poems) (Tel Aviv: Makhborot le-Sifrut, 1966), 72. Vogel wanted *Hayyei nissuim* to be translated into German. That he failed was a great disappointment to him.

10. Shaked, "Minor Centers," 484–486.

11. S. Halkin had his novel, *Ad mashber* (Unto Breakdown), published by Am Oved; Wallenrod's and Lisitsky's major novels were published by Mossad Bialik. See also Robert Alter, "The Inner Immigration of Hebrew Prose," *The Legacy of Jewish Migration: Eighteen Eighty-One and Its Impact,* ed. David Berger (New York: Brooklyn College Press, 1983), 97–106.

12. The main critics to introduce Halkin and Preil to the younger gen-

eration included D. Miron, M. Megged, T. Carmi, J. Ewen, G. Shaked, M. Peri, N. Zach, Y. Feldman, and Y. Schwartz.

13. Y. H. Brenner, "The Palestinian Genre and Its Accessories" (in Hebrew), *Ha-poel ha-tzair,* vol. 4, no. 21, 10 Aug. 1921.

14. I. Even-Zohar, "The Function of the Literary Polysystem in the History of Literature," *Papers in Historical Poetics* (Tel Aviv: Porter Institute, 1978), 11–23.

15. Archives of Yitzhak Lamdan in *Genazim* (Archives of the Association of Hebrew Writers) in Tel Aviv.

16. Gershon Shaked, "The Twin Who Emigrated: The Writings of L. A. Arieli-Orloff" (in Hebrew), *Siman keriah* 5 (1976): 481–491.

17. Haiim Rozen, *Ha-ivrit shelanu* (Our Hebrew) (Tel Aviv: Am Oved, 1956).

Bialik here and now

In 1913 Ben-Zion Eisenstadt (b. Kelts, Belorussia, 1883; d. New York, 1951) published an article in the Hebrew periodical *Eshkol* entitled "Heroes of Modern Hebrew Poetry." In it he discussed a very weighty question: Who among the contemporary poets were worthy of inclusion within the Hebrew literary canon? "It is a palpable and bitter truth," Eisenstadt wrote, "that even talented modern poets such as Shaul Tchernichowsky, Zalman Shneour, and Yaakov Kahan have repudiated eternal life, our infinite life, to concern themselves with the passing moment and hour, or, at most, with limited and well-demarcated times. They have not taken up the everlasting form stamped and engraved upon our 'eternal tablets' but have cried out for the other, artificial visages, which lose their force and pass away with time."

In the course of his discussion, Eisenstadt wrote of Hayyim Nahman Bialik: "Hebrew prophecy is a matter of certainty, clear and absolute, positive and necessary and not skeptical, and the judgment of national tradition will not elevate Bialik, for the prophet alone is the true poet. Nor will it accord him the honor given to the first among our great poets, for he is not at all among their number but far behind them on the path of salubrious faith, which is the basis of our national poetry in exile." In conclusion, the critic lauded a "truer poet," who outweighs all the false ones. The true poet in question is Yehezkel Lewitt (b. Mogilev, Belorussia, 1878; d. New York, 1945), who wrote in Hebrew and Yiddish. According to Eisenstadt, he is "a high priest, faithful to the saints of his people and its greatness—in that temple of our poetry, whose wisdom is so beautiful and pleasant, whose words are so true and elevated. The apprentice priests in the 'temple' of our poetry would do well to seek wisdom from his lips, which bring forth precious stones and pearls, whose value is inestimable!"

A few years earlier, in 1903, another distinguished critic, Samuel Leib Zitron, had made similar comments. He wrote in "Passages" (an exchange of letters on the old and the new in literature and life), which appeared in *Eshkol* the year after the publication of Bialik's first collection of poems: "You ask me whether we have national poets in our literature, poets of rebirth? To my regret I must answer your question in the negative: No! No!"

In these and other critical writings the same question reverberates again and again: To whom will "the judgment of national tradition" (in Eisenstadt's words) accord the honor of being a true poet, the poet worthy of inclusion in the literary canon? What are the criteria? Above all, the question we must ask is: How is it that, of all the poets of his generation, Bialik is the one who has survived? Why Bialik and not Yehezkel Lewitt? The latter, so highly praised by the critics of his generation, has vanished from the literary and even the historical consciousness of the current generation. Moreover, one can ask, what is Bialik's particular merit that makes him worthier than such important poets as Shaul Tchernichowsky, Yaakov Steinberg, and Yaakov Fichman? While these are certainly remembered, some more than others, none has achieved canonization. They are not national treasures but simply reserves to draw against—some of them widely read, others less so.

In antiquity the process of canonization was straightforward. Authority was vested in a well-defined group whose prestige was universally acknowledged. That group would praise or condemn books and authors according to various considerations: "At first it was said that Proverbs, the Song of Songs, and Ecclesiastes were apocryphal; they were known to include parables until the members of the Great Assembly came and interpreted them" (*Avot derabbi nathan* 1). Once authority of that stature disappeared, it was replaced by an amorphous and anonymous process that might be called "the judgment of national tradition."

One wonders, therefore, why this judgment chose Bialik from among all his contemporaries. He would have been rejected had it used the yardstick of Eisenstadt, Zitron, and their heirs. It is erroneous to hold that Bialik was simply an outstanding poet of rebirth, or one likely to fortify those pioneers waging physical and cultural

battles. In contrast to one poem such as "May They Be Strength-
ened," one finds dozens of his poems that are far from "gracing the
soil of our land" or lauding the spirit of its pioneers or warriors. It
was not one of the "decadent" poets, such as Yaakov Steinberg,
David Vogel, Meir Wieseltier, or Yona Wallach, who wrote the following lines:

Why should we dread death—his angel mounted on our shoulder
His bit in our mouth
With a cry of rebirth, with joyful shouts and laughter,
We totter to the grave.

("Word")

It is thus difficult indeed to justify Bialik's inclusion in the literary canon if we measure his poetry only against the values of national renascence. By that yardstick, the "judgment of the national
tradition" would more likely prefer the poetry of either Tchernichowsky or the later Yaakov Kahan. And if Eisenstadt, Zitron,
and their descendants had been members of the Sanhedrin, they
would not even have considered Bialik, for fear of inflicting permanent damage upon the souls of the young. Many sensitive readers
might well prefer Steinberg or Fichman, for they are closer to the
delicate soul of lyric poetry than is Bialik, whose verse is not pure
and refined. Readers of "refined taste" would certainly prefer other
poets, just as they would doubtless prefer a writer of prose such as
Uri Nissan Gnessin to Y. H. Brenner. We are, therefore, no nearer
to solving the riddle of why Bialik remains with us here and now.

II

To that end, one should turn to the five long poems that are generally considered to be Bialik's masterpieces (an opinion that he
shared) in hopes of identifying certain basic features that can help
unlock the riddle. Critics have offered many, sometimes contradictory, reasons for Bialik's status in Hebrew poetry, each seeking his
own reasons for preserving Bialik from generation to generation.[1]
Many see him as a poet of renascence; others, as a poet of destruction. Some extol him as a prophet; others, as a secular leader. Some
find pathos and sarcasm in his poetry; others discern the ironies of
ambiguity. Some see him as the innocent young yeshiva boy; others

find in him the shadowy, instinctive world of a culture that has repressed its darker urges. What emerges from the plethora of interpretation is a sense that the desire to explain is more powerful than the explanations themselves. The collective unconscious has struggled to maintain its ties with the poet who has apparently expressed something very basic within the soul of his audience over the past hundred years.

Works that are better or more interesting from a stylistic point of view do not necessarily become canonical; rather, it is those that respond to a certain central expectation in the soul of the audience. Lionel Trilling, a critic steeped in the teachings of Freud, argued that the artist gives form and substance to the collective neuroses of his society.[2] The great artist is the one who best heeds and expresses such neuroses—for there is some relationship between the infrastructure of the work and the psychic and social substratum of the intended audience.

In order to examine the essence of that substratum, we shall turn to Bialik's five long poems: "The Perpetual Scholar" (1895), "The Dead of the Desert" (1902), "In the City of Slaughter" (1904), "The Pool" (1905), and "The Scroll of Fire" (1905). Each has been interpreted in different ways and there is not one line that has not been burdened with learned exposition and commentary. All five are universally acknowledged to have achieved canonical status—in a way that the long poems of Tchernichowsky, Shneour, or Fichman have not.

Characteristic of the five works is that all employ symbols that are ambiguous and multivalent, symbols that convey simultaneously both a value and its antithesis. Such a revolutionary conception of a social group's symbolic world does not present values as sacred or absolute. Rather, revolutionary works cast doubt upon the underlying symbols, forcing the audience to cope with a twilight situation, a crisis from which a new reality may be born. The audience must struggle with an ambivalent or polyvalent situation, a dichotomy that is left unresolved.

In the first poem, "The Perpetual Scholar," depicting the life of a young yeshiva student, the narrator's ambivalence regarding the symbols is evident; and the ambiguity may be more apparent than in the later works. The poem does more than describe a type or cry out against it and its world. The poet makes us ask several basic questions. Is this work an elegy for a world in which the contemplative study of Torah (meaning general Jewish learning) can no longer coexist with everyday life? And/or is it a satire about an individual who tries to perpetuate a superannuated way of life? In other words: Is the "Perpetual Scholar," the symbol of the ideal figure of the traditional society, a *hero* because he successfully overcomes his instincts and keeps everyday life separate from the Torah; or is he simply a *victim* precisely because he still has suppressed feelings that others have succeeded in overcoming? Moreover, the ideal of keeping Torah separate from life is no longer valid, and the main hope of the younger generation is to change their attitudes:

> If only one generous spirit breathed within you
> And cleared the "Path of Torah" we have rebelled,
> And paved the way of life to the Yeshiva.

("The Perpetual Scholar")

Values central to the world of the audience are questioned. Toward the end of the poem one sees signs that the dichotomy might be resolved, but, in fact, no such definitive resolution is evident in the text. The ideal of a life of Torah and the opposite of that ideal are presented ambiguously as the poem frequently expresses contradictory positions.

None of Bialik's works conceives the ambivalence of his intended audience better than "The Dead of the Desert," the story of the remnants of the first generation of the Exodus from Egypt, cursed to remain in the desert as the "living dead." Bialik depicts their rebellion against the curse of the Almighty. The questions that the poem poses were of metahistorical significance in 1902 and remain so today. The poem questions whether it is the situation of the "living dead" or the disruption of that apparent contradiction through rebellion that is against the order of the universe.

> Since God denies us,
> His ark refused us,
> We will ascend alone.

("The Dead of the Desert")

Such issues are not fully resolved in the course of the plot, and, to the extent that there is some resolution, it is rather strange. The end of the rebellion bears witness to its beginning. In 1904 Bialik wrote:

> With a cry of rebirth, with joyful shouts
>   and laughter,
> We totter to the grave

("Word")

These lines seem to give a blunt expression to the experience embodied earlier in "The Dead of the Desert." The rebellion does not end in redemption and rebirth but in the suppression of the rebels. The silence that takes over the desert after the rebellion is more dreadful than that which had preceeded it. It is the Arabs who remain to tell the story of the "people of the writing."

What, then, is the general message of that poem? Secular rebellion against the curse of God and history? An elegy to a failed rebellion? An apocalyptic vision of the dangers inherent in the forces that seek to return to history after being concealed for so many years? The apotheosis of the heroic rebels who are ready to fight a final battle regardless of the tragic results? The symbolic plot, therefore, poses difficult questions, ones that still retain their force nearly a century later. History has yet to furnish simple and unequivocal answers.

"In the City of Slaughter" raises questions that are no less troubling. The poem cannot be interpreted simply as a response to an historical event. It does not "represent" the Kishinev pogrom of 1903; nor is it a reaction to that event alone. The original title of the poem, "The Burden of Nemirov," which Bialik adopted because of the censor, is no less appropriate than the ultimate one. Kishinev is merely another Nemirov: [1] The two events are simply the twin tips of the iceberg of an historical paradigm that already had a long past and was also to have a long future. The early years of this century seem like a small-scale dress rehearsal for the 1940s. For the post-Holocaust audience passages of the poem ring with a believable and self-evident reality that makes other literary passages pale in comparison.

"In the City of Slaughter" offers a philosophy of history that attempts to interpret the ambiguity of the victims' role in their fate. It poses an astonishing question: Who is to blame—the murderers, the ways of the world and the Almighty ("The sun shone, the acacia bloomed, and the slaughterer slaughtered"), or perhaps the victims themselves? Furthermore, is not the acceptance of the victim's situation as a divine decree worse than the murder itself? In other words, are the victims not more contemptible than the murderers?

> To the graveyards, beggars! Dig up your fathers' bones
> And the bones of your holy brethren, and fill your packs
> And shoulder them. On your way now, you shall
> Peddle them at every fair.

("In the City of Slaughter")

This question of the status of the victim in historical consciousness continues to nag at us to this day, for the reader's self-image is linked to his assessment of the victims and the survivors. He identifies with them and yet attempts to repress the very thought of them— anything to avoid having to cope with the dreadful images that Bialik forces on his audiences.

The social ramifications of "The Pool" are more latent than those of the other poems. It is the story of a pool in the woods and its transformation at different hours of the day (morning, noon, night, and in the time of a tempest). The poem deals with the bonds between exterior and interior, between the observer (the pool) and the world observed (time and the landscape). The observer is placed outside time, like the dead of the desert, and that situation is the source of both his strength and his weakness. The observing pool (with a mirror function) is autonomous and independent, yet subservient and dependent. The aesthetic position of the involved and the noninvolved creates this ambiguity: "Reflecting all things and containing all / transfigured as she transformation finds." This correlation between dependence and independence is the psychological problem of the social group dwelling outside of time. The poet himself does not judge whether that is desirable or undesirable but leaves matters at an eternal standoff: "Considering the riddle of two worlds / twin worlds (but which one prior, to me unknown)."

Bialik's poetry often emphasizes the deep inner bond between the private myth or neurosis of the poet and the myths and neuroses of his readers. In the case of a personal poem such as "The Pool" (and in the series of poems entitled "Orphaned"), the same fateful connection is particularly conspicuous. Each one of the poems discussed can be interpreted in the light of the personality of the poet, but, similarly, each also relates to some fundamental problems of the intended audience. It is precisely that relationship that accounts for the ongoing vitality of Bialik's work.

The correlation between the social group, the poet, and the basic thesis of the poem is particularly evident in "The Scroll of Fire," a work that has been given various mythical interpretations, most of them having a certain validity. The ambivalence—the suggestion of polarity—is more evident than in the earlier ones. Two archetypical figures representing two extremes are set in opposition: "the young sad-eyed youth" and "the fair youth with the pale eyes." The poem opens with an apocalyptic description of the destruction of the Temple and the burning of the symbols of God's kingdom on earth. A double exile follows from this destruction, for it is also an exile from eros—from fecundity and continuity. Existence is marked by ambivalence: half-life, half-death. After the destruction, young people were sent into exile; and the sexes, stranded in different places on an island, had the urge to reunite but could never again meet.

The poet presents two reactions to the historical situation that followed the separation of the sexes: despair, the decision to perpetuate destruction, preferring the absolute negation of an ambiguous existence; and hope, the wish to seek out a ray of lost light. Here, too, the alternatives are not unequivocal. The "sad-eyed youth" disappears in the river of loss and oblivion, but the fair youth with the pale eyes "wandered in the world like an errant star in eternal space, naked and barefoot and near-sighted. He had nothing but the great fire in the depths of his heart, and the weariness of the dawn in the abyss of his eye." This dichotomy between absolute despair and hesitant, romantic hope is an eternal element of the human condition. As explored by Bialik, it has not lost its relevance; nor have the other dichotomies that he laid bare.

III

The underlying symbolic infrastructure of each of the five poems implies the dichotomy between destruction and rebirth. The fervor of rebirth, the power of poetic speech, and the force of renascent expression struggle on some level against the ever-present forces of destruction and decline, although for Bialik the poet, one concludes, the trauma of destruction usually conquers the angels of rebirth.

"The Perpetual Scholar," for one, is a doomed figure. Any hope derives from the (unlikely) possibility of a transformation that will revive the living dead and return him to the cycle of life:

> How abundant the ears to be harvested in joy
> If only a single generous spirit breathed in you.

The image of the living dead recurs throughout Bialik's poetry. It stands at the center of "The Dead of the Desert": The living dead giants try to be fully alive but die once more. The protest of the giants is voiced in the passionate outcry:

> We are the brave!
> Last of the enslaved!
> First to be free!

Dialectically, the plot leads from destruction to rebirth and back to destruction; thematically, the nexus between life and death dominates: death in life and life in death.

The paradoxical dichotomy between the dead who live and the living who are dead reaches its fullest expression in "The Scroll of Fire," in which the state of destruction is conceived of as death in life. A barrier separates the young men from the young women, precluding continuity or fertility. Thus, exile is, in essence, a sterile, hopeless situation that precludes continuity or fertility. This state of death in life brings in its wake either rebellion that ends in total destruction (like the "lad with the angry eyelids" or the "dead of the desert") or an intense quest to recover the fire of life. Longings are expressed in the heightened language, in the bold representation of the living dead that contains in its intensity a kind of redemption.

IV

Ambivalence, polarity, dichotomy—what has all this to do with our initial query regarding Bialik's lasting power?

We now know that the collective experience of Eastern European Jewry laid bare by Bialik in the early twentieth century would come increasingly to characterize Jewish existence in most of the Diaspora during the rest of the century: in essence, the experience of destruction and rebirth. We of this generation are accustomed to calling ourselves "the generation of the Holocaust and rebirth"; but these events do not apply only to a discrete historical period that began in the 1930s and ended in the 1940s. Bialik, who died in 1934, before the onset of the Holocaust, deeply felt that the processes of destruction and rebirth were in a dormant, potential state. The poet removed them from a state of social potential and gave them expression in poetry. Jews of his generation were perhaps not conscious of how intensely Bialik felt the internal, spiritual and the external, historical dialectic of their age. But his inclusion in the literary canon was not long in coming because that generation knew, in the depths of its soul, that the poet expressed truths that they dared not feel or express. He breathed the breath of actuality into what at that time was only a vague potentiality, a potentiality that would become an even more dreadful actuality decades later.

If Bialik is still with us here and now, it is because the historical process that was made concrete in his works is still not played out; to our sorrow, it has yet to exhaust itself. The ambiguity of the basic symbols still worms its way, and we still live in a period that the poet Nathan Alterman, who was far closer to Bialik than would seem at first glance, called a time of "life on the razor's edge."

NOTES

1. In the following interpretations I draw upon the work of a long line of commentators, including Fischel Lachower, Dov Sadan, Baruch Kurzweil, Yonatan Ratosh, Adi Zemach, Dan Miron, Menahem Peri, and many others. The interpretations are not meant to stand by themselves but rather to offer additional explications of why Bialik is still with us today.
2. Lionel Trilling, "Art and Neurosis," in *The Liberal Imagination: Essays on Literature and Society* (New York: Doubleday, 1953).
3. Thousands of Jews were massacred in this Russian town during the Chmielnicki persecutions of 1648.

Where shall we hide? Our house is destroyed, and our enemies cover the highways. If a miracle was done for us, and we escaped, must we depend on miracles?

S. Y. Agnon, As Day Dawns

by a miracle
Agnon's literary representation of social dramas

I

Any historical or social description contains a story. Any presentation of historical or social facts assumes knowledge of the facts and connects those facts according to certain principles, whether conscious and explicit or unconscious and implicit. Thus, even in a historical account—in Aristotelian terms—matters are not described as they actually are but as they ought to have been by necessity and probability. Historians not only choose among facts according to literary criteria but also connect them according to those criteria.

One may concur with Hayden White that a historical narrative posits some social order against which historical forces rise up (so that a precondition for "narrative" history is the existence of a state with laws), and, therefore, any true historian seeks to find and transmit some sort of moral lesson from the sequence of events he describes.[1] Or one may agree with Victor Turner that a given social structure acts according to a certain dramatic order inherent in the structure itself: beginning in disruption, reaching a crisis, and, finally, either achieving reconciliation through the reintegration of the social forces or else culminating in a rift that indicates a perverted social reality that cannot be reformed. Ritual and folk tales, first, and literary stories, later, concretize that drama in literature.[2]

By the same token, one might use terminology that is more essentially sociological (Marxist vocabulary, for instance), but that also relates to historical facts and usually tells similar "stories" (even though the materials may derive from other societies and historical periods).[3] The basic assumption is that the overt facts are merely a superstructure overlying a deeper social and economic structure that is represented by those facts.

Just as history is literary—one can locate the story concealed behind any historical account—literary works that relate to historical materials organize those materials according to their own original story. It is perhaps nothing new to say that a story is a story.

Historical accounts and social descriptions usually refer to various elite groups who represent and enact certain processes. In a work of the imagination, the elite group, which has extraliterary reference, is replaced by imaginary figures that lack such reference (although fiction also includes prototypes and authentic characters that do seem to have extraliterary reference).

Despite the foregoing, it must be emphasized that in literature, as in history, general extraliterary references enable the reader to fill in gaps and flesh out the world of the novel. (It is assumed that the reader understands the setting and period depicted as a specific historical time and place.) The social novel, in turn, defines, formulates, and, principally, focuses such references to evoke a "drama" taken to represent events that occur in the extraliterary world. Thus extraliterary associations seem to correspond to the strictly literary associations represented in the fiction. The social novel imposes a fictional viewpoint on history, so much so that frequently our image of a historical period is fashioned more by literary than by historical sources. Through literature readers modify (even if only briefly) the model they ordinarily accept. The general image of a period, place, or personage is shaped by historical accounts, based on facts alone, as well as by fiction. Each new literary work modifies the image.

II

Several of the following remarks, based on the theoretical premises just presented, have already been made in different contexts by such eminent critics of Agnon as Baruch Kurzweil, David Canaani, and Dov Sadan.[4] Here, however, I shall attempt to present certain basic assumptions, old and new, that might perhaps receive fresh meaning in the present context; for while it does not always present new details, the approach described above does place this complex of assumptions in a new conceptual framework.

In his six major novels, S. Y. Agnon dealt with at least three of the main periods in the social history of the Jews from the early 1800s through the 1940s. He portrayed the world of the shtetl during three periods in *The Bridal Canopy, A Simple Story,* and *A Guest for the Night.* He depicted the new society in the Land of Israel in *Only Yesterday* and *Shirah* (posthumously published in 1971). And he focused on German Jewry in *Mr. Lublin's Shop* (posthumously published in 1975).

Each of these novels has a social significance of its own. Each serves as a kind of synecdoche by means of which the author sought to fashion, pattern, and interpret the model of the society that it portrays. Several of Agnon's models might seem rather surprising to someone habituated to looking at that reality in a cut-and-dried fashion derived from routine literature or from some other purportedly factual source. Whether all the ways of seeing revealed in these different novels combine to produce a general model is a question to be addressed toward the end of our investigation.

The Bridal Canopy was Agnon's first novel. Begun in the 1920s and first published in 1931,[5] it depicts the world of the shtetl in the early nineteenth century as a society cut off and enclosed within the borders of the religious community. In the forefront of the novel stands the family of Reb Yudel Hassid, the protagonist. The central social problem addressed in the novel is the balance between matter and spirit. At the outset, Reb Yudel Hassid is presented as a spiritual idler, a scholar who is unconcerned with his family's material sustenance. He eventually sets out on a fundraising journey for the dowry of his daughters—leaving his family in order to support them—and thereby to restore the balance between matter and spirit. The family's chances for survival are thus based on a strange welfare system (dowries for poor brides) that provides a certain type of needy person with communal support.

As it happens, the trip is a total failure: The unbalanced protagonist attains no equilibrium whatsoever. He himself repeatedly slips over to the materialist extreme by spending most of his time at meals, at telling and hearing stories, and at other pleasures. Toward the end he returns to Torah study, which again does not support him. Until the close of the novel he is, therefore, unable to sustain his family by his own resources. It turns out that two paths are open to him. He can save his family either by fraud or by a miracle. The miracle is that the fraud becomes truth: The first Reb Yudel is falsely identified as the *other* Reb Yudel Nathansohn. The latter, a very rich man, is supposed to have a daughter (which he has not) with a "fat" dowry, and so the son of a wealthy family is ready to marry poor Reb Yudel's daughter. Subsequently, by a miracle, poor Reb Yudel discovers a treasure in his home that makes him into a sort of wealthy Reb Yudel Nathansohn. In this way, opposite poles in the dichotomy of matter and spirit are melded.

And if the novel deals with the survival of a family, it is also, by extension, concerned with society's continued existence, which is also precariously dependent on either a miracle or fraud. It is not surprising, then, that Agnon believes that this doomed society, in its parlous state, can be saved only in the imagination, not in the proper advancement of the plot. The fertility ceremony concluding the novel does not draw upon the true power of the society but, rather, upon the force of fraudulence and a miracle.

Indeed these depictions of traditional society—with its mistaken identity and fraud, material and spiritual bankruptcy—characterized Agnon's work from the very beginning. Without doubt they are already present in the novella *And the Rugged Shall be Made Level* (first published in 1912), which is far more similar in structure to *The Bridal Canopy* than appears at first glance.

III

A Simple Story relates to the same society one hundred years later, at the turn of the twentieth century. Traditional society, which has lost its authority and force, has been replaced by a semisecular society that operates according to economic, rather than halakhic or spiritual, norms. Or, in a distortion of the well-known saying from *The Ethics of the Fathers:* "Who is content with his lot? The rich man . . ." According to Agnon, the members of that society are concerned, more than anything else, with retaining and maintaining their financial assets: The survival of the Jewish bourgeoisie hangs in the balance. As in *The Bridal Canopy*, marriage is the yardstick by which the community's values are measured. Hirshl, the protagonist, attempts to defy the social convention that wealth must wed wealth. "Any marriage which is not a decent one" in this regard is considered to be a kind of sin against the accepted norms of the parents' world, norms that are quite close to those of Thomas Mann's *Buddenbrooks*. To Hirshl's parents, orderly existence and the maximal increase of property supersede all other values. Unable to withstand the tension of the conflict, the young man loses his mind and is sent by his family to those entrusted by the society to cure maladies that do not permit its members to function according to its demands. Psychology thus functions to rehabilitate society's errant sons so that they can maintain the culture of property. Through the "miracle" of psychology, the social order is saved from disintegration: Hirshl, having finished his treatment, is fully prepared to meet society's economic and communal demands.

In both *A Simple Story* and *The Bridal Canopy*, society hovers on the brink of disintegration. And in both the unity of the family is preserved by an external power, a deus ex machina, in the guise of a "treasure" or a psychological institute, without which the bonds of society would collapse.

IV

A Guest for the Night can be viewed from two opposing angles. It is a novel about a man who leaves his family and also about a man and his family who leave a place of safety in the Land of Israel so that the head of the family, at least, can relive his own traditional past in the Diaspora. The protagonist is unable to create a substitute for his family in the old house of study.

Incidentally, in the city of Scibucz, the marriage of Rachel and Yeruham—the one and only couple that starts a family—is the exception that proves the rule: This is a story about disintegrating families. Anyone trying to return and strike roots in that society becomes part of its disintegration; it is a society destined for decline because it no longer even has the power to struggle for unity.

The hero-narrator's effort to bring back old times in such a place is artificial, without purpose, and without a future: He is merely "a guest for the night." The only way out of that cul-de-sac—the Eastern European shtetl—is to leave. As in Agnon's other novels, the society depicted here has nowhere to go. The only exit, in the form of a deus ex machina, is rather simple: the return of the protagonist to his home and family. So although this is not a novel of Jewish renascence, it does have a Zionist message of sorts. But that miracle is possibly *only for the guest,* not for the inhabitants of Scibucz: Implicit in the miracle is the prophecy of disaster for the multitude.

Analyzing these works, one is forced to conclude that the dilemmas they pose are not subject to any true—or natural—solution. They are resolved, in ironic fashion, by miracles that, if anything, oppose the plot. The social drama should end in hopeless defeat because of defects that cannot be corrected. The author must therefore use external countermodels in order to bring elements of rebirth into the pattern of destruction. But they are all merely temporary solutions, ironic miracles that permit the few to exit from the hopeless situations in which the many are trapped.

V

Like the other novels, *Only Yesterday* also begins with the protagonist leaving the bosom of his family and his homeland to find a new identity—following in the footsteps of his ancestor Reb Yudel Hassid in *The Bridal Canopy.* This novel of maturation and character formation represents as well the effort of part of the shtetl society to find a new identity and a new homeland for itself. Yitzhak Kummer, the main character, along with "our other brethren, men of our redemption" have a romantic, personal vision of renewal and renascence in the Land of Israel, a kind of Arcadia. What emerges is that the effort at maturation fails. The protagonist, who had tried to separate himself from his family in order to achieve some degree of erotic and personal freedom, forfeits those liberties in Reb Faish's ultra-Orthodox house. In other words, the one who sought a new identity, loses his identity. And unidentified powers of madness (in the guise of Balak the dog) overcome him and eliminate him. Moreover, it is the very desire to cut himself off from his former self that provokes the powers that destroy him. This story takes a rather dim view of the efforts of the Second Aliyah to strike roots in the Land of Israel, an effort that was doomed to failure because the generation was unworthy. The main character, "like our other brethren, men of our redemption," had insufficient spiritual power to attain the freedom, independence, and maturity that would permit him to meet the challenges and overcome the hardships of existence in the new Land of Israel.

In this novel, too, the proper development of the plot leads into a cul-de-sac, and again the author attempts to offer some measure of Zionist redemption by means of a *mythical miracle:* the rain after the drought and after Yitzhak's burial. It serves as a sign, as it were, that now that the victim has been sacrificed, the sin has been atoned for and the land will once more flourish. Again, a causal sequence stands in opposition to the inner logic of the plot and derives from another source, implying that only by means of a miracle can society be saved. The force of miracles, the need for miracles, permeates these novels. Thus we have seen the treasure that cancels out the false identity of matter and spirit; the psychologist who exorcises the demon of rebellion; the gates that open to the guest, allowing him to leave the "hotel" and return to his home and family; and here in *Only Yesterday,* a society unable to cope with its conflicts that might be saved through a suprahuman miracle, even though, or perhaps because, the individual is condemned to death.

VI

There is, of course, a parallel between *The Bridal Canopy* as a journey and *Only Yesterday* as a journey, between the successful failure of Reb Yudel and the failed success of his grandson Yitzhak Kummer. Similarly, it is possible to discern a strange parallel between Hirshl's desperate efforts to break through the boundaries of family in *A Simple Story* and the effort made by Herbst (a sort of Hirshl thirty years older) to shatter its framework in *Shirah.* Herbst lives in

the Land of Israel during the thirties, in a society in transition between settlement and state, a society of those remaining after a
large part of the Second Aliyah had disappeared—left—and those
added in the waves of immigration after World War I. Agnon *chose*
to represent that society through a remote professor, an academic
scholar who specializes in the study of the royal graves of Byzantium, and whose life is more immersed in the past than in the daily
life of the present. Like the other professors in the novel (Welt-
fremd, Neu, Bachlam), Herbst's life is very different from the dyna-
mism of others in the Jerusalem of the 1930s and 1940s, the city of
Taglicht, Zohara, Tamara, and Heinz.

Various and sundry groups and institutions of the Yishuv occupy the background of the work: the Haganah, Revisionist dissi-
dents, kibbutzim, Neturei Karta (ultra-Orthodox anti-Zionists),
Oriental Jews, and more. The oppositions between past and present, foreground and background, are central to the literary structure. The protagonist tries to flee from the restrictive norms of his
society, from his family, and from his obsessive preoccupation with
the dead past (the cemeteries of Byzantium), to a present that offers
both life and poetry (Hebrew *shirah*). The quest poses a question:
Can one be devoted to the past and live in the present? Or, is it
possible to build a bridge between the dynamic, perhaps overly dynamic, present and the preoccupation with the dead past, which
has become the intellectual's raison d'être in the new land? This opposition not only provides the social and spiritual infrastructure of
the novel but also represents one of the central conflicts of the
modern Land of Israel.

Following the logic of the plot, another of Agnon's protagonists
reaches a dead end, unable to break out of the confines of the fam
ily or of his listless spiritual life. The novel, which the author left unfinished, has two conclusions, each leading into a cul-de-sac. The
ending as published presents the return to mundane, trivial existence, a conclusion somewhat similar to that of *A Simple Story*. The
quest for redemption and for escape from one's bourgeois fate fails
because social conventions overpower the yearning for rebellion.

There is an alternative ending to the novel that had been part of
the original manuscript and that was published earlier, in 1956, as a
story entitled "Forevermore." In it the desire to escape from the
conflict leads to a world entirely removed from the present: the

leper asylum. There, in the realm of "eternal time," every conflict is resolved by acknowledging that the life of suffering is eternal law.

From the social point of view, it seems that the author prefers the ahistorical situation of exile to the entrance into history that characterizes life in the Land of Israel. If "Forevermore" is in fact an alternate ending for *Shirah*, that story symbolizes the fate of a society that has let its miracles slip through its fingers. It is an extreme expression of the failure of personal rebirth in old age (personal rebirth implied by the artistic attempt to bring the tombs of history back to life), and perhaps the failure of social rebirth of a nation which, in old age, feels the flush of life.

VII

In the novel *Mr. Lublin's Store*, the depiction of social reality through the plot (or lack of plot) reaches its literary peak. To Agnon, the West offers only hopeless suffocation and a dead end from the Jewish point of view and in every other respect as well. This plotless story is about characters who are mired in the slough of German life but are incapable of leaving it. Eastern European Jews (Lublin, Stern) have nowhere to go back to. Once again, the only people who might be able to save themselves are those who can break out of the vicious cycle of hopelessness produced by a chain of "German" plots with no redemptive endings. These plots depict the German local world: The Jews there are permanent outsiders, marginal victims of impersonal processes.

By exception, then, one who has come from the Land of Israel can go back. In this case, as in the novella *Ad henna* (Unto Here), the miracle of leaving Germany is a possible solution only for the chosen few but not for the entire community, which is apparently condemned to remain behind.

VIII

Again and again, in his "Diaspora" novels, Agnon depicted the drama of a society trying to stay alive by means of obsolete values and with no economic infrastructure to sustain those values.

The Jewish framework is validated only insofar as it supports the struggle for survival of this bourgeois society. It is in a state of disintegration; its structures have been shattered and destroyed; and it has not the slightest chance for rehabilitation. The only hope for its members is to abandon it completely.

Agnon presents a social group that tries to restore itself to life in this way—through a new identity, a new land, and a new system of values—in *The Field*, his never-written novel about life in the Land of Israel during the Second Aliyah. But the individual within the group lacks the strength to undergo the far-reaching transformation that the new society demands, and he is destroyed in the effort to effectuate it. In *Shirah*, Agnon portrays the drama of an intellectual in a dynamic society trying to justify his present life through an obsessive bond to the past. The disparity between eras causes him to try to detach himself from the existing structures of work and family and live for the moment. In each of these dramas, as in the ones discussed earlier in this essay, the normal causal structure of the plot leads to a dead end; and the author usually resolves his drama by means of a counterplot that derives from the realm of the irrational: miracles, depth psychology, myth, and other similar devices. These works do not end happily, with reconciliation, but rather with acknowledgment of the irreconcilable gap between the powers that are at odds with each other.

Agnon tries to grapple with the dead end by drawing upon powers from elsewhere, as it were. And within the body of his stories he holds out the promise, either explicitly or implicitly, of a book that would depict the countervailing positive process. For example, he mentions the story of Bluma Nacht in *A Simple Story*; and the story of our brethren who work the lands of the Lord in *The Field* is previewed at the end of *Only Yesterday*. His other novels and stories hint at an alternate story, one that was not written, such as the story of the key of the synagogue transplanted from the shtetl in the Land of Israel as a sequel to *A Guest for the Night*, and the story of the renewed life of Dr. Levi's library after it reaches the Land of Israel as a sequel to *Ad henna*. All of these plots are miraculous, and the author hints at them without bringing them to realization. They are likely to appear at the end of a story, deriving from a different plot and leading to yet another plot (such as the Reb Yudel's voyage to the Land of Israel).

What emerges from a general examination of the plots of these novels is that Agnon "argued" that only by means of irrational counterplots (or a rational counterplot contrasting with an irrational act based on nostalgia, such as the return to the doomed shtetl) can this generation grapple with the conflicts it confronts. According to his perception of the nature of things and logic, recent generations of Jewish society are trapped in a cul-de-sac, and each generation, everywhere, is similarly threatened. One might say that the final lesson of Agnon's view of history is that the society exists by virtue of miracles; and we have nothing else on which to depend.

IX

The preceding remarks are not an attempt to investigate the thematics of the works discussed. Nor is the claim made that these works actually represent reality. It is Agnon's very personal interpretation of historical reality that is elucidated by this general examination of the patterns of the plot and the organizational principle behind the depiction of the historical material. And his world view, in turn, influences our own interpretation of the extraliterary world—a model as valid as any other model certainly. One can even lose sight of the fact that Agnon's world is fictional—so well made and persuasive is it in its comprehensiveness, so convincing in its fidelity. We believe that it exists as depicted; we trust that it mirrors nonfictional reality. Indeed, his depiction may seem even more reliable than those we obtain from other literary or nonliterary sources, and we read reality according to the rules imposed upon us by his fiction. By a miracle, Agnon's world becomes our own.

NOTES

1. Hayden White, "The Value of Narrativity in the Representation of Reality," in *On Narrativity*, ed. J. T. Mitchell (Chicago: The University of Chicago Press, 1981), 1–23.
2. Victor Turner, "Social Dramas and Stories About Them," in ibid., pp. 137–164.

3. Maynard Solomon, ed., *Marxism and Art: Essays Classic and Contemporary* (New York: Knopf, 1973).

4. Baruch Kurzweil, *Masot al sipurei shai agnon* (Essays on the Stories of S. Y. Agnon) (Jerusalem: Schocken, 1962); David Canaani, "The Revealed and the Hidden" (in Hebrew), in *Beinam levein zemanam* (Between Themselves and Their Time) (Merhaviah: Sifriat Poalim, 1955), 9–36; Dov Sadan, *Al shai agnon: masa, iyun ve-ḥeker* (On S. Y. Agnon: Essay, Study, Research) (Tel Aviv: Ha-Kibbutz ha-Meuḥad, 1959).

5. Henceforth I shall not refer to the many interpretations of each of these novels. It is sufficient to note that this article could not have been written without the assistance of earlier research. Matters have been largely summed up in Hillel Barzel's introduction to the collection of articles in Hebrew on Agnon: Hillel Barzel, ed., *Shemuel yosef agnon: mivḥar maamarim al yetsirato* (Tel Aviv: Am Oved, 1982). Regrettably, that collection does not include the extremely important articles of A. M. Lipschutz and Gustav Krojanker. Cf. also the short survey, Gershon Shaked, *Ha-siporet ha-ivrit 1880–1980* (Hebrew Narrative Fiction, 1880–1980), vol. 2 (Tel Aviv: Keter, 1983), 180–184.

first person plural
literature of the
1948 generation

I

The earliest Hebrew writers in Eretz Israel—the majority of them native-born, or "sabras"—were the first children of a culture in formation. Born in the 1920s and raised on a Hebrew vernacular and a Hebrew literary tradition, they built upon the foundations for a new society that had been laid by their parents. Most of these young writers identified with the ideals of the parent generation— the pioneering elite of the Labor movement.

The world view of these writers took shape during the British Mandate period, a time when the Yishuv, the young Jewish settlement in Eretz Israel, was enduring repeated clashes with its Arab neighbors (the riots of 1921, 1929, 1936–1939) and ambivalent relations with the British authorities. The Holocaust and the founding of the State provided the historical climaxes in their development; but it was the War of Independence in particular that afforded them their most intense existential experience. Not without reason were they called the "1948 generation" or the "Palmah generation," after the vanguard brigade of the Jewish armed forces during the 1940s.

The 1948 generation was educated to fulfill the pioneer ethos of their parents by means of the formal and informal educational systems of the Yishuv—especially the "workers' stream," which was controlled by the Histadrut, and the pioneer youth movements Ha-Noar ha-Oved, Maḥanot ha-Olim, and Ha-Shomer ha-Tzair. Indeed, most were educated according to a curriculum that broke completely with those that had molded the youth of the heder, the yeshiva, and the gymnasium. Jewish studies in Israel came to be based mainly on a secular depiction of the Bible, a popularization of nonhalakhic literature, such as Bialik's *Sefer ha-Aggadah,* and an overemphasis on the struggle for independence in the history of the Jewish people, especially in First and Second Temple times. This tendency was marked by an increasing dissociation from religious traditions and from the social values of the Diaspora.[1] Indeed, the acute distaste for the image of the "Diaspora Jew" was ultimately institutionalized in the "Canaanite movement" established in the 1940s by a group that included Yonatan Ratosh and Aharon Amir. Touting an ideology of the "Hebrew nation" based on ancient pre-Judaic roots in the land, this movement denied the historical legitimacy of the 2000-year-long Diaspora experience of the Jewish people. Albeit small, its ideological influence extended far beyond its actual political power.[2] For the Palmah generation, educated under this influence, the transition from a voluntary Yishuv, with its pioneering ideals, to an established state, based on bureaucracy and civic obligation, occasioned an existential crisis.

II

We can in part form an image of this sabra generation from the literary legacies of some of those who fell during the struggle against the British and in the War of Independence. The diaries and letters of this young elite reflect a spirit of complete identification with the values of the parent generation. From these writings, several general and salient lines emerge, bridging the differences between the world of young intellectuals like Yehiam Weitz or Rafi Maletz, who were reared on the classics of music and literature, and the world of others with narrower horizons. Thus, S. Yizhar wrote in the introduction to a collection of letters by his friend and schoolmate Yehiam Weitz, who fell in 1946:

And this small and discontinuous testimony, sometimes bright and sometimes weak, sometimes complete and sometimes fragmented—testimony of ten years of growth of one sabra, and in whom is an example of this entire generation, testimony that is heard by anyone who listens, and tells of the internal and of the gentle, and of the depressions, indeed real depressions, that lie within the breast of a young man whose exterior is pleasant and sarcastic and is seasoned with spice and caprice.[3]

That generation shared a vision at once romantic and realistic. It was a generation with a mission, as Eldad Penn (son of the painter Abel Penn) wrote in his diary on 3 January 1946:

It is possible to come to two conclusions: The first is that since man's life is so short, he must enjoy it as much as he can; and the second is that precisely because life is short, man dies with half of his desire still unfulfilled. Therefore one should be devoted to a sacred and important goal that will be above life, and sacrifice himself for its sake. Sometimes the first feeling overcomes me and sometimes the second. But of late, it seems to me that the second feeling is overtaking me, it appears that I am coming slowly to the realization that the value of life in itself is small if it does not serve something higher than its own self.[4]

Penn's words give voice to the many similar thoughts expressed in *Yevilei esh* (Scrolls of Fire, 1952), an anthology of writings of soldiers killed in and before the 1948 war. The dominant literary legacy of this generation—love of country, passionate idealism, and readiness to sacrifice—was the fruit of the Zionist education tendered at home, in the youth movement, and in school. For these young people, there was no doubt that only Zionism could ensure Jewish survival as a nation; they saw American Jewry's failure to acknowledge this solution as a national tragedy. Although they were the children of war, they saw themselves as the key link in the chain of Jewish history. They set their sights high, as befitted a society of pioneer immigrants and their children who, in the words of a popular Hanukkah song, came "to dispel the darkness."

The drastic change—the crisis—in perceptions did not come about immediately after the 1948 war. Yet a letter from Yehiam Weitz (written in London on 25 May 1939) already reveals that disappointment inhered in their romanticism, which by its very nature made demands that could not be realized in flesh and blood:

. . . Because the new generation—if there is something good in it, it is due to the climate of Eretz Israel and due to its nerve. The rest of their characteristics, all the rest, are not "different" nor are they "new" nor are they "pioneering" nor are they so "healthy." We don't have peasants, we don't have simple folk, we don't have young people who go out to work and who have no Jewish fantasies of a career, young people who, instead of agonizing over their culture, simply live it and make it—we don't have this kind of youth. Teachers who know how to give their souls for their belief, willing to "break their heads" and to instill in their students a love of learning—we have practically none of these. In their place there are all those followers with Mapu in their bones. Not writers who write about truth, but rather all those who are still picking through the pile of ashes of the shtetl. The newspapers, instead of creating a culture of a nation—create a culture of the intellectuals of Israel. The municipalities, instead of doing something—stand and think all the time how to push the workers into a corner, and shall I begin to lament the Arab question? Shall I say now that if we have a function in Eretz Israel—is it to slowly and steadily undermine the social order of the Arab inhabitants of Palestine? To approach and to meddle and to make peace constantly with the simple Arab, to open schools for him—secretly, if he fears the overt—to try everything, to crucify incessantly and shamelessly every thief and bribe-taker?[5]

These words, though written by a member of the Palmah generation, in fact summarize the basic values of the Second Aliyah (1905–1909): its work ethic, its simplicity and frugality, its touchstones in cultural questions, and its approach to Arabs. (They are indeed close in spirit to Brenner, who had expressed disgust with the "intellectual," with the "small town" mentality, and with the artificial.) Yet the young generation, including Yehiam, does not—cannot—fulfill even these values, let alone the grander values of their own age.

The images that derive from the romanticism of the pioneering movement—return to the earth and adoration of the "noble savage" in the persons of the Arab and the sabra—carry within themselves the seeds of irony, the gap between the vision and its realization. The disillusionment with the dream, which became a central subject in Hebrew fiction after the 1948 war, derives not only from the actual nature of the Yishuv and the state; it is also a function of the nature of the romantic vision: It could not stand up to the test of reality.

III

To some extent the flesh-and-blood sabra was the model for the fictional sabra. But in many cases, it seems, the authors did not fully understand the prototype. The literary figure was a linguistic creation, and the language of the authors was always highbrow. The highbrow linguistic register shaped the simple young man in a high mimetic mode. It is a peculiarity of the 1948 generation that its principal storytellers did not draw upon the bounty of the Hebrew vernacular, in spite of its metaphorical wealth and its vitality. Although it was an available linguistic "option" for them, they did not seem to feel a need for it. If they did, it was only for use in dialogue; otherwise, the language of reality left no mark on their work. Rather, their linguistic tradition derives in the main from the conventions of the European-born fathers of modern Hebrew literature.

By the time of the 1948 generation, two central traditions had emerged: (1) the highly stylized language that evolved from Mendele, Agnon, and Berkowitz, based primarily on the language of the sages (participles, conjunctions, and vocabulary), regular phrases, and literary idioms, and (2) the "new trend" language of the Steinman-Shlonsky group and their periodicals, *Ketuvim* and *Turim*, which tried to promote neologism as a replacement for traditional idiom. Neither tradition was deeply influenced by the developing spoken language. The "classical formula" writers tried to describe a new experience with old tools. The "new formula" writers tried to invent a new language by means of artificial, internal linguistic processes; the relationship of that creation to the living language was much like the relationship of innovations of the Academy of the Hebrew Language today to the contemporary linguistic reality.

Writers of the 1948 generation could be found in both camps. The second approach in particular, which did not integrate the spoken dialect except in dialogue, created a discrepancy between dialogue and description. Slang was not an integral component of the literary style. Even to today, writers have rarely given literary expression to the language of the mass immigration, as distinguished from the Sabra slang; and when they have, it is similarly used mostly for dialogue and not for narrative passages.

IV

One may see in this linguistic artificiality symptoms of broader literary woes. Consider the words of the editor of one of the early periodicals of this generation, *Daf ḥadash,* first published in September 1947:

The latest generation is mainly a generation of continuers, a generation of completers of circles. They received everything ready-made: a homeland that they were not troubled to conquer; a language that they absorbed with their mothers' milk; and tools that others had taken the pains to shape.* The relationship between them and what surrounded them—which in the final analysis determines their world view and literary approach—became a matter of accepting a *fait accompli* and not a struggle for revival, which was characteristic of its predecessors and cast their tools. The latest generation could have been thankful that it was not again compelled to battle over an alphabet of expression and form. Perhaps this fact helped it to grow its wings, but it took away their flying license. With what may this be compared? To a powerful and perfected motor whose starter has been removed. In the same way, Hebrew literature was, in the last ten years, a literature of description, of "local color," without any missions or great goals. This phenomenon, which is distressingly prevalent in the literatures of the world, gave birth to the adventure novel, a story whose plot covers up, with suspense, trickery, and spectacular descriptions, the hollowness from which it suffers. From all the great trouble in the world, the woes of decadence and destruction and from the whole tremendous struggle for renewal, Hebrew literature has taken not a jot. The voice of the Hebrew writer has disappeared, and if the voice of literature is heard, it is mainly in the realm of poetry. In the central being of the life of the public, such literature leaves no impression.[6]

And indeed, it is hard to find outstanding innovations in the works of the 1948 generation, in spite of its extensive exposure to English and American literature, which became their second culture (as opposed to the fathers, who were raised on Slavic and Franco-German literature). Indeed, the Anglo-American influence was not well received by the Marxist critics of the time. In 1947, for example, Amos Elon, then a dedicated Marxist, wrote:

It seems that this literature [Anglo-American] of decadent capitalism cannot serve as a conceptual basis for a nation in renewal. The decadence of Hemingway, Arthur Koestler and Sartre the French, cannot be a guiding light. But where has their influence reached if you open *Yalkut ha-reim* [Friends' Magazine]—a mouthpiece of our young writers—and are greeted with "the spirit of Hemingway" hovering over the pages of the magazine?[7]

* *Although they did fight, they generally were only carrying out the will of their fathers.* —G.S.

Still, although that literature prevailed from a quantitative stand-point, it was not the only voice. Russian literature, which was widely translated into Hebrew during and after World War II, con-tinued to exert an influence and was published by the same Labor movement publishing house that put out the works of the young generation. Nevertheless, it must be emphasized that the European influence was an indirect one during those years when Shlonsky and members of his generation reigned in the field of translation. Shlonsky himself translated Gorky, Gogol, Sholokhov, Simyonov, and others, from Russian literature as well as the tales of Till Eulen-spiegel, *Colas Breugnon*, Shakespeare, and others. Of all the many translations produced, the body of Soviet literature undoubtedly had the greatest impact on the "contents" and forms of Hebrew works because its ideological underpinnings paralleled those of the young Israeli intellectual elite. Like the "Socialist realist" Soviet au-thors,* the young Hebrew writers sought (at the outset) to present the hero as a pioneer and builder and the plot as a semidocu-mentary depiction of the building of Israel. This tradition of "the emigrants-immigrants" has its roots in the literature of the Third Aliyah as well, in the works of Ever Hadani, Yosef Aricha, and Shlomo Reichenstein, who wrote of those who came "to build and be rebuilt."

Furthermore, one cannot ignore in this matter the impact of po-etry on fiction. If Shlonsky, Goldberg, and Penn had an influence mainly on language forms and innovations, Alterman also had a great influence on the content of fiction, its world view. As embod-ied in *Ha-tur ha-shevii* (The Seventh Column, 1947) and especially *Simhat aniyyim* (The Joy of the Poor, 1941) and in *Shirei makkot mits-rayim* (Poems of the Egyptian Plagues, 1944), his is a secular exis-tential ethos, a code of behavior, a set of values that transcends even death. What the dead man sings in the voice of the poet are songs of complete fidelity—to wife, to father, to friends, to city, to youth, and to nation. Alterman's poems epitomized the national consensus of the Jewish Yishuv in Eretz Israel: struggle against the British and the Arabs, the "purity" of arms—which never should be misused—illegal immigration, and admiration of the working

---

The major trend in Soviet criticism demanded that writers always depict the ten-sions and struggles of their homeland positively.

settlement. These values achieve metaphysical dimensions above life and death in his "balladist" poems. The religious roots of this generation had indeed been severed, and until the 1950s it had no significant affinity with the Jewish Diaspora experience. These had been exchanged for myth that centered on transcendent secular values, higher than life and death, as embodied in *Simḥat aniyyim*.

V

Young fiction began to flourish immediately after S. Yizhar published *Be-faatei negev* (In the Wastelands of the Negev, 1945) and *Ha-ḥorshah asher ba-givah* (The Grove on the Hill, 1947)—Moshe Shamir published *Hu halakh ba-sadot* (He Walked Through the Fields, 1947), and Yigal Mossinsohn published *Aforim ka-sak* (Gray as Sackcloth, 1946). From then on, this fiction had come of age and had to react to various and contradicting critical expectations.

True, there were critics who were full of praise. Shlomo Nitzan insists that Yizhar's *Ha-ḥorshah asher ba-givah* is a story without characters. He does not protest against this tendency but, rather, accepts and "interprets" it: "Our collective period, which is increasing and deepening in its collectivity, loses track of its individuals and transforms them from units of life into functions." Furthermore:

The Magic Mountain of Thomas Mann is a great book about human beings as individuals. Nowadays, in the days of the collective organization, the totality comes to the fore, the bloc as a unit, and only from within this tight totality are the individuals perceived in a blur and lacking an essential nature (for example, *For Whom the Bell Tolls*). Here is a bloc of people that branches out into its extensions—its individuals. Of course it is possible to rebel against such a vision of Man and to argue about it. But one cannot deny its existence. . . .

Man was a unit of life and became a function. In any case, his life ceased to be "internal and meditative" and became active. But activity not as a sacrifice or a duty, not as a means to something—rather as a way of life, as a style, as a fulfillment of his being. And it could be that since man himself is a function, that is, that constantly and in every aspect of his life he is a part of something—this is the natural way of life. And so, by living his own life, he still builds something outside of him, and all matters are interrelated and the march of time goes on.[8]

The critical premise was that the era itself had lost contact with the individual, and therefore the power and role of literature was to present the collective in general. The blurring of the image of the individual in the works of the young writers did not stem from lack of talent or understanding. It derived from the power of reality; for some writers and critics such a novel was a fitting expression for a society whose gaze was directed at the collective and not at the individual. This critical expectation was not only a validation of works already published but also a demand for more works of a similar nature.

Not all the critics felt this way, however, and from the late forties to the sixties, harsh criticism poured down from the political Left and Right. Characteristic of the left-wing critics was Azriel Ukhmani, who bemoaned the fact that the fiction of the young generation was influenced by English and American culture, rather than by Russian. Preferring plots that lacked an "artistic-ideological form," meaning that the art should be an expresson of the "right" socialistic ideology, he argued that the books of Moshe Shamir are faulty, that *Hu halakh ba-sadot* is defective from the standpoint of ideas, and that in *Tahat ha-shemesh* (Under the Sun, 1950), "everything is incidental and not based on a real psychological foundation." According to Ukhmani, "A realistic novel dealing with the class struggle is not a symbol and not a parable, it is life and reality rooted in time and social relationships." Shamir found refuge in the simplicity of the schematic and did not produce a social-realistic novel. The root of evil, according to Ukhmani, is in Shamir's affinity with Norman Mailer (*The Naked and the Dead*), an author whose rebellion is seen as liable to lead to fascism. Sexual revolution, in other words, is not social revolution; obscene language and drunkenness are not the whole man. Ukhmani concludes: "The time has come for our storytellers to be liberated from slang as an end in itself, from licentiousness as identical with the rebellious." He demands a return to man and to pathos. The new hero need not be introspective, but he has to advance the social revolution in a constructive way.[9]

Right-wing criticism set out from different premises but reached similar conclusions. Baruch Kurzweil, for example, charged that this is monotonic fiction, lacking epic depth, capable only of bas-reliefs and in most cases only sketches, limited in its subject matter, afflicted with a lot of pseudo-sophistication, and tending to immediate expression of every experience—even before it is ripe for literature. This is semireportage ("literalization of life," in his language), abounding in sexuality and actualism (as in the work of Yigal Mossinsohn), lacking cultural and historical depth. So its successes, such as they are, are mainly lyrical (for example, Benjamin Tammuz, Ḥolot ha-zahav [Golden Sands, 1950]).

Several of Kurzweil's premises were further developed by Mordechai Shalev in a series of articles in the journal *Sullam*. Shalev's basic contention was that the Israeli fiction of the 1950s lacks vision and is cut off from unconscious experiences. It abounds in talk without dramatizing the deeds of the heroes; and in its imitation of external reality, it does not expose the spiritual roots of the sabra but detects only his sadistic aspects. It is, then, an empty literature with empty heroes. In its images there is "an emotional struggle in only two voices," very simplified in its outlook. "Marxism in this sense," Shalev observes, "does for the writers and youth collectively what everyone does individually—casts off natural emotional chaos in favor of a compulsory, rational arrangement, as it were." The literature of the younger generation is closer in his eyes to the works of the Hebrew Enlightenment of the nineteenth century than to the literature of revival of the twentieth century. And from this standpoint it is a "powerful reaction to the non-experimental era that preceded Bialik."[11] The problem of this literature is that it has no affinity with the mysterious world of myth and the soul. And in order to be resurrected it must not join the collective vision with personal tension but, rather, find the natural human basis common to them both; "its weaknesses stem primarily from the loss of touch with the subconscious, the source of tension, conflict, and vision."[12]

Already in 1952, these critics from the Left and the Right were zealously supported by one of the representatives of the 1948 generation itself, Matti Megged. Megged stressed that the "reduction" that was perhaps compulsory in life was not also compulsory in literature. The writers described their heroes externally only, thus failing to depict a process of organic maturation.

The absence of the man is conspicuous. If the image is given only in its external/incidental outlines, devoid of roots as compelled by the plot, by force of events, in any event it is not given fundamentally. And as we distance ourselves from a living acquaintance with these characters, we also lose touch with them, lose the ability to identify with them the way they were depicted in literature.[13]

Twenty years later Amalia Kahana-Karmon (a writer who is a chronological peer of the 1948 generation but whose writing belongs to that of a later type) tried to probe the relationship between this generation and those who depicted it in literature. To her, the weakness of the fiction was a function of the strength of reality. Regarding the relationship between literature and life, Kahana-Karmon argues very cogently that the realistic romantics, who were ready to sacrifice themselves on the altar of their homeland, could only create a collective and conformist literature:

My theory is this: The literature of 1948 deals with imperatives of transcendental reality. With ideal good, ideal evil, and so on. And there is very little interest in reality as it exists. Reality as it exists with its sea of neutralities, apathetic to imperatives, the code of delicacy of the time, compelled them to grasp reality in a general and schematic way. . . . This compulsiveness causes a certain shallowness precisely in the area to which we are currently sensitive. It led to denial of essentials, that is, life itself in all its variety. . . .

At first glance a certain paradox exists. Taken as individuals, most of these people who are supposed to be expressing in literature the spirit of the time are splendid people. In all that concerns rectitude, backbone, broad shoulders, intellectual honesty, respect for one's fellowman and for the public, responsibility, sense of proportion. From these standpoints not a few of the "geniuses" of the generation that followed are at best backward in comparison. On the other hand, how did it happen that precisely to those among them who were the good boys, its devoted and obedient sons, their era—splendid in itself—did something awful? The answer, it seems to me, is this: 1948 was a short era in which conformity was definitely justified, and nothing could be worse than this for a writer, this entrapment in a bear hug. Not even the bear is aware that you are engulfed in his hug.[14]

In these words it is possible to find the connection between the images that were revealed to us in the diaries and letters of the fallen soldiers and the criticism expressed about the writers who created a literary world in their image. Not ideological treachery and not cultural shallowness—rather, fidelity to the great deed that is beyond ideology and culture produced the writers of this generation.

VI

The Israeli authors who began their careers in the 1940s and are still writing today started out—expressly and consciously—in the realistic tradition. While they created fictional situations and fictional characters, they also integrated into their works much extraliterary documentary material about the history of the settlement and the wars of Israel. Most of the negative criticism of their work appeared after 1948, when many of the fiction writers who had fought in the War of Independence published books reporting on the war. With these books in front of them, critics and readers as well were no longer satisfied with mere reflections of reality. The point of departure for most critics was that the literature of this generation was not "literary" enough. It was more journalistic than fictional. Statehood generated an upheaval that brought about a change in values, a change in the typology of the fictional hero, and a change in forms of storytelling. The 1948 war was the climactic and tension-releasing experience of this group of writers. In their reportage it was transformed from a traumatic experience to an object of nostalgia. The upheaval that followed was in the transition from a movement to a state: from Haganah, Palmah, and Irgun to the Israel Defense Forces; from a group of "comrades" to bureaucrats; from mutual aid to a network of "pull" (protektzia).

It was social satire that accompanied this transition, this reversal, this great awakening from the romantic dream—notably with a series of short articles called Uzi ve-shut (Uzi's Opinion), a daily feature in Haaretz that began its run in 1949. Written by Benjamin Tammuz and Amos Kenan, the column reflected the gentle humor of the former and the almost grotesque sarcasm of the latter. The articles caught on because, clearly, they filled a tremendous popular need to react to the growing sense of empty rhetoric and the collapse of truth. In one such piece (14 Jan. 1951) the emotional and spiritual "revolution" of the 1948 generation was portrayed as a parody on the biblical expulsion from the Garden of Eden:

A story about Adam and Eve:

Once upon a time, Adam and Eve were in the Garden of Eden. It was a really beautiful place with many trees and water and all kinds of animals, and a band of ministering angels playing all kinds of jazz, and Adam and Eve would dance. And the angel Gabriel would tell them the problems of the world, and they would eat tinned meat.

Until one day, Eve was very sad. Even eating half a kilo of bananas and plums did not help her, so she went to visit her friend the snake. The snake lived in a high and nice tree and he was altogether a creature with a good head. So he said to her: Eve, don't be a fool. What good is this boring Garden of Eden? What you need is a state. You should have your own state. You see this tree? This is the Tree of Knowledge. If you eat an apple from it you will get a state and everyone will recognize you. You will even be able to make peace proposals to China.

So Eve ate an apple and came to Adam and tempted him, and he also ate. When God heard this he got really mad and said, "You wanted a state? Take your state." And he threw them out of the Garden of Eden. And only one fish went to accompany them and they called it *fillet*,[i] since they were filled with wonder.

Adam and Eve lived happily ever after and the snake went to America as an emissary to take up a collection and tempt the Jews to give money and changed his name to a Hebrew one; and his name at the moment is Nachshon.[ii]

The departure of the innocents and dreamers from the lost paradise of the Yishuv into the hell of the state would become a central subject of the new fiction. Satire, such as that of Tammuz and Kenan, was the first literary expression to explore the prototypes of the new Israeli society. Kenan transformed stereotypes from the Yishuv period into contemporary caricatures, and soon enough these motifs were assimilated into "legitimate" literature, in the

[i] *A pun: "Fillet" is written here as if it had the same root as the word for "amazement"; it also alludes to the imported frozen fish fillets that were a staple during the austerity period.*
[ii] *A pun: This is an affectionate diminutive (the word for snake is "nachash") and also a word for pioneering (and hence a name proudly given to some children in the preceding period), specifically associated with the struggle for the establishment of the state, as in the famous "Operation Nachshon."*

works of Aharon Megged, David Shahar, Tammuz, Nitzan, Yehudit Hendel, and others.

Satire, therefore, preceded narrative fiction, and poetry as well, in reflecting the psychological processes that were irrevocably developing, at first secretly and invisibly but later openly and noisily. This is a satire that contrasted the utopian Zionist vision with the actuality of life in the State of Israel. It also established a language of differentiation, capable of depicting a variety of individuals and types. Uzi is one of the first sabras to have recourse to a spoken language—not the language of a literary elite spiced with Arabic and not a language based on consciously prescribed lexical changes. It was, rather, a language that selected and combined words in new and diverse ways. Different is the language of Yerahmiel the Mapainik; and different yet again is the language of Rav Moshe Hakatan, a member of the ultra-Orthodox Neturei Karta sect; Eliezer Gaoni, the Marxist; and of Rav Kalonymus, a member of the religious Zionist Mizrachi party. These parodies of linguistic "idioms" indicated the various new linguistic possibilities for fiction.

Another contribution to satire came from Ephraim Kishon, who on 14 May 1952 issued a call "to the masses of the nation" in the daily newspaper *Maariv*. He announced that he was launching a satiric column of his own and stressed its general and nonpartisan nature: He was offering merchandise to all comers. In this Kishon differed from Kenan, who was interested primarily in the old guard, the people of the "old" Zionist Yishuv. Kishon, by contrast, looked at the country as a mixed bag, a melting pot of the old guard and—especially—recent immigrants. In his language Kishon built on the work of Kenan and others; he found the slang already there and used it for his own needs, shaping it to suit his new audience.

Nevertheless, it must be noted that Kishon's point of departure is completely different from Kenan's. The two often hit the same targets but from a different angle and with different weapons. Both described the growing emptiness of political life at a time when ideology had lost its meaning—and its authority—yet continued to be a factor in the social life of the country. The ideological Yishuv had struggled over every theoretical detail; the new immigrants could not understand what all the struggles were about.

Kishon's satire does not measure the present by the values of the past as did Kenan's. His point of departure is European; he criticizes the world of Eretz Israel in the light of the most perfect of possible states. He does not write for a small elite; his situations are known to every Tel Aviv petit bourgeois who knows more than elementary Hebrew. His satire is directed against all those little cells of the establishment that create misery for the average Israeli in the street. He is, in other words, the ombudsman who represents the "little citizen" against the forces of discrimination and disorder. He addresses issues that concern the quality of life: the selling of milk that has gone sour; the snobbery of the "people of the book" who do not buy books in Hebrew and who secretly enjoy American pornographic magazines; the Israeli habit of competing over how big everyone's apartment is; bureaucracy; the absurd politicization of social life; and the economic mess. He also goes after the enemies of Israel. In general, Kishon's satire is gentle: Israel is for him, in sum, the best of all possible worlds. He does not criticize the state in the name of those values it has betrayed, as Kenan does, but in the name of the values of "normalization."

It seems to me that the elegiac-satiric tone, this strange mixture of yearning for a myth and of a sorry struggle with a distorted reality, has become the dominant tone in Hebrew literature of the past thirty-five years. It is much more Kenan's—Uzi's—view than Kishon's. The changes that were generated in fiction in the late 1950s with the appearance of the new "young guard" (e.g., Sadeh, Yehoshua, Amichai, Appelfeld, Oz) can be understood only in the context of the social "upheaval" of the 1950s, which found its first direct expression in parody.

VII

At the outset, the writers of this new fiction focused on their own generation, but after the "psychological upheaval" of the 1950s they sought to break out of that narrow world in order to understand where their generation came from, where it was going, and to whom it would ultimately have to account for its actions. To some extent, this even complied with the critical expectations of both the Right and the Left.

The writers of the "realistic" literature of the 1940s and 1950s—the Palmah generation—are still creating to this day. Influenced by the upheaval wrought by the establishment of the state, they tried in their writing to break through the barriers of time and space. They dealt with the image of the generation of the fathers—sometimes nostalgically, sometimes critically. Some—Hanoch Bartov, Nathan Shaham, Aharon Megged, Benjamin Tammuz—sought to describe their formative world, the world of childhood and growing up in the period of the Yishuv. Others, such as Yehudit Hendel and Mordekhai Tabib, set out to describe groups and communities that were out of the "Ashkenazi" mainstream. And several, including Moshe Shamir, turned to history and tossed today's problems into the background to focus on yesterday instead.

In spite of the wealth of subjects, materials, and fiction techniques (on a sufficiently high level and usually according to realistic conventions), this literature did not always attain outstanding achievements. Only in the 1960s and 1970s did several of the writers attempt to stray from the realistic tradition. Megged tried his hand at a surrealistic format; Alexander and Yonat Sened turned to the "nouveau roman"; Tammuz eschewed the lyrical story in favor of the symbolistic-mythic novel; Yehudit Hendel moved from the realistic story, by way of the impressionistic novel, to the peak of the impressionistic world outlook. However, in spite of all the changes in schools and techniques, many of the storytellers did not succeed in reaching full concretization of human conflicts: The criticism directed at them from the Right and the Left was not entirely unjustified. Paradoxically, despite their realistic point of origin, many could not create a truly realistic style; and although for the first time they could put their finger on the mentality of the native, they could not penetrate beyond the mentality to the old images of new people in a new land. They did not penetrate into the very unique and individual characters of their "heroes." Like writers of the 1930s, the very external and stereotypic tradition of the provincial genre still dominated the scene.

Of special importance is the work of S. Yizhar, perhaps the only one untouched by this process of change: All of his works are populated by the same set of heroes. The vast majority of them are products of the kibbutz or moshav, sensitive and tentative, raised on values of the Labor movement and love of the Hebrew language. Thus his *Yemei tsiklag* (The Days of Ziklag, 1958) differs from *Efrayim ḥozer le-aspeset* (Efraim Goes Back to Alfalfa, 1938), neither in epic scope nor in the characterization—only in quantitative scope. (*Yemei tsiklag* is a great panoramic novel of more than 1000 pages. *Efrayim* is a novella thirty pages in length.) Yizhar is faithful to open space, the landscape, and his friends. But he could not find roots in the past of the founding fathers. More than his friends, he feared that reality limited his consciousness, leaving the realm of the romantic as the only avenue of escape. In one of his last stories, *Ha-nimlat* (The Fugitive) (in *Sipurei mishur* [Stories of the Plains], 1963), his hero, following a runaway colt, tries to break out of the confines of the landscape and the homeland. His heroes had no alternative. They could not change and adapt themselves to the changing country, and they could not leave their beloved countryside. The only way out was the romantic skies. Only there was the last resort of the romantic never-never land of the old pre-state Yishuv. "From here, one can only see up to the orchards. As if they are the edge of the world, as if this is the bridge of the earth, border to the ocean. . . . Make a horse of me and I will gallop there, full of the itch to open beyond the closed protection. Beyond the border of the world" (p. 49). And also:

And what remains? What remains is that he who ran away, ran away and he who remained, remained. What remains is that we are all here without anything to do but with gloomy thoughts, and he who ran—wherever he was running to, he is there. . . . (pp. 56–57)
   Where, you ask? Obviously: to the sun. Straight into it. Where else? Through its bright open gates. Into its fiery gold, of course, where if not to the sun? To the sun. To the sun. And without returning. Hallelujah! (p. 63)

   The work of Yizhar exemplifies the artistic problems of the 1948 generation: It grew up without conflict with its fathers, cut off from its historical roots, and with a negative attitude to Jewish religious traditions. It could take root in the open space of the homeland, the values of the place and the time, there and then, and the new type of people who blossomed in this freedom—Perhaps from this comes the importance of the "sabra," the native-born Israeli, as symbolized by a plant. (And indeed, Yizhar's most impressive artistic achievements lie in the descriptions of space and the conquest of the desert with words—in essence, striking verbal roots in the homeland.) From their adolescence, these sabras were nurtured by the youth movements (more than by families), knew their friends better than their fathers, and looked to their peers as models (as with Yehiam Weitz). More than seeing their fellow man as he was, they saw him as he was supposed to be. At the outset, attempts to break out of these limits were unsuccessful. After the upheaval, members of the 1948 generation did not again accept the image of a simple ideal. The old values declined and were undermined, and the generation of the War of Independence had to face its own unadorned image in the mirror. Yizhar was the only one among them who recognized the limits and felt the terrible suffocation of this kind of freedom and this social group. And since his heroes are not able to imagine any other place, here and now, they long for a domain that does not exist, like Icarus who longed for the sun. This is a kind of passion for "the islands of gold we dreamed about" [Bialik], a passion that can be fulfilled in death alone. Yizhar's silence after this story is not a coincidence. The realm that does not exist beyond freedom is a realm of great silence.

NOTES

1. See "Jewish Heritage: Revolt and Transformation in Israeli Culture," in this volume.
2. Baruch Kurzweil, "The Essence and Sources of the Canaanite Movement" (in Hebrew), in *Sifrutenu ha-ḥadashah: hemshekh o mahapekhah?* [Modern Hebrew Literature: Continuity or Revolution?] (Tel Aviv: Schocken, 1960), 270–300.
3. S. Yizhar, Introduction to Yehiam Weitz, *Mikhtavim* (Letters) (Tel Aviv: Am Oved, 1948), 7–8.
4. Eldad Penn, *Gevilei esh* (Scrolls of Fire), Reuven Avinoam (Tel Aviv: Ministry of Defense, 1952), 360.
5. Yehiam Weitz, to his father, in *Mikhtavim*, pp. 202–203.
6. Hayim Glikstein, "The Rebellion of the Young" (in Hebrew), *Daf ḥadash* (1947):6.
7. Amos Elon, "Sarcasm in Israeli Youth" (in Hebrew), *Bashaar* (May-June 1947): 11.

8. Shlomo Nitzan, "The Subconscious of an Age" (in Hebrew), *Itim* 3 (20 Oct. 1947).

9. Azriel Ukhmani, "Summing up our Literature" (in Hebrew), *Orlogin* 1 (Dec. 1950): 29.

10. Baruch Kurzweil, "On the Possibilities of Israeli Narrative Fiction" (in Hebrew), *Haaretz*, 4 Apr. 1947; "Some Remarks on the Essence of the Israeli Narrative Fiction" (in Hebrew), *Haaretz*, 27 Oct. 1953; "Cultural and Cognitive Landscapes in Israeli Narrative Fiction" (in Hebrew), *Haaretz*, 11 Dec. 1953.

11. Mordekhai Shalev, "An Escape from the Soul" (in Hebrew), *Sulam* 1, no. 9 (1950):28.

12. Mordekhai Shalev, "A Literature Without Human Beings" (in Hebrew), *Sulam* 10 (1950):23.

13. M. Megged, "The Sabra in our Literature" (in Hebrew), *Massa*, 7 Apr. 1952.

14. Amalia Kahana-Karmon, "What Has the Year '48 Done to Its Writers?" (in Hebrew), *Yediot aharonot*, 4 May 1973.

15. A. Kenan, "Uzi ve-shut" (in Hebrew), *Haaretz*, 14 Jan. 1951.

questionable exclamation points
on the political meaning of contemporary Israeli fiction

I

It is characteristic of good literature (and of all good art) that it questions the existing pattern of society. Just as it wishes to overturn accepted forms, it also attempts to reverse meanings by the model it creates. The very essence of literature lies in this attitude of opposition, even more so in the regimen of Israeli life in the seventies and eighties, where everything cries out for its opposite, and every truth for its contrary.

In its challenge to contemporary Israeli society, the fiction of the last decade, and perhaps the fiction of the past few decades, indulges and tortures itself with the illness of nostalgia. "The painful return" is typical of a very wide range of authors, from Megged to Ben-Ner. Shamir's hero Uriah, in *Kivsat ha-rash* (1957; *The Poor Man's Ewe*, 1959), had already sought to return to the Land of Israel of Adullam, which preceded the establishment of the ancient kingdom of Judah. Megged had the same approach in *Hedva ve-ani* (1954) with his Shlomik, who wished to return to *Ha-ḥalom ha-yarok* (The Green Dream) of the lost kibbutz Arcadia. In numerous stories—such as *Ir yamim rabim* (1972; *City of Many Days*, 1977) by Shulamith Hareven, *Ha-sipur al dodah shlomtsion ha-gedolah* (1975; *The Story of Aunt Shlomzion the Great*, 1978) by Yoram Kaniuk, *Ha-dod perets mamri* (Uncle Peretz Takes Off, 1972), by Yaakov Shabtai,

Ha-gevirah (The Mistress, 1983) by Yitshak Orpaz, and *Mavet ba-geshem* (Death in the Rain, 1982) by Ruth Almog—one senses the same tone of longing for "Israel the beautiful," a society that once seemed to exist but is no more. The past is the opposite of the present, the founders are human beings, and the sons, grasshoppers. The Israel of orchards is contrasted to the Israel of contractors (to use Ruth Almog's expression); the pure pioneers' Israel, to the Israel that has indentured itself to various and sundry golden calves. The *Erets rehokah* (Distant Land, 1981) by Yitzhak Ben-Ner is not necessarily New Zealand, to which one of the heroes of the novel wishes to emigrate, but the Land of Israel as a dream that never came true or as a reality that has been deformed. The "political" elegy—the converse of political satire—is the regressive vision, as it were, of those who wish to return to their social childhood, to the time of their political innocence. It is a clear expression of the directions in which Israeli society has developed: If we examine the literature carefully, it may turn out that it is "conservative" rather than "revolutionary," that it seeks to restore a lost paradise rather than find a new one. For Israeli writers of the seventies and eighties, utopia is the reality of the past—the present nothing but a great and ugly dystopia.

II

Longings of that kind are not, of course, simply expressions of psychological "regression." Essentially, they are manifestations of political opposition to the order of life in Israel. By "order of life" I do not refer to one political party or another (such as Likud or Labor), but to the order of the new "wealth," which has taken over all our idealistic ways of life, corrupting them and rendering them ugly. In fact, most of the authors are guided, in their longings, by the basic values of pioneering Zionism, which sought to alter the nature of the Jew by changing the conditions of Jewish life—the "absorption model." What the nostalgia of most of the writers implies is that conditions have actually changed but the Jew has not. That is one of Hanokh Levin's principal "messages" in his "Jewish bourgeois" plays, such as *Hefetz* (1972), *Neurei Vardale* (Young Vardale, 1974), and *Shitz* (1975).

Several stories written in recent years have reexamined the "absorption model," which until then had generally been viewed in a positive light. Sammy Michael and Aharon Appelfeld are two striking examples of authors from opposite extremes of the ethnic gamut who challenge in their novels the conventional model of absorption. Sammy Michael is a writer of Oriental-Iraqi background. In his "homeland" he was a member of the Arab-Iraqi Communist party. He became a Zionist quite lately, only shortly before his emigration to Israel after the War of Independence. Appelfeld is a refugee, a survivor of the Holocaust, who came to Israel after World War II. Both have, to say the least, ambivalent feelings about the first years of their emigration. In Michael's *Shavim ve-shavim yoter* (All Men Are Equal: But Some Are More, 1974) and Appelfeld's *Mikvat ha-or* (The Burnings of Light, 1980), the present is juxtaposed with the past so as to make us aware that the roots of the present (and of present consciousness) lie therein. Formerly that experience did not reach the level of public awareness, since those being absorbed did not yet have a *self-conscious* sense. Mute, lacking voice and language, they were unable to express their experiences.

The works of Appelfeld and Michael provide a sort of retroactive response to Hanoch Bartov's *Shesh kenafayim le-ehad* (1954; *Each Had Six Wings*, 1973), a work that was created as a tribute to the good will of the "absorbers" in the absorption process. Michael's and Appelfeld's works reevaluate the process from the point of view of the "victims," those being absorbed. Both writers explore the feelings of estrangement and alienation experienced by newcomers to Israeli society, feelings that are mediated by the individual's past. Sammy Michael's "All Men Are Equal: But Some Are More" is a semidocumentary naturalistic novel. It is a diary of a young Jew of Iraqi-Bagdadian origin during the Six Day War. While being on an armored truck with two Ashkenazis and one Yemenite, he reacts in a very intense way to the Ashkenazi commander of the truck. In his diary, he recollects the events of the war, but mostly his and his family's traumatic experiences in the first years of their emigration and how these humiliations have shaped his relationship with the Israeli establishment, which has changed since his first terrible encounters with the haughtiness of the absorbers. At the end of the novel the "hero" is cited by the commander-in-chief and is accepted in the hardest way (suffering, blood and war comradeship) by the Israeli establishment. Appelfeld's alienated heroes relate to the absorbers negatively, as "guards" or "preachers": The institutions of Youth Aliyah, in other words, are only another incarnation of the internment camps. These heroes do not strike roots in the new land, as in *Ha-kutonet ve-ha-pasim* (1983; *Tzili: The Story of a Life*, 1984). What emerges is that these authors reject the model of the "ingathering of exiles" and the "melting pot" and offer an alternative model in its stead. So, while these works do not demand revolutionary change, they do propose a new model that differs from the accepted "political" positions.

III

The critic Nissim Calderon addresses another important book, Yaakov Shabtai's *Zikhron devarim* (1977; *Past Continuous*, 1985), from a political perspective, suggesting a connection between that work and the political upheaval that brought the Likud to power in 1977. Calderon sees in the novel a fine allegorical expression of the rise and fall of the Labor movement, whose values of family steadfastness and stubborn dogmatism stifled its children and ultimately reached a dead end. From this perspective, the existential cul-de-sac of the characters in *Zikhron devarim* is only the literary superstructure of a social and political dead end.[1] I do not wish to deny or contradict his interpretation but, rather, to add to it from a different point of view.

The critic Dan Miron noted a certain affinity between *Zikhron devarim* and S. Yizhar's *Yemei tsiklag* (The Days of Ziklag, 1958).[2] It is marvelous and surprising that both of these works, one written twenty years after the other, focus on the identical social stratum: Yizhar's model is the group of (mostly) Ashkenazi youth, members of the bourgeois social elite of their generation at the supreme hour of trial, the War of Independence; Shabtai's group of young people—younger by a generation than Yizhar's heroes—(apparently) have similar social roots. Nevertheless, despite the similarity, these two authors develop their material in very different directions.

Yizhar's characters are types, two-dimensional and uniform in their psychological makeup, undifferentiated latitudinally—from one another—or longitudinally—from their fathers. Only on a superficial level is there any individuality: They have different hobbies and dream about girls with different names, but there is an essential sameness in their basic "political" and "social" attitudes, in the romantic innocence that molds their thoughts, and in their powerful and unmediated connection with open spaces and nature. There is no "longitudinal" difference among them in that they are not the products of personal history. Yizhar does not link them to their fathers, nor does he emphasize that different sons have different fathers. Indeed, his social model is one of sons with no fathers and no past, romantic in their visions and rather uniform in their deeds. This is a "collective" that is rich in its power to view the landscape but poor and thin in its spiritual resources.

Yaakov Shabtai, by contrast, emphasizes differences, both latitudinal and longitudinal: His three heroes (Goldman, Caesar, and Israel) are distinct personalities vis-à-vis each other and, even more so, in relation to the novel's other protagonists; they are also very distinct in their relations to their parents. Although both writers present a positive image of "Israel the beautiful," Shabtai's Israel is not a uniform monolith. On the contrary, it is a varied and divided land, demographically both beautiful and ugly, with a rich and "crazy" reservoir of people—almost to the point of an infinite differentiation that borders on disintegration. Yet it can also produce "family," or tribal, loyalty that preserves a certain degree of unity.

Shabtai was one of the first Israeli writers who discovered urban neighborhoods and, through them, the rich and varied pluralism of the Jewish population of Israel—so different from the mythic pioneer figures who had previously been central. Their heroes are motivated by a far more subtle, varied, and complex set of factors. The familiar model that had formed the image of the Israeli as young hero had, in other words, disintegrated. Its artificial uniformity was replaced by a new model—the native-born Israeli—who was the product of an actual environment, the child of real parents, and of a particular time and place. These are characters devoid of both heroism and joy; they would not have pleased the "1948 gener-ation," who hoped to create heroes but ended up instead with the suffering souls that are laid bare in the work of Shabtai and other questioning writers of the seventies and eighties. His "older brother" Yizhar, however, has viewed the situation as a whole cloth of blue and white, whose children were born—spontaneously—of the sea into a "youth movement" society. Such literature had re-sponded to the expectations of the founding generation, which sought to raise children who were as remote as possible from the old image of the Diaspora Jew. In this opposition of polar extremes, "Israel" symbolized what was new, healthy, and upright, whereas "Diaspora" stood for the old, sickly, and stooped. The new Israeli would have nothing to do with the ambivalences of an earlier gen-eration: During the late forties and fifties, the public rejected char-acters with dual identities and demanded from their writers the new prototype, the youth of the Land of Israel, irrespective of whether or not it was a faithful depiction of reality. These writers, especially Yizhar, produced a non-Oedipal literature of idealized relationships between the generations.

The second generation of Zionism, Shabtai's, has ceased to see itself as a unified group of adolescents. It perceives itself, instead, as a group of alienated adults. Ambivalence, even dual identity—having skipped a generation—has again become a central subject of Hebrew literature. There can be no doubt that this new con-sciousness emerged from experience and then brought readers to observe that experience from a new point of view. The new figure who appeared in the late 1960s gradually took over a central posi-tion in the literature of the 1970s and 1980s—the figure of the up-rooted Israeli. In essence, the model of alienation and affliction—the preheroic model—reemerged from the deep unconscious of the nation's soul: Appelfeld's survivors, Yehoshua's observer, Oz's kibbutzniks, Amichai's schizophrenic hero, Sadeh's anti-hero, the alienated and forlorn heroines of Amalia Kahana-Karmon and Ruth Almog, to name but a few examples. These figures are up-rooted, detached from the soil and from their fellow man: Once again alienation and isolation, which the writers of the 1940s had tried to overcome through fellowship, comradery in arms, and by flattening differences and individuality for the sake of the greater good, came to dominate Hebrew fiction. Here, then, we seek to explore the political significance of this change.

IV

Yitzhak Ben-Ner has tended to confront current political issues ever since his collection of stories *Aharei ha-geshem* (After the Rain, 1979). A splendid example of the author's attempt to relate to the current experience is the collection of stories that he tried to unify into his 1981 novella, *Erets rehokah* (A Distant Land, 1981). The entire work relates to what has happened in Israeli society after the political upheaval of 1977 and in the light of Sadat's historic visit to Jerusalem that year. Indeed, this book is almost a *roman à clef*: Its extraliterary point of departure is the Labor party scandal of the Yadlin Affair, to which the addressee relates as a benchmark in reality against which to measure the fiction. Here we must be aware of the theory of representation: The actual social event or prototype is not represented in the work, but the two "events"—the real and the fictional—suggest to the addressee a comparison between his model of reality (social corruption) and the literary model. The book, the created model, operates as a kind of literary embodiment of oppositional "questions"—once again, not political opposition to a given government but opposition to the social order—to challenge the commonly accepted, comfortable model of the "Land of Israel." What happened, it asks, to the children of little Tel Aviv— the Tel Aviv of the 1930s and 1940s—who grew up freely and abandoned the path of their elders? What happened to the lovely kibbutz girl, who became the innocent victim of Bohemian rascals and fell prey to the cultural Americanization of a disintegrating society? How did the basic values of society change, turning a society of immigrants into a society of emigrants (or of those who wish to emigrate)? In Ben-Ner's social novel we find no new "revolutionary" truth. On the contrary, he idealizes and lauds the Zionist past as against the degraded, corrupt present. And in his novel *Protokol* (1983) he again speaks up for the basic values of traditional Zionism—the "good old" model. His is a satirical criticism of Israeli society measured against the yardstick of nostalgia and elegy. His stories are elegies that bare satiric claws, or satires motivated by elegiac longing. In this regard, despite striking differences in form, Yitshak Orpaz's trilogy (*Bayit le-adam eḥad* [A House for One, 1974], *Ha-gevirah* [The Mistress, 1983], and *Ha-elem* [A Charming Traitor, 1984]) is of a piece with Ben-Ner's stories.

V

One author who has not been satisfied merely to diagnose the social situation and juxtapose it with a past ideal is A. B. Yehoshua, whose career started earlier than Shabtai's and Ben-Ner's. It seems to me, once again, that any attempt at a political reduction of his work sins both against his work and against politics. Nevertheless, I am committing that reduction—but with the understanding that it is to elucidate only a specific, *limited* aspect of his work. I emphasize this point before my discussion of several of his works because the temptation to reduce his work to political allegory is so great (and some critics, such as Yosef Oren, have taken that path with great success).

Yehoshua too juxtaposed an antimodel to the "Zionist" model, but his goal was to challenge the accepted model—not to idealize it. He raised all the questions about Israeli society that we always wanted to ask and never dared, bringing them up from the collective unconscious to the consciousness of a literary "model"; he actualized all the political doubts and hesitations that have disturbed our sleep in our secret nightmares. Already in his first stories in the collection *Mot ha-zaken* (The Death of the Old Man, 1962), he began asking "provocative" questions; but the inner censor buried them under several layers of allegory. The stories seemed to remove the problems that plague the society's collective unconscious from the confines of reality so that the reader could relate to them *as if* they did not refer to him. Appropriating his content from the traditional *model*, Yehoshua played havoc with it, reorganizing it into a new configuration, portraying everything in its opposite. He asked major questions about the established truisms of Zionism: the revival of the nation and the legitimacy of the right to the land. It is certainly the case that many of his predecessors, including Yizhar, Megged, Shamir, and Tammuz, were aroused by the flaws of the Israeli establishment to speak out against moral corruption and the betrayal of Zionist or general human values. But none of them ever questioned the fundamentals—the legitimacy of the Zionist experience.

Not so Yehoshua. He struggles with some of the basic assumptions of the Zionist establishment, in his story "Mul ha-yearot" ("Opposite the Forests," 1968), as he had done in *Bi-tehilat kayits 1970* (1974; *Early in the Summer of 1970*, 1977). The central symbols in the former story are a forest planted by the Jewish National Fund and the ruins of an Arab village. The forest guards are the "viewer from the house of Israel" and an Arab whose tongue has been cut and helps the watchman-viewer in his work. The Arab and the ruins are the antithesis within the Zionist thesis. The Arab burns down the forest in the passive presence of the "viewer." The model presented by that story raises challenging questions that probe the very foundations of the Zionist idea. Who has a right to this land? The ones who planted the artificial forest or the ones whose village is buried beneath it? The one who views, as it were, and protects the forest with a devious heart or the one who burns it down with all his heart? Yehoshua, then, brings to the surface the very questions that the "ruling" elite had repressed, that it did not (in fact) dare to ask itself, the dark side of the Zionist experience, the demon that doubts and hesitates and hides behind the certainties. (We find something similar, but in a less sophisticated form, in Tammuz's story "Taharut sehiya" (Swimming Contest). The creative consciousness here creates the antimodel of existence, which is latent in experience just as an antithesis is latent in a thesis.

In his two novels, *Ha-meahev* (1977; *The Lover*, 1978) and *Gerushim meuharim* (1982; *A Late Divorce*, 1984) Yehoshua presents figures who are the opposite of the typical Israeli "heroes." One is a young Sephardi man who emigrates, returns, is conscripted against his will during the Yom Kippur War, deserts the army, and joins "the religious Ashkenazis," who likewise are deserters from the Zionist establishment. The other is a young Arab, a citizen of the state of Israel who works in a garage owned by a Jew and who wishes to integrate into Israeli society. He succeeds in penetrating it only by means of his virility: He seduces his boss's daughter just as the Sephardi religious deserter seduces the same man's wife. Where the other characters are impotent, these two are vital— unlikely "heroes" who are a far cry from Yizhar's idealized image, the son of the pioneering settler, the descendant of King David, the Maccabees, and the Zealots. Here marginal figures in the Israeli landscape have taken center stage, the way having been cleared for them by the decline of the "average" Israeli, who has lost the dominion of his virility. Those other forces, therefore, come to dominate him.

Yehoshua forces us to look out at the light from a vantage point within the shadow, at a literary model that is the obverse of the accepted one in life and literature. He subjects both the new and the old heroes to his revolutionary criticism, as the former displaces the latter. He forces us to reexamine all of our assumptions—but not in the name of a glorious past that has been degraded. Rather, he challenges us to look toward the anxieties of the future, which are liable to take over our present and our past.

In *A Late Divorce* we actually have a more positive point of departure. The (somewhat indirect) social message of that book is that despite the collapse of values and the disintegration of the Israeli "family," the "native" Israeli is bound to his homeland like a neurotic to his illness or a husband to his "crazy" wife. It may be impossible to live here, but there is nowhere else, because, according to Yehoshua, the Israelis are trapped by unconscious guilt feelings they have for their "old spouse." Divorce is actually impossible because of the neurotic attachment to the "wife and mother." Their "motherland" will never let them go; they are "trapped" unconsciously and engaged consciously by a neurotic loyalty to their sick parentage. In this, Yehoshua picks up on Brenner's notion. Here is where you have to live and die. As much as one may wish to be redeemed from that bond with this mad country, it is impossible to sever it.

In the past few years it has been possible to discern, in the infrastructure of works by various writers, attempts to lay bare the roots of the forces active in present-day Israeli life. Some of the recent novels of Benjamin Tammuz, like *Yaakov* (1971), *Ha-pardes* (1971; The Orchard, 1984), and *Rekvium le-naaman* (Requiem for Naaman, 1982), attempt to serve such a social function. They are different from his novels of social criticism (the trilogy, *Ḥayyei elyakum* [The Life of Elyakum], *Be-sof maarav* (1966; *Castle in Spain*, 1973), and *Sefer ha-ḥazayot* (The Book of Imaginings), which depicted concrete instances of corruption by promenading a picaresque "Felix Krull"* through Israeli life (like David Shahar, in his novel *Yeraḥ ha-devash ve-ha-zahav* (Gold and Honey Moon). The later novels attempt to reach the essence of the Jewish-Arab problem (*Yaakov*) and the rise and fall of a Zionist "family," which has in this novel a literal and a symbolic meaning—family and the Jews in Israel.

VI

Other authors, such as Kaniuk (*Ha-yehudi ha-aḥaron* [The Last Jew, 1981]), Alexander and Yonat Sened, and Amos Oz look backward or inward in order to understand the mind and dynamics of the world in which we live. Their works are not, of course, limited to their social meaning, but it can be read both between the lines and in the lines themselves.

The glimmer of acceptance of the country as it is and not as it should be, hinted at in Yehoshua's *A Late Divorce*, reappears in a very different way in the novel of the Seneds. Alexander and Yonat Sened are a married couple who write their novels together. They are also old-time settlers in Revivim, a southern kibbutz in the desert. One of their last novels, *Kevar erets noshevet* (A Land Inhabited Already, 1981), is a kind of antithesis both in name and content to their first, *Adamah lelo tsel* (Earth with No Shadow), which was published in 1950. The material of those two novels is the kibbutz, and both of them relate politically to that "establishment" as a kind of synecdoche for all of Israeli society. In *Adamah lelo tsel* the kibbutz is a kind of utopian ideal. Although the pioneer's struggle with the wilderness and hostile forces does not, in fact, bring him to Arcadia, by fulfilling his own ideals, his way of life in some fashion is an embodiment of utopia. For the same authors, thirty years later, the kibbutz dweller no longer embodies the utopian ideal. *Kevar erets noshevet* is a utopia that has become tainted reality: The kib-

Cf. Thomas Mann's picaresque hero from his novel of the same name.

butz as consumer society must now struggle against inner forces rather than outer ones. The ambusher lurks within, not in the desert. It is a little world of gossip, loneliness, and bereavement, with which one must live, to which one must become reconciled. Not necessarily the best of worlds, but also not the worst, it is the only one that actually exists among all the possible worlds. This is not a work of nostalgia, of longing for another utopian dream. Nor is it a work that presents "utopia" as an antiutopia. Rather it represents the voice of maturity, of adults who have come to terms with their sentimental longings and who are reconciled to reality. We *must* view the Seneds' later novel in the light of their first one, the one serving as a countermodel to the other. And the countermodel, it seems, is not actually the opposite of but, rather, a kind of complement to the "original."

Amos Oz also has tried to penetrate to the mystic foundations of Israeli Jewish society and to accept its contradictions in several of his works. In a few of his first stories (in *Be-artsot hatan* (1965; *Where the Jackals Howl,* 1981), he also substituted an anti-hero for the accepted heroes. But unlike Yehoshua, for instance, he did not use marginal figures in order to bring the margins to the center. He discovered, instead, that there are also "margins" in the center itself. Thus, the *antiparatrooper* in "Be-derekh ha-ruah" ("The Way of the Wind," from the collection *Where the Jackals Howl*) or the antihero in "Minzar ha-shatkanim" ("The Trappist Monastery," from the same collection) are the most precious sons of the establishment, but they are unable and unwilling to pass the test of manliness and heroism to which that establishment subjects them. These stories are not antiwar stories but, rather, antihero stories. Oz's nonheroes, who were born within the Israeli establishment, do not differ in essence from Appelfeld's, who came here from abroad. Azaria in Oz's *Menuhah nekhonah* (1982; *A Perfect Peace,* 1985), who comes from outside and enters the establishment, seems like a parody of the establishment even though he adapts to it. He is similar to Appelfeld's heroes in *Mikhvat ha-or,* alienated although they are apparently absorbed.

Oz has tried to write historiosophical stories, meaning stories that encounter the basic assumptions of Jewish history, for example, *Ahavah meuheret* (1971; *Late Love,* 1975), and *Ad mavet* (1971;

Unto Death, 1975). *Unto Death* attempts to understand the historiosophy of dread. We learn that the source of anti-Semitism is a society's need to find scapegoats for its frustrations. Oppression produces frustration, and frustration demands a victim. But in sacrificing the victim, the oppressor brings his own end nearer: Having "wasted," as it were, his best powers and energies on destruction, sapping his vitality, he withers away. This ambivalent process that describes anti-Semitism hints at the historiosophy of Israeli existence as well: It could also be seen as the basis for the forces at work among the "Crusaders" of our age.

Oz's two most recent works, a collection of novellas called *Har ha-etsah ha-raah* (1976; *The Hill of Evil Counsel,* 1978) and the novel *A Perfect Peace* are stories that might possibly be termed metapolitical; that is, they do not relate to the present but attempt to reveal, by means of the distant or the recent past, the forces at work in the foundations of the historical drama of the Jewish people. *The Hill of Evil Counsel,* a collection of three novellas that juxtaposes rational, sane fathers—men of modest aspirations who wish to build up the Land of Israel step-by-step, a dunam here, a dunam there—and romantic Polish mothers, including the romanticism of the underground that casts its spell over them. The boy protagonist stands between those two extremes, molded by the clash of opposing forces: the skeptical, ironic father (in two different novellas) and the mothers (again in different novellas) and friends: British admirals and members of the underground. The hero of the last novella, Nussbaum, the sane visionary or visionary scientist, is an amalgam of opposites. All these characters appear before the young, impressionable boy in the years before the War of Independence, when the future of this society lay in the balance.

Underlying Israeli existence, then, are the basic forces of sane rationality and (Slavic) romantic and passionate visions: the archetypical, mythical struggle between the rational and the irrational, intellect and emotion. Here history merely brings to the fore those forces that vie with one another within the mythical infrastructure. It does not produce innovation but only actualizes what had existed in potential. The present is only a revelation of the primordial past, prior to history and consciousness.

For Oz, in other words, the opposition between the Revisionist movement and Labor Zionism is more than a historical dispute between parties. It is a psychohistorical confrontation that doubtless exists within every nation and people—although it is here manifested in the young national movement. Oz wished to express something similar in *A Perfect Peace*, where rational forces (Levi Eshkol and the fathers, who are even imaginative in their rationalism) clash with irrational forces (other fathers and some of the children), who are liable to destroy the framework of Zionist existence.

Notwithstanding his attempt to create metahistorical models and to understand historical processes in their mythic depths, Oz, in his creative works (and in his public political positions), opts in the end for the rational, in preference to the forces that oppose. There is no question that Oz has a deep understanding of the complex mixture of the Zionist endeavor—the visionary, irrational romanticism of messianic fanatics and the rational pragmatism of sober pioneers. He depicts the paradoxical tension in the Jewish revival movement (or in the nation's collective subconscious) between the right-wing revisionists, whose slogan is "to die or to conquer the mountain," and the political system of the labor movement pioneers, who aim to accomplish Zionist goals piecemeal (as the pioneer song goes: "acre after acre").

VII

In returning to our point of departure, I reiterate the point that explicitly political works do not necessarily convey the most interesting or the most profound sociopolitical messages. Just as there are trivial works in other literary genres (various suspense stories and romances), there are also trivial works in the sociopolitical realm. Such works may respond to the immediate demand of the public for political reinforcement or for opposition. The political poem from the Six Day War, "Nasser meḥakeh le-rabin" (Nasser is Waiting for Rabin), is one such direct political litany that fulfills a "positive" function in strengthening the received opinions of the political consensus. Many of the political poems about the War in Lebanon are overtly political (and simplistic to the same degree), meant to strengthen the antiestablishment consensus of those who oppose the government. Such literature can fulfill a worthy—if nonliterary—function. Political litanies, satires, and trivial novels mobilize support for one side or another in the political arena and are directly involved in current disputes.

However, my intention in this essay was to discuss not that kind of writing but, rather, social novels endowed with political significance. A story, of course, is not just a political utterance. It is first of all a *story*, and its literary quality is doubtless more important than all of its political, and its nonpolitical, messages. Without doubt, however, it also has political significance, since it builds a model of reality related to its time and place. Still, those who read *Ha-shavui* (The Prisoner, 1959) by Yizhar respond to its messages because of its stylistic and emotional power and because it is *not* merely a political story, despite the fact that a political message was also conveyed, whether the author wished it to be or not. I am not saying anything very new, then, in asserting that great literature is always political, even though not all political literature is great.

Like all good literature, Hebrew fiction during the 1970s and 1980s, only a small part of which has been mentioned here, looked more like a question mark than an exclamation point. It asked "big" questions and posed important challenges; it created a *world* that no longer permitted its readers to relate to their society and environment with complacency.

NOTES

1. Nissim Calderon, *Be-heksher politi* (In a Political Context) (Tel Aviv: Siman Keriah, 1980), 26–46.
2. Dan Miron, *Pinkas patuah* (Current Israeli Prose Fiction: Views and Reviews) (Tel Aviv: Sifriat Poalim, 1979), 22–23.

It may be that it is impossible to live here, but one must stay here, one must die here, sleep . . . There is no other place . . .

Y. H. *Brenner,* From
Here and From There

no other place
on Saul Friedländer's *when memory comes*, 1979

On 10 November 1938, a nine-year-old boy was alone in a large apartment on a respectable street in Vienna. His mother had gone out. His father had been deported to a concentration camp in April. The boy did not know that there was rioting outside. Sensing the approaching dusk by the shadows on the lofty walls, he crawled under the piano in a corner. To calm his fears he played. He tried to take refuge in fantasy; but his fear overwhelmed him. There was shouting on the floor above. He turned on all the lights and set two chairs against the front door. Soon there was knocking. The boy was afraid to open the door. When the men came bursting in he did not know where to hide. None of the tricks he had learned from his books were of any help. Finally, he crawled back under the piano.

The boy never saw the men's faces, only their five pairs of boots. Taking no interest in him, they emptied the apartment of its contents—rugs and paintings, silver, and finally furniture, piece by piece. It was only when they turned to the piano that they noticed the child clinging to one of its legs. They worked him over with their boots; they said and did things that the boy does not want to remember.

When it was all over, the boy curled up within himself, surrounded by the bare walls of the now empty apartment. He could not turn on the lights because the raiders had taken all the bulbs. Huddled in that darkness, mortified and alone, the boy discovered his own private kind of Zionism. How different it was from the Zionism of those pioneers in the sunny fields of the Jezreel Valley.

That boy was myself, and the personal account I have given is relevant to Saul Friedländer's work *When Memory Comes*,[1] a book that has stimulated me to reflect on what happened to me, to Friedländer, and to many others. Indeed, it demands a response from all who are personally acquainted with its themes: childhood lost and childhood regained; the fate of European Jewry and Jewish destiny; the European, the Israeli, and the Jew—their identities and their relationship to one another. Most importantly, it raises the question of how the past molded that "vision" of a perfect society that, in Friedländer's words, "could never be eliminated" (p. 145).

A cruel historical and cultural experience molded the consciousness of the Holocaust survivors. The more complex that experience, the more complicated that consciousness. The survivor's consciousness has not yet freed itself of the distant pre-Holocaust past, and that, perhaps, has had a greater impact than even the Holocaust itself. From Friedländer's book, as from many others of the same genre, it appears as if that consciousness does not at all want to be relieved of the past—that it finds its neurotic condition comfortable. The trauma of the Holocaust did not lead to an existential revolution in the psyche of the Jewish intellectual survivor but, rather, to his taking up a permanent position among the pieces of his shattered self.

The first question that arises on reading Friedländer's book is what existential decision was made by the survivor—here the European-Jewish intellectual represented by Friedländer—in the aftermath of the trauma that utterly shattered the foundations of his existence. Friedländer's experiences are similar to those of Kafka, Herzl, and many others of his generation. They were sons of the assimilated Jewish "Austro-Hungarian" (Czech) bourgeoisie whose parents foresaw for them a life of tranquillity, cushioned by material comfort and sweetened by culture. They were educated to be members of that society and of the international intellectual elite. What the average American Jewish parent wants for his children (at a time when American culture has become international) is what our parents had wanted for us. But as the Dreyfus affair marked a turning point in Herzl's life, so, on a different scale, the Holocaust

of European Jewry ended the smooth flow of our lives and con-
founded our parents' plans. The survivors, it seemed, had to draw
up new plans.

II

But is this in fact what they did? It appears from Friedländer's book
that although the trauma left its mark on him, what he really wants
is to turn back the dislocated wheel of time and begin again on that
day when the Germans marched into the city and he and his family
fled to France. Since that day he has seen and experienced much.
He was a persecuted child in a Jewish orphanage and a Catholic
child in a Christian school. He was separated from his parents
when they were sent to the death camps. Ultimately he made his
way to Netanya and Ben Shemen, where he absorbed some of the
spirit of Eretz Israel and the Zionist youth movement. He served in
the Israeli Army and bound his destiny to the land. But in the final
analysis, although he is in the East, his heart remains in the West.

Friedländer writes in French, which has remained his principal
literary language. He spends half his time in Europe, whose culture is of great importance to him. He calls himself a "Jew," like
those who call themselves "Jews of the Spirit"; like those "refined
Jews" of Germany—Franz Rosenzweig, Hermann Cohen, and others—who, in looking for the core of the pomegranate, threw out
the seeds together with the peel.

Judaism, as it appears in the "Jewish" sections of *When Memory
Comes*, is for Friedländer the fullest realization of universal moral
values, the antithesis of provincialism or parochialism (pp. 103–
104). Accordingly, he has higher regard for the writings of Buber
than the folklore glimpsed in Ben Shemen and Netanya. Buber's
ideas also differ from the "Biblical austerity and the cold rigor of the
Law" and, most importantly, they are in sharp contrast to "the superficial, the banal, the transitory aspects of Israeli life" (p. 105).
Like reformers who tend to interpret away every real experience by
symbolization, Friedländer interprets the State of Israel as a sort of
allegory of humanity's woeful course: "I tell myself that the Jewish
state may perhaps be only a step on the way of a people whose par-

ticular destiny has come to symbolize the endless quest—ever hesitant, ever begun anew—of all of mankind" (p. 183). Most certainly for Friedländer, the state per se is not enough; it achieves legitimacy only if it fulfills a universal mission, something on the order of being the proverbial "light unto the nations."

According to this interpretation, one concludes that Friedländer is trying to undo what time has wrought and to return to his roots, trying to regain what history took away from him and what he later lost by a willful act (when he abandoned his identity as a Catholic child to return to the fold of Judaism, p. 139): in effect, trying to regain the Europe that had been lost. He did not come to terms with his historical fate; nor did he fully internalize his decision to emigrate to Eretz Israel. Rejecting Israeli "culture," which he belittles in various sweeps of his pen, he remains fundamentally a European. (Thus, when his young Israeli peers go out each morning on their business, he can be found immersed in French literature or in reconstructing a map of the Paris Métro.)

The concept of "Jew" actually serves Friedländer as a kind of semantic cover for the concept of "European." Since most Europeans belong to a specific national and cultural milieu, the Jew is the only all-European European. In this Friedländer resembles George Steiner. He exchanges the Austro-Hungarian bourgeois experience (international, polyglot, and multicultural) for a new experience that is nothing but a metamorphosis of the old. Even as an Israeli, Friedländer is a European whose Judaism serves as a window dressing.

III

The tragedy in twentieth-century Jewish autobiography is that the writer's life never ends where it began, even though spiritually he is drawn back to his place of origin. History has created the basis for a collective novel that, were it truly fiction, would sound like melodramatic kitsch. Whose ears would not be set atingle upon hearing of Friedländer's numerous incarnations: Pavel who became Paul, who went on to become Shaul, and who in the end chose the name Saul, a kind of hybrid of the two? The trouble is that all this is reality and not fiction.

It was Tolstoy who said that all happy families are alike and that only miserable families differ from one another. The normal lives of children, from Switzerland to New Zealand, are all alike; the fate of Jewish children in the 1940s, from the banks of the Volga to the English Channel, differ. Each has his or her own tragic tale, as exemplified by Friedländer. His memoir is more than that; it is, as well, a work of distinct literary talent, of subtlety and clarity. The descriptions of his father, both in his prime and during the crisis, and of the Eastern European Jewish family that adopted him after the Holocaust are literary gems. They have a Proustian quality in their easy movement from past to present—the past casting its shadow over the present, the present illuminating the past.

In addition, the accounts of the odd, persecuted little Jewish boy in the Jewish orphanage and of the same child suppressing his Jewishness and discovering Christianity in the monastery are written with such delicacy and keen perception that one wishes this autobiography had stuck to its story without digression—remaining autobiography and nothing else. If not for its need to offer a self-justification and to proclaim a universalist Jewish message for future generations, this book would be among the finest works on the lost childhood of the Holocaust generation.

The "narrative time" of the book is 1977, that historical moment when Egyptian President Anwar Sadat came to Jerusalem and the Jews found themselves once again at a turning point in a history rich in turning points. The time Friedländer writes about, the "narrated time," begins with Hitler's rise to power in 1933, the year of the author's birth. The book thus maintains a constant tension between past events (especially between 1933 and 1947) and the present. The author only sketchily describes the years of his development in Eretz Israel, and he omits his personal life (his marriage and children) and the years of study and teaching in Geneva and Jerusalem (making only a few comments about what happened to his students after the Yom Kippur War).

This selectivity regarding subject matter is determined by the fact that the book is not merely autobiographical in the most basic sense; it is also an attempt to clarify, by recounting the author's personal experience, the interplay between historical and existential fate and the individual's sense of identity. What is the relationship of a victim to the identities that fate has imposed on him and that, given the choice, he would never have chosen for himself? This is the complex question to which Friedländer is seeking an answer.

Pavel Friedländer was the son of an assimilated family who, although they included some Zionist "black sheep," were Czechs of the Mosaic persuasion: His father would no more have dreamed that his son would be baptized a Catholic than that he would renew his life in Zion. Friedländer's choice of materials thus focuses on those stations that represent the convergence of identity, historical fate, and the individual's appreciation of his own identity. Consciously or not, in his search for the thread running through his life, he chooses those points in his life that illuminate and reflect the mutual relations between these. In his last metamorphosis, Friedländer is again a kind of *Luftmensch* who finds detachment and suspension more comfortable than bonds of any kind. The decision "to be a Zionist" that brought him to Eretz Israel grew out of his personal experiences during the Holocaust: He refused to become only passive once again and demanded that the Jews "take their fate in their own hands." This Zionism did not work out well for him, perhaps because it stemmed from purely logical premises and not, according to Friedländer's own account, from a renewed contact with "buried emotional layers" (p. 160).

What is also surprising in Friedländer's selection of subject matter is that the years 1947–1977 in Eretz Israel are almost nonexistent, as if they had simply vanished. Friedländer vividly describes his 1948 voyage to Israel on board the *Altalena*. But what happened to him between that time and his departure for Sweden in the sixties? What ties were formed between him and the country and its people, and why did he return to it after each of his wanderings abroad, even though he felt so alienated from it?

IV

The answer to this question is to be found by asking a larger question: What is Eretz Israel to those cultured European Jews for whom history has decreed exile? Is it not some kind of Devil's Island to which history expelled them while they, like Dreyfus in his time, long to get back to the European motherland, to have their honor restored, to regain their positions in the cultural avant-garde? Is the scale of our tiny country not drawn to their cultural dimensions? Even the trauma of the Holocaust has not led this group (which includes the cream of German Jewry and the intellectual elite of European immigrants) to prefer a life of independence in the jungle to one of slavery in the *Académie Française*. Confronted with the tension between cultural nostalgia and historical memory, they frequently opt for nostalgia. It is not my intention to judge Friedländer or the larger group he represents—those exiled from their countries or those living like exiles in their country—but only to point out what seems to me a basic phenomenon of Israel's cultural life.

The first set of questions suggests other, related questions that are implicit in Friedländer's book. Is this intellectual elite prepared to live in Israel only on the condition that its population be extraordinary, a "light unto the nations"? And since this people is not a beacon but instead adapts to its oriental surroundings, do these men of the spirit take up arms against, or abandon, the provincial banality of the Levantine country in which they find themselves?

Friedländer's tone betrays the arrogance of the European intellectuals in Israel who are prepared to tolerate the narrow and insecure boundaries of Eretz Israel only on condition that they be compensated for the loss of Europe's expanses by the extraordinariness of the people. As long as the state is renowned for its cultural and social achievements, members of this elite can comfortably identify with it; when the state's standing declines on the moral and cultural exchange, the same individuals prefer to dissociate themselves from it. In other words, one lives in Israel as in a kind of exile, a victim of circumstance stranded by fate, which has left its indelible mark of Cain. This type of intellectual finds himself in a quandary. As much as he would like to erase the trauma of the past and reconcile himself with the Europe that turned its back on him, he cannot.

v

Y. H. Brenner, in *From Here and From There* (1911), wrote in pessimistic tones of the Jewish people, Eretz Israel, and their interrelations. He was forced to conclude, nevertheless, that although "it

may be that it is impossible to live here . . . there is no other place."
Brenner himself saw only the foreshadowing of the trauma that was
yet to come: Homel and Kishinev were but dress rehearsals for
Auschwitz and Bergen-Belsen. Still, he observed life in Eretz Israel
with a fiercely sober eye. Not romantic pioneers, but the realities of
Arab labor, the French-Levantine culture, and the sons of the farm-
ers who were emigrating provided the substance of his writings.
(Only the occasional odd idealist tried to work the land and to
better himself.) Brenner—who rejected the term "chosen people"
and even proposed that it be dropped from the prayer book—nonetheless believed that Israel was the place for a Jew to live, under all
circumstances, and unconditionally. In Israel, the struggle for
gradual change in the way of life of the individual could proceed.

VI

When Memory Comes is not a mere memoir; it is an apologia pro vita
sua. As such, it invites a response. Friedländer has taken a stand—
however equivocal—on the fundamental issues of Jewish existence,
and he obliges the reader, too, to clarify his own stand. Like
Friedländer, I too lost the foundations of my existence. Yet despite
my own ambivalences—the longings for the West, the love for and
aversion to the Eretz Israel of today—it seems to me that the commitment must be unequivocal. Friedländer suggests that it is possible to return to the old territory and strike roots of sorts, living a
kind of dual existence. I would argue that once the ground is destroyed there is no recovering it.

Baruch Kurzweil (who came from an altogether different background), like Friedländer, yearned all his life for the "world of yesterday." He once told me that he could not forgive Hitler for having
destroyed his spiritual world and for having cast him into a culture
not his own. The past certainly cannot be erased: One carries—
everywhere and forever—a lifetime's accumulation of wounds and
cultural wealth. But when the world of yesterday is destroyed,
whoever looks back, like Lot's wife, assures that his soul will never
arrive in the promised land. Never. The state of ambivalent detachment is perhaps more interesting and complex than that of attach-

ment, just as illness is more interesting than health. Perhaps the internal state cannot be altered and one must learn to live with it, as Friedländer has tried in his memoir and in his life. But to the extent that identity depends on consciousness, as he proved at a certain stage in his life, a person has no choice but to decide. And if one has fled the ruins of Sodom, there is no other place but here.

NOTE

1. Saul Friedländer, *When Memory Comes*, trans. Helen R. Lane (New York: Farrar, Straus, and Giroux, Inc., 1979).

selected bibliography

Abramson, Glenda, and Parfitt, Tudor, eds. *The Great Transition: The Recovery of the Lost Centers of Modern Hebrew Literature*. Totowa, N.J.: Rowman and Allenheld, 1985.

Alter, Robert. *After the Tradition: Essays on Modern Jewish Writing*. New York: E. P. Dutton and Co., 1969.

Appelfeld, Aharon. *Masot be-guf rishon* (Essays in First Person Singular). Jerusalem: The Jewish Agency, 1979.

Arnold, H. L., ed. *Text und Kritik: Joseph Roth*. Munich: Edition Text und Kritik, 1974.

Avinoam, Reuven, ed. *Gevilei esh* (Scrolls of Fire). Tel Aviv: Ministry of Defense, 1952.

Band, Arnold J. *Nostalgia and Nightmare: A Study in the Fiction of S. Y. Agnon*. Berkeley: University of California Press, 1968.

Barzel, Hillel, ed. *Shemuel yosef agnon: mivhar maamarim al yetsirato*. Tel Aviv: Am Oved, 1982.

Berger, David, ed. *The Legacy of Jewish Migration: Eighteen Eighty-One and Its Impact*. New York: Brooklyn College Press, 1983.

Brenner, Y. H. "The Palestinian Genre and Its Accessories" (in Hebrew). *Ha-poel ha-tzair*, vol. 4, no. 21, 10 Aug. 1921.

Brod, Max. *Franz Kafkas Glauben und Lehre*. Winterthur: Mondial-verlag, 1948.

Bronsen, David. "Austrian versus Jew: The Torn Identity of Joseph Roth." *Leo Baeck Institute Year Book* 18 (1973): 220–226.

———. *Joseph Roth: Eine Biographie*. Munich: D.T.V., repr. 1981.

Calderon, Nissim. *Be-heksher politi* (In a Political Context). Tel Aviv: Siman Keriah, 1980.

Einsiedel, Wolfgang von. "Nur ein Roman (zu Wassermanns 'Fall Maurizius')." *Die Schöne Literatur* 10 (Oct. 1928): 478–481.

Even-Zohar, Itamar. *Papers in Historical Poetics*. Tel Aviv: Porter Institute, 1978.

Fichman, Yaakov. *Ruhot menagnot: sofrei polin* (Singing Winds: Writers in Poland). Jerusalem: Mossad Bialik, 1953.

Halkin, Simon. *Mavo la-siporet ha-ivrit* (An Introduction to Hebrew Fiction). Jerusalem: Mifal ha-Shikhpul, 1958.

Holtz, Avraham. *Isaac Dov Berkowitz: Voice of the Uprooted*. Ithaca, Cornell University Press, 1973.

Kahn, Ludwig W. *Literatur und Glaubenskrise*. Stuttgart: Kohlhammer, 1964.

Karlweis, Martha. *Jakob Wassermann: Gestalt, Kampf und Werk*. Amsterdam: Querido, 1935.

Kaznelson, Siegmund. "Um jüdisches Volkstum (zu Jakob Wassermanns Bekenntnisbuch)." *Der Jude* 4 (1921): 49–52.

Kressel, Getzel, "The 'Storm' of the Young in *Ha-shiloah*" (in Hebrew). *Gilyonot* 26 (1952): 359–363.

Krojanker, Gustav, ed. *Juden in der deutschen Literatur*. Berlin: Weltverlag, 1922.

Kurzweil, Baruch. *Sifrutenu ha-hadashah: hemshekh o mahapekhah?* (Modern Hebrew Literature: Continuity or Revolution?). Tel Aviv: Schocken, 1960.

———. *Masot al sipurei shai agnon* (Essays on the Stories of S. Y. Agnon). Jerusalem: Schocken, 1962.

Lachower, Fischel. *Toledot ha-sifrut ha-ivrit ha-hadashah* (A History of Hebrew Literature). Tel Aviv: Devir, 1946–1948.

———. *Al gevul ha-yashan veha-hadash* (On the Border Between Old and New). Jerusalem: Mossad Bialik, 1951.

Lessing, Theodor. *Der jüdische Selbsthass*. Berlin: Zionistischer Bücher-Bund, 1930.

Lewisohn, Ludwig. *What is this Jewish Heritage?* New York: B'nai B'rith Hillel Foundation, 1954.

Magris, Claudio. *Weit von Wo: Verlorene Welt des Ostjudentums*. Vienna: Europaverlag, 1974.

Miron, Dan. *Pinkas patuah* (Current Israeli Prose Fiction: Views and Reviews). Tel Aviv: Sifriat Poalim, 1979.

Mitchell, J. T., ed. *On Narrativity*. Chicago: University of Chicago Press, 1981.

Ozick, Cynthia. *Art and Ardor*. New York: Knopf, 1983.

Pongs, Hermann *Franz Kafka: Dichter des Labyrinths*. Heidelberg: Rothe, 1960.

Rosenfeld, Sidney. "The Chain of Generation: A Jewish Theme in Joseph Roth's Novels." *Leo Baeck Institute Year Book* 18 (1973): 227–231.

Roth, Philip. *Reading Myself and Others*. New York: Farrar, Straus and Giroux, 1976.

Rovit, Earl, ed. *Saul Bellow: A Collection of Critical Essays*. Englewood Cliffs, N.J.: Prentice-Hall, 1975.

Rozen, Haiim. *Ha-ivrit shelanu* (Our Hebrew). Tel Aviv: Am Oved, 1956.

Sadan, Dov. *Al shai agnon: masa, iyun ve-heker* (On S. Y. Agnon: Essay, Study, Research). Tel Aviv: Ha-Kibbutz ha-Meuhad, 1959.

———. *Avnei-bedek* (Touchstones). Tel Aviv: Ha-Kibbutz ha-Meuhad, 1962.

———. *Bein din le-heshbon* (Report and Account). Tel Aviv: Devir, 1963.

Schulz, Max F. *Radical Sophistication: Studies in Contemporary Jewish American Novelists*. Athens, Ohio: Ohio University Press, 1969.

Shaked, Gershon. *Bein tsehok le-dema* (Laughter and Tears). Tel Aviv: Massada Press, 1965.

———. *Ha-mahazeh ha-ivri ha-histori be-tekufat ha-tehiyah* (The Hebrew Historical Drama in the Twentieth Century). Jerusalem: Mossad Bialik, 1970.

———. *Omanut ha-sipur shel agnon* (The Narrative Art of S. Y. Agnon). Tel Aviv: Sifriat Poalim, 1973.

———. "The Myth of Rebellion: An Interpretation of 'The Dead of the Desert' by H. N. Bialik." *Hebrew University Studies in Literature* 2 (Spring 1974): 92–116.

———, ed. *Bialik: yetsirato be-rei ha-bikoret, antologia* (Bialik: Critical Essays on His Works, an Anthology). Jerusalem: Mossad Bialik, 1974.

———. *Ha-siporet ha-ivrit 1880–1980* (Hebrew Narrative Fiction, 1880–1980). Vols. 1 and 2. Tel Aviv: Keter and Ha-Kibbutz ha-Meuhad, 1977–1983.

Shlonsky, Avraham. *Yalkut eshel* (The Eshel Anthology). Tel Aviv: Sifriat Poalim, 1960.

Sokel, Walter H. "Franz Kafka as a Jew." *Leo Baeck Institute Year Book* 18 (1973): 233–238.

Trilling, Lionel. *The Liberal Imagination: Essays on Literature and Society*. New York: Doubleday, 1953.

Werses, Samuel. *Sipur ve-shorsho* (The Story and Its Roots). Tel Aviv: Massada Press, 1971.

Wiener, Meir. *Tsu der geshikhte fun der yidisher literature in 19 jahrhundert* (Remarks to the History of Yiddish Literature in the Nineteenth Century). Vol. 2. New York: YKVF, 1946.

Wisse, Ruth. *The Schlemiel as Modern Hero*. Chicago: University of Chicago Press, 1971.

Zohn, Harry. *Wiener Juden in der deutschen Literatur*. Tel Aviv: Editions "Olamenu," 1964.

Zweig, Arnold. *Bilanz der deutschen Judenheit*. 1933. Reprint. Cologne: J. Melzer, 1961.

index of writers

Agnon, S. Y., 12–16, 18–20, 26–27,
  88–89, 91–93, 108–109, 116, 119,
  133–143, 149
Ahad Ha-am, 86–87, 93, 97, 104, 116
Almog, Ruth, 166, 170
Aloni, Nissim, 84
Altenberg, Peter, 59, 89
Alterman, Nathan, 89, 115, 132, 151–152
Amichai, Yehuda, 85, 93, 102, 106, 109,
  159, 170
Amir, Aharon, 146
Appelfeld, Aharon, 17–18, 108–110, 159,
  167–168, 170, 176
Arendt, Hannah, 7–8
Aricha, Yosef, 117, 151
Arieli-Orloff, L.A., 118
Asch, Sholem, 5

Babel, Isaac, 100
Barash, Asher, 84, 89
Baron, Devorah, 89
Bartov, Hanoch, 89, 160, 167–168
Barzel, Hillel, 13
Bavli, Hillel, 118
Beckett, Samuel, 89
Bellow, Saul, 71, 74–78, 108–109
Ben-Ner, Yitzhak, 165–166, 171–172
Ben-Shaul, Mordecai, 89
Berdyczewski, M. J., 26–27, 61, 68, 85,
  93, 108, 111
Berkowitz, I. D., 26, 68, 89, 90, 149
Bertini, K. A., 118

Bialik, Hayyim Nahman, 61, 84, 89–90,
  104–105, 108, 111, 119, 123–132, 154
Björnson, Björnstjerne, 88–89, 92
Börne, Ludwig, 88
Brainin, Reuben, 87–88
Brenner, Y. H., 5, 11–12, 26–27, 68, 85,
  87, 89, 93, 97, 116–117, 119, 125, 148,
  174, 187–188
Brod, Max, 4, 7, 23, 39, 59, 63
Bronsen, David, 40
Buber, Martin, 24, 59, 183
Bunin, Hayyim Isaac, 118

Calderon, Nissim, 168
Canaani, David, 135
Canetti, Elias, 108
Cervantes, Miguel de, 89–90
Chekhov, Anton, 89–90
Cohen, Hermann, 183

Dostoevsky, Feodor, 89

Efros, Israel Isaac, 118
Ehrenstein, Albert, 59
Eisenstadt, Ben-Zion, 123–125
Eliraz, Yisrael, 106
Elon, Amos, 150
Eulenspiegel, Till, 151
Even-Zohar, I., 117
Eytan, Rachel, 119

Feierberg, M. Z., 85, 87
Fichman, Yaakov, 112, 124–126
Flaubert, Gustave, 89
France, Anatole, 88–89
Frankel, Naomi, 70
Freigerson, Zvi, 118
Freiman, Avraham, 118
Friedländer, Saul, 181–189
Friedman, Bruce J., 71
Frisch, Max, 11
Frischmann, David, 84, 87–89
Fürst, Max, 7

Gilboa, Amir, 106
Ginsburg, Pesah, 89
Glickman, Moshe, 97–98
Gnessin, Uri Nissan, 89–91, 93, 119, 125
Goethe, Johann Wolfgang von, 39, 87, 89
Gogol, Nikolai, 151
Goldberg, Lea, 89, 151
Goldmann, Lucien, 9
Gordin, Jacob, 89
Gordon, A. D., 99, 101
Gorky, Maxim, 151
Gouri, Haim, 106
Grade, Chaim, 69
Graetz, Heinrich, 4
Greenberg, Uri Zvi, 99
Guarini, Giovanni Battista, 83

Hadani, Ever, 117, 151
Halkin, Simon, 89, 90, 114–115, 118
Hameiri, Avigdor, 117
Hamsun, Knut, 88–89, 92
Hanani, J., 118
Hanokh, Gershon, 101
Har-Even, Yaakov, 118
Hareven, Shulamith, 165
Hayyug, Moshe, 118
Hazaz, Haim, 84–85, 91–92
Heine, Heinrich, 88
Hemingway, Ernest, 88
Hendel, Yehudit, 158
Herzl, Theodor, 98, 182

Horowitz, David, 101
Horowitz, Yaakov, 84, 89

Jacobsen, Jens Peter, 88–89, 92
Jens, Walter, 7, 9, 15
Jong, Erica, 77

Kabak, A. A., 89
Kafka, Franz, 1–20, 23, 31–32, 39–41, 59, 64–67, 74, 109, 182
Kahan, Yaakov, 123–125
Kahana-Karmon, Amalia, 109, 155, 170
Kahn, Ludwig, 86
Kaniuk, Yoram, 165, 175
Kariv, Avraham, 118
Kasher, S., 118
Katznelson, Berl, 105–106
Kenan, Amos, 156–159
Kimhi, Dov, 88
Kishon, Ephraim, 158–159
Kraus, Karl, 23
Kurzweil, Baruch, 13, 119, 135, 153–154, 188

Lamdan, Yitzhak, 99, 118
Lasker-Schüler, Else, 59
Lee, R., 119
Lelchuk, Alan, 77
Lenski, Hayyim, 118
Letteris, Meir, 89
Levin, Hanokh, 89, 93, 166–167
Lewisohn, Ludwig, 59, 62–63
Lewitt, Yehezkel, 123–124
Lisitsky, Ephraim, 114–115
Luzzatto, Moses Hayyim, 83

Maeterlinck, Maurice, 88–89
Mailer, Norman, 153
Malamud, Bernard, 71, 73–78
Maletz, Rafi, 146
Manger, Itzik, 108
Mann, Thomas, 137
Mapu, Abraham, 113–114

Megged, Aharon, 106, 158, 160, 165, 173

Megged, Matti, 154

Mendele Mokher Seforim, 84, 91, 97, 111, 119, 149

Merzhekovsky, Dmitri, 89

Michael, Sammy, 167–168

Miron, Dan, 119, 168

Moked, Gabriel, 13

Mordekhay, B., 118

Mossinsohn, Yigal, 152, 154

Nitzan, Shlomo, 89, 152, 158

Ogen, I., 118

Oren, Yosef, 172

Orpaz, Yitshak, 166, 172

Oz, Amos, 102, 108–110, 159, 171, 175–178

Ozick, Cynthia, 59–60, 72–73

Pagis, Dan, 106, 109

Penn, Eldad, 147, 151

Peretz, I. L., 5, 84–85, 88–89, 111

Peri, M., 119

Pines, Meyer, 4

Pomerantz, Berl, 118

Pongs, Hermann, 7, 8, 10

Potok, Chaim, 70

Preil, Gabriel, 115, 119

Rabinov, Y., 118

Rabinowitz, Yaakov, 100, 107

Rapoport, Ben-Zion, 118

Ratosh, Yonatan, 103, 146

Rawnitzki, Yehoshua Hana, 105

Reichenstein, Shlomo, 151

Remarque, Erich Maria, 89

Reuveni, Aharon, 88

Rodin, Elisha, 118

Rolland, Romain, 90

Rosenzweig, Franz, 183

Roth, Henry, 68–69

Roth, Joseph, 39–52, 64–67, 69, 71, 108–109, 114

Roth, Philip, 71–72, 74–78, 108

Sadan, Dov, 119, 135

Sadeh, Pinhas, 85, 159, 170

Schiller, Johann, 39, 87, 89

Schirmann, Jefim Hayyim, 105

Schnitzler, Arthur, 7, 23, 59, 63, 89, 100, 114

Schulz, Max, 59

Sened, Alexander, 160, 175–176

Sened, Yonat, 160, 175–176

Shabtai, Yaakov, 106, 165–166, 168–172

Shaham, Nathan, 89, 160

Shahar, David, 158, 175

Shaked, Gershon, 119

Shakespeare, William, 89, 151

Shalev, Mordechai, 154

Shalom, Shin, 99

Shami, Yitzhak, 70

Shamir, Moshe, 16–18, 84, 89, 105, 109, 152–153, 160, 165, 173

Shenhar, Yitzhak, 84, 89, 118

Shlonsky, Avraham, 88–90, 98, 100, 104, 114–115, 149, 151

Shneour, Zalman, 123, 126

Shofman, Gershon, 12, 26–27, 90, 93

Shoham, Mattityahu, 113–114, 118

Sholem Aleichem, 5, 69, 77, 90

Sholokhov, Mikhail, 151

Shrira, S., 118

Silberschlag, Eisig, 118

Simyonov, Konstantin, 151

Singer, Isaac Bashevis, 69–70, 72–73, 108

Smilansky, Moshe, 116

Sokel, Walter H., 7

Spielhagen, Friedrich, 89

Stein, Menahem-Edmund, 118

Steinberg, Judah, 85

Steinberg, Yaakov, 12, 119, 124–125

Steiner, George, 184

Steinman, Eliezer, 93, 149

Stendahl, M. H. B., 89

Sternheim, Carl, 59

Stifter, Adalbert, 89

Tabib, Mordekhai, 160
Tabkai, A., 118
Tammuz, Benjamin, 154, 156–158, 160, 173–175
Tchernichowsky, Shaul, 123–126
Tishby, Isaiah, 105
Tolstoy, Leo, 89, 185
Tramer, Hans, 59
Treivish, Joseph Eliyahu, 89
Trilling, Lionel, 126
Turner, Victor, 133
Twersky, Yohanan, 118
Tzessler, Joseph, 118

Ukhmani, Azriel, 153

Vogel, David, 69–70, 93, 114, 119, 125

Walden, Daniel, 68
Wallach, Yona, 125
Wallenrod, Reuben, 114–115, 118
Wassermann, Jakob, 7, 24–35, 59, 64, 66–68, 71, 89

Weininger, Otto, 59, 62–63
Weitz, Yehiam, 146–148, 162
Werfel, Franz, 23, 59
White, Hayden, 133
Whitman, Walt, 89
Wieseltier, Meir, 109, 125
Wilde, Oscar, 89
Wilkansky, Meyer, 116
Wolfowski, Menahem Zalman, 89

Yehoshua, A. B., 17, 19–20, 93, 108–110, 159, 170, 172–175
Yizhar, S., 16, 18, 89, 108–109, 118, 146, 152, 160–162, 168, 170, 172–173, 179

Zach, N., 106, 109, 119
Zarchi, Israel, 117
Zemach, Shlomo, 116, 119
Zitron, Samuel Leib, 124–125
Zohn, Harry, 59
Zweig, Arnold, 59
Zweig, Stefan, 7, 23, 39–52, 89, 114